Tompkins Cortland Community College

Presented by

TOMPKINS CORTLAND COMMUNITY

COLLEGE   FOUNDATION

1987 GAYLORD

Historic Landmarks
of Black America

West

Wash.

Ore.

Ida.

Mont.

N.D.

S.D.

Wyo.

Neb.

Nev.

Utah

Colo.

Kan.

Cal.

Ariz.

N.M.

Okla.

Texas

Hawaii

Ontario

Minn.

Midwest

Wisc.

Iowa

Ill.

Mich.

Ind.

Ohio

Ontario

N.Y.

Pa.

Maine

Vt.

N.H.

Mass.

Ct.

R.I.

N.J.

Md.

Del.

Northeast

Washington, D.C.

W.Va.

Va.

Mo.

Ky.

Tenn.

Ark.

N.C.

S.C.

Miss.

Ala.

Ga.

Southeast

La.

South
Central

Fla.

Historic Landmarks of Black America

by George Cantor

Foreword by Robert L. Harris, Jr., Consulting Editor
Africana Studies and Research Center, Cornell University

Gale Research Inc. · DETROIT · LONDON

While every effort has been made to assure the reliability of the information presented in this publication, Gale Research Inc. neither guarantees the accuracy of the data contained herein nor assumes any responsibility for errors, omissions, or discrepancies. Gale accepts no payment for listing, and inclusion in the publication of any organization, agency, institution, publication, service, or individual does not imply endorsement of the editors or publisher. Errors brought to the attention of the publisher and verified to the satisfaction of the publisher will be corrected in future editions.

The paper used in this publication meets the minimum requirements of American National Standard for Information Sciences—Permanence Paper for Printed Library Materials, ANSI Z39.48-1984. ∞™

Library of Congress Cataloging-in-Publication Data

Cantor, George, 1941-
    Historic landmarks of Black America / by George Cantor; foreword by Robert L. Harris
        p.   cm.
    Includes bibliographical references and index.
    ISBN 0-8103-7809-4 : $29.95
    1. Afro-Americans—Monuments—Guide-books.   2. Historic sites—United States—Guide-books.   3. United States—History, Local.
4. United States—Description and travel—1981- —Guide-books.
I. Title.
E185.53.A1C36   1991
917.304'928—dc20   91-12543
                                                                                        CIP

Copyright © 1991
Gale Research Inc.
835 Penobscot Building
Detroit, MI 48226-4094

ISBN 0-8103-7809-4

Printed in the United States of America

Published simultaneously in the United Kingdom by Gale Research International Limited
(An affiliated company of Gale Research Inc.)

ON THE COVER:
Harlem's Apollo, the world-famous theater where many black artists—Ella Fitzgerald, Nat King Cole, James Brown, Michael Jackson—got started. Photo: New York Convention and Visitors' Bureau.

To Jaime and Courtney, and the better world that they'll make.

C O N T E N T S

HIGHLIGHTS • xi
PREFACE • xiii
FOREWORD • *A Brief History of Black America* • xv

C   H   A   P   T   E   R   1

The Midwest   1
Illinois • 4
Indiana • 13
Iowa • 17
Michigan • 19
Minnesota • 31
Ohio • 33
Wisconsin • 48

C   H   A   P   T   E   R   2

The Northeast   51
Connecticut • 54
Delaware • 59
Maine • 61
Maryland • 62
Massachusetts • 70
New Hampshire • 82
New Jersey • 83
New York • 88
Pennsylvania • 103
Rhode Island • 112
Vermont • 114

C   H   A   P   T   E   R   3

The South Central States   117
Alabama • 120
Arkansas • 144
Kentucky • 149
Louisiana • 157
Mississippi • 168
Missouri • 182
Tennessee • 192

C H A P T E R 4

The Southeast 205

Florida • 208
Georgia • 215
North Carolina • 226
South Carolina • 235
Virginia • 244
Washington, D.C. • 266
West Virginia • 276

C H A P T E R 5

The West 281

Arizona • 284
California • 290
Colorado • 296
Hawaii • 303
Kansas • 305
Montana • 313
Nebraska • 316
New Mexico • 318
Oklahoma • 322
Oregon • 326
South Dakota • 328
Texas • 330
Utah • 334
Washington • 336

C H A P T E R 6

Ontario 339

TIMELINE • 347
FURTHER READING • 355
INDEX • 361

HIGHLIGHTS

Historic Landmarks of Black America is designed for students seeking information on landmarks and events in African-American history and for travelers planning visits to sites of historical interest. Features of the book include:

▶ historical sketches on more than 300 sites related to African-American history, including:

- monuments
- plaques
- parks
- archives
- historical museums
- art museums
- houses
- birthplaces
- grave sites
- theaters
- churches
- libraries
- colleges & universities
- battlefields
- forts

▶ sites chosen on the basis of their interest to the traveler and their historical significance

▶ selected sites related to African history, such as the National Museum of African Art in Washington, D.C.

▶ sites in 46 states plus Ontario

▶ practical information for planning visits to each site, including:

- location
- season
- hours
- admission fees
- exhibits and facilities
- special programs
- accessibility for the handicapped
- telephone number

▶ regional organization, with states listed alphabetically within each region

▶ more than 100 illustrations of people, places, and events

▶ a map of the United States on which each site is represented

▶ six regional maps

▶ an introduction outlining the history of African Americans

▶ a timeline noting important dates in African-American history that are related to the sites in this book

▶ a selected bibliography of further reading, including histories, literature, biographies, and studies of popular culture and religion

▶ an index of people, sites, and events mentioned in the text

P R E F A C E

Anyone who ever has written about travel knows the American Guides. They were turned out, one for each state, during the Depression by the Works Progress Administration as a federal project for unemployed writers and editors. More than merely travel guides, the books are an invaluable source of information about local history and folklore. They also are snapshots of an older America that, even then, was in the process of disappearing under the impact of revolutions in transportation and mass media. Sometimes, however, in reading through them, you are brought up short by the realization of how much attitudes have changed since they were written.

While researching this book, for example, I came across this passage in the South Dakota Guide:

> After the Civil War, two companies of hand-picked Negroes were stationed at Fort Sisseton. Despite the fact that every man was over six feet tall and an athlete, they did not relish their situation. First, they were afraid of the Indians; next, they were ridiculously out of place when wintery winds swept tons of snow across the prairie; then, too, and worst of all, they were given the job of digging up the bodies of soldiers who had been buried there for removal to another fort....
>
> One big, husky Negro was standing on a rough box in a grave, loosening the dirt around the sides. A board gave way and the Negro's foot sank into the body of a dead soldier. A superhuman leap vaulted him out of the grave to the solid ground where he emulated the feats of Jessie Owens and Ralph Metcalf for speed. He never returned to the fort, and his whereabouts have never been entered upon the records.

Besides the condescending racial tone conveyed in this passage, it is atrocious history. Any assertion that the all-black infantry and cavalry units formed within the U.S. Army after 1866 "were afraid of the Indians" is ludicrous. If anything, the Indians feared them.

They were called Buffalo Soldiers and for twenty-five years they served in the thick of these frontier wars; they fought against the Cheyenne on the Great Plains, the Apache in the deserts of the Southwest, the Sioux in the "wintery winds" of the frozen Dakota

Territory. These were the men who rode to the rescue of the trapped cavalry platoon at Beecher Island, Colorado; who served at Fort Apache and broke the strength of Geronimo and Vittorio; who pursued Pancho Villa through Mexico. Twelve of them were awarded the Congressional Medal of Honor.

But you will search in vain through almost all of American popular culture, its movies and songs and novels, for descriptions of their exploits. It's as if these black troopers had vanished without leaving so much as a footprint behind.

In much the same way, so many elements of African-American history have been ignored by general travel guides. The traveler interested in getting a fuller understanding of American history, one that includes black people as an integral part of the progress and passion of that story, will come away empty-handed. That is the traveler to whom this book is directed.

Writing this book has been an education. In researching the landmarks that appear in these pages, I found an America that is unknown to most Americans. Names that were only dimly recognized were fleshed out, given substance, fitted into the flow of Americana. I relived the epic struggle for civil rights, reviving memories of events I had witnessed in my own lifetime and trying to describe their importance to the contemporary traveler. I saw the American story from a new perspective. Research for much of this material involved my returning to familiar places, but fitted, as it were, with a new set of glasses, that enabled me to see things clearly that were out of focus before.

This is not the first travel book I've written but it was by far the most difficult, because so many of these historic sites have not been identified and publicized by their state travel offices. What I found especially interesting was that some of the most helpful agencies were located in the South. The state travel offices of Alabama, Virginia, Tennessee, Kentucky, and Mississippi were particularly helpful. So were those in Missouri and Ohio, as well as those in the cities of St. Louis, Boston, Detroit, New York, Philadelphia, Baltimore, Los Angeles, and Oakland. Unfortunately, a number of state travel offices seemed entirely unaware of the wealth of historic attractions in their own backyards.

I know that the informed reader will find omissions here. What I tried to do was concentrate on those places which have something tangible remaining for the traveler to see. The selection of historically black colleges was especially difficult. I tried to choose those most directly connected to major historic events, those associated with famous individuals, or those with especially notable campuses. Inevitably, some were passed over.

But the main purpose of *Historic Landmarks of Black America* is to help the history-minded traveler locate and experience a facet of this country that has too often turned up missing from the general itinerary. It is a place of astonishing variety and rich texture. It is America, too, and an America well worth knowing.

George Cantor

A Brief History of Black America

by Robert L. Harris, Jr.

Africana Studies and Research Center
Cornell University

As this indispensable guide attests, African Americans have made a deep and lasting imprint upon the history and landscape of the United States. From the early exploration and settlement of the country, to its westward expansion, military campaigns, economic development, cultural achievements, and social advances, African Americans have played critical roles. Nevertheless, black contributions and achievements have not always been recognized and appreciated by the larger society, and sometimes have been forgotten by African Americans themselves. This guide, whether used as a reference to the tragedies and triumphs of black Americans or as a directory to historical sites and monuments, helps to preserve the record of black accomplishment and to introduce readers to memorable places where they can gain further knowledge about the black experience.

THE COLONIAL PERIOD

Although African Americans participated in the early exploration, settlement, and westward expansion of the United States, they were brought from Africa primarily for their labor. They filled a need, especially in the South, for workers to clear fields, build homes, tend livestock, and cultivate crops. The southern climate and soil were conducive to large-scale agricultural production, whereas northern conditions were suitable only to small-scale family farming. As a result, the plantation system became the basis of the southern economy, while the northern economy was based on commerce and, later, industry.

The first Africans, other than those who accompanied the early Spanish explorers, arrived in what is today the United States in 1619, a year before the Mayflower landed at Plymouth Rock. Those first Africans, about twenty in number, landed at **Jamestown, Virginia,** probably as indentured servants. Indentured servitude was the method by which southern planters acquired workers. In return for an agreement to work for a specified term, most often three to seven years, the planter paid the servant's passage to the colonies. At the end of the term, the indentured servant was entitled to freedom and a small parcel of land. At first, most indentured servants came from

England; however, as their cost increased due to smaller supply in England, planters turned more to Africa for laborers.

Because of what appeared to be an almost inexhaustible supply of labor from Africa and the ability to distinguish Africans from other workers by their color, the planters began to rely more on Africans and to lengthen their terms of service until they were enslaved for life. At this stage, slavery was based more on class and religious differences than on the allegations of racial inferiority that apologists later used to justify slavery. During the seventeenth century, some black families became Christians, acquired land, and interacted with white settlers on a basis of relative racial equality. As slavery became entrenched during the late seventeenth and early eighteenth centuries, it was presumed more frequently that a black person was a slave, and the colonies began to restrict the mobility and activities of free Africans.

Until the 1740s, white ministers did not spend much energy converting Africans to Christianity, and slaves, except those who worked in white households, had little contact with the white population. Africans were thereby able to retain many of their own customs and practices. They employed the "ring shout" in religious worship, for example, wherein they moved in unison in a counter-clockwise direction, shuffling their feet, clapping their hands, and chanting songs, often in their native languages. They used "call and response" in their religious services, narrowing the psychological distance between the preacher and the congregation. These practices, drawn from their African heritage, would endure well into the twentieth century and influence the development of spirituals, blues, jazz, gospel, rhythm and blues, rock and roll, soul, and indeed all popular music in America.

For a time, the colonists believed that Christianity and slavery were incompatible, and that conversion to Christianity would free Africans from bondage. By the early eighteenth century, however, most of the colonies had passed laws making it clear that conversion to Christianity did not require emancipation. Planters and ministers began to promulgate the idea that Christianity made better and more faithful slaves, that the Bible sanctioned slavery, and that it was their duty to rescue Africans from heathenism. The effort to convert slaves did not erase African culture, but rather helped to foster the growth of an African American culture that merged African traditions with the realities of life in a new sociocultural environment. Witness, for example, the practice of decorating graves with some of the last articles used by the deceased as preserved at the **Hampton Spring Cemetery** in Carthage, Arkansas, where African Americans arranged shards of pottery on graves in a pattern similar to that found in West Africa. Similarly, the custom of placing masks on graves to prevent evil spirits from interfering with the soul's journey to the afterlife and to remind the living of their ancestors was retained at the **Effigy Cemetery** in Jackson, Alabama.

In 1714, there were approximately sixty thousand Africans in the colonies, or about fourteen percent of the total population. By 1754, the number had grown to almost three hundred thousand, or twenty percent of the colonists. The black population was growing at a faster rate than the population as a whole, especially in the South, and became cause for some concern. In South Carolina, for example, Africans outnumbered whites by two to one.

Partly out of fear of slave uprisings, as well as the outbreak of the French and Indian Wars (1754-61) and growing estrangement from Great Britain due to the imposition of various taxes, the colonies began to curtail slave importation. In October, 1774, the first Continental Congress agreed to discontinue the slave trade by December. One of Thomas Jefferson's early drafts of the Declaration of Independence included an indictment of King George III for imposing the "traffic in human flesh" on the colonists; that bill was stricken at the insistence of Georgia and South Carolina. Nevertheless, the Revolutionary War and its rationale based on "natural rights of man" weakened slavery in the new nation. Drawing phrases from the Declaration of Independence, African Americans petitioned colonial legislatures for their freedom.

THE REVOLUTIONARY WAR PERIOD

The Continental Army at first barred black soldiers from enlisting in the war for America's independence. But after the British Governor of Virginia, Lord Dunmore, issued a proclamation in November, 1775, offering freedom to those slaves reaching his lines, the patriots reversed themselves and invited black men to join their forces. Some five thousand Africans fought with the patriots against the loyalists. General Nathanael Greene organized the First Rhode Island Regiment, the only all-black unit to fight in the Revolutionary War. In the rest of the Continental Army and in the colonial militias, black men fought alongside white soldiers. After the War for Independence, the military segregated black troops, a policy that lasted until the Korean War (1950-53).

Hundreds of black men gained freedom by fighting in the Revolutionary War, and other steps were taken to end slavery: the new government barred slavery in the Northwest Territory; each Northern state enacted measures by 1804 to abolish slavery; and the Constitution provided for the termination of the slave trade in 1808. At the same time, the Constitution defined slaves as only three-fifths of a person for purposes of Congressional representation and declared that slaves could not become free by fleeing from a slave state to a free state or territory.

Given the racial prejudice and discrimination that was manifest toward African Americans, black people developed their own institutions. They formed mutual aid and benevolent societies to provide for illness, disability, and burial expenses, as well as lectures, subscription libraries, and apprenticeship programs for black youth. They established independent black churches, such as the African Methodist Episcopal Church (AME). Richard Allen, Absolom Jones, and William White left **St. George Methodist Episcopal Church** in Philadelphia in 1787 when they were rudely pulled from their knees during prayer and directed to the gallery newly reserved for African Americans.

Allen and others founded **Bethel AME Church** in Philadelphia, which joined with other newly formed black congregations in 1816 to establish the AME church as an independent denomination. Black Baptists also started churches beginning in **Savannah, Georgia** in 1779, but they did not coalesce into a general body until 1886, with formation of the National Baptist Convention. African American institutions developed primarily in the North, where the free black population encountered fewer restrictions than in the South. Northern African Americans did not enjoy racial equality, but they did have more rights than their southern counterparts.

EARLY NINETEENTH CENTURY: SLAVE RESISTANCE

Between the mid-1790s and 1808, the last year of foreign slave trade, the southern states imported almost one hundred thousand slaves. This was the largest infusion of Africans into the U.S. during the course of the slave trade, which brought approximately 450,000 Africans to the United States, as well as over 4,000,000 to the Caribbean, 3,700,000 to Brazil, 1,500,000 to the rest of South America, and 225,000 to Central America. In all, slave traders brought almost ten million Africans to the Americas over a three hundred year period.

In the United States, the end of legal participation in the foreign slave trade stimulated a thriving domestic slave trade, as slaves were sold from the older and more exhausted lands of the upper South to the newer and more fertile areas of the lower South. The **Franklin and Armfield Office** in Alexandria, Virginia, now a National Historic Landmark, was the largest slavetrading firm in the South. Although it was unlawful to import slaves from Africa, some slave dealers illegally transported Africans to the U.S. and sold them into bondage. In 1859, the last known slave ship from Africa, the Clothilde, became stranded on its route to Mobile, Alabama, and the Africans escaped to an area north of the city called **Africa Town,** where their descendants live today. One of the last survivors of the ship, Cudjoe Lewis, died in 1935.

The rapid infusion of Africans over the fifteen-year span from 1793 to 1808 created unrest among the slaves. The newly imported Africans had fresh memories of home and freedom and did not succumb as easily to enslavement as those slaves born in the U.S. In August, 1800, Gabriel Prosser planned a slave uprising in Henrico County, Virginia. An estimated one thousand slaves gathered six miles outside Richmond, Virginia for an assault on the city. A violent storm interrupted their plans, which slave informants had already revealed to white authorities. Some thirty-five slaves, including Gabriel Prosser, were executed for participating in the plot.

Many slaves escaped to Florida, a Spanish territory, until it became part of the United States in 1821. After the War of 1812, about three hundred escaped slaves and a group of native Americans seized control of an abandoned British outpost north of **St. Augustine** that became known as "Fort Negro." American forces captured the fort in 1816. Today its ruins are being excavated for important information on black and Indian life during the early nineteenth century. Africans fought with the Seminole Indians against the United States during the First Seminole War, 1817-18. The Second Seminole War, 1835-42, was precipitated by the capture of Morning Dew, Chief Osceola's black wife, as a fugitive slave. Among Osceola's two thousand warriors were about three hundred black men. It took American troops seven years to subdue the Seminole, who were finally removed to the West. Ironically, black soldiers would fight to contain this same tribe after the Civil War.

Slave unrest was epidemic during the early nineteenth century. Revolt and rumor of revolt constantly occupied the South. In 1822, Denmark Vesey, a former slave in South Carolina who had purchased his freedom in 1800 with earnings from a lottery, organized the largest slave conspiracy in American history. He planned an attack on **Charleston** and sought assistance from the newly independent black nation of Haiti. Among Vesey's closest lieutenants were the Africans Monday Gell, an Ibo, Gullah Jack, Angolan, and Mingo Harth, Mandingo. Vesey conspired to attack the city in July, seize weapons, kill any whites who resisted, and set the city ablaze as a signal for slaves from the surrounding areas to enter Charleston. An estimated nine thousand slaves were involved in the plot, which was revealed to white authorities by two black men. Thirty-five African Americans, including Vesey, were killed for their participation in the conspiracy, and thirty-seven were banished from the state.

The bloodiest slave rebellion in the United States took place August 21, 1831, in Southampton County, Virginia. Nat Turner, a mystic and talented slave who could read and write, believed that God had ordained him to end slavery. Together with six other slaves, Turner killed his own slave master and marched toward the county seat of Jerusalem (now **Courtland**), attacking plantations and murdering their white residents. Turner's band of rebels had grown to about sixty by the time they were met by the militia. About fifty-seven whites were killed in the uprising, and more than one hundred slaves lost their lives during the rebellion and afterward as whites sought revenge. Turner escaped for two months before he was captured and executed.

Perhaps the most celebrated case of slave resistance took place in 1839 aboard the ship *The Amistad*. The vessel was sailing from Havana to Port Principe, Cuba, with a cargo of fifty-four slaves. During the voyage, the slaves, under the leadership of Joseph Cinque, rose up, killed the captain and his crew, and demanded that the ship sail to Africa. The navigators pretended to sail toward Africa by day but steered the ship northwest at night for two months, finally landing on Long Island. The Cubans who survived demanded a return of their "merchandise" in a trial that reached the United States Supreme Court, with former president John Quincy Adams representing the captives. The court ruled in 1841 that the Amistad Africans should be set free, and they returned to Africa. The cemetery in **Farmington, Connecticut,** where the slaves stayed during the trial, contains a memorial for one of the captives, who accidentally drowned before the trial ended. The famous black artist,

Hale Woodruff, painted a series of frescoes at **Talladega College** in Alabama, depicting the Amistad revolt. The largest body of records on African-American history and race relations is housed at Tulane University in New Orleans and named the **Amistad Research Center.**

These slave uprisings, especially the Nat Turner revolt, sent shock waves throughout the South. The slaveocracy was under seige internally from slave unrest and externally from the abolitionist movement. To protect its "peculiar institution," the South closed black churches, made it illegal for three or more African Americans—slave or free—to meet without white supervision, declared it a crime to teach a black person—slave or free—to read and write, and invested every white man with the power to regulate the activities of African Americans. Most pernicious was the justification that apologists gave to defend slavery. Prior to the 1830s, southerners upheld slavery as a "necessary evil" that was distasteful but important to the region's economic development. Once under attack, especially by white abolitionists, southerners justified slavery as a "positive good." They used racist pseudoscience to argue that Africans were an inferior race, that Africa was a backward continent, and that slavery rescued Africans from savagery, barbarity, and heathenism. They cited the curses of Cain and Ham in the Bible as divine sanction for the servitude of black people. Slavery was held up as the natural condition of black people and freedom an aberration. Free African Americans would supposedly degenerate physically and spiritually without the beneficent protection of slavery.

THE UNDERGROUND RAILROAD AND ABOLITIONISM

As the South became an armed camp against slave uprisings, flight from bondage became the most viable route to freedom. More than one hundred thousand slaves may have escaped north via the Underground Railroad. Homes in dozens of cities, especially along the Mason-Dixon line, served as stations on the Underground Railroad, sheltering fugitive slaves until it was safe for them to travel farther north or to Canada. The most prominent conductor on the Underground Railroad was Harriet Tubman, born a slave in Maryland, from which she escaped at the age of twenty-eight. She returned to the South some nineteen times and rescued approximately three hundred slaves. She was among the thousands of African Americans who had to live in Canada for a time after passage of the fugitive slave law of 1850, which required legal authorities to cooperate with slave holders in returning their "property." That legislation placed the lives of many northern African Americans in jeopardy because they could not conclusively prove their freedom. Some fifty thousand African Americans moved to Canada during the 1850s and settled in the Ontario towns of **Amherstburg, Chatham,** and **Dresden.**

To support fugitive slaves and to protect themselves from being kidnapped into slavery, northern African Americans formed vigilance committees to look out for slavecatchers and to rescue black men and women claimed as escaped slaves. On October 1, 1851, slavecatchers in Syracuse, New York, seized Jerry McHenry, a longtime resident of the city and well-known fugitive slave. African Americans snatched him from the courthouse after a hearing and tried to free him, but they were overtaken by the police who recaptured him. That evening a large crowd of blacks and whites gathered at the jail, where they stormed the building, freed McHenry, and sent him to Canada.

Northern African Americans were in the vanguard of the struggle against slavery. Through the pulpit, newspapers, pamphlets, self-help organizations, and state and national conventions, they sought both to end slavery and to demonstrate their capacity for racial equality. In 1827, Samuel Cornish and John Russwurm published the first black newspaper, *Freedom's Journal,* in New York City. The most important and longest running black newspaper before the Civil War was the *North Star,* which Frederick Douglass edited in Rochester, New York. Born a slave in Maryland, Douglass escaped in 1838. He settled first in New Bedford, Massachusetts, where he joined the abolitionist movement. Through his autobiography, the *Narrative of Frederick Douglass* (1845), lectures, and antislavery activities, Douglass became the best known black abolitionist, indeed one of the major spokesmen for black America during the nineteenth century.

Douglass was not without rivals before the Civil War, especially Martin R. Delany and Henry Highland Garnet. Douglass, like the great white abolitionist William Lloyd Garrison, editor of the *Liberator,* advocated moral suasion to end slavery. Garnet proposed political agitation and slave rebellion as a means to free the slaves. In his 1843 address to the Buffalo National Black Convention, Garnet spoke directly to the slaves, advising them: "Arise, arise! Rather die freemen than live to be slaves! Let your motto be resistance; no oppressed people have secured their liberty without resistance." As the noose of racism and segregation tightened during the 1850s, Garnet and other black leaders, especially Martin R. Delany, advocated that African Americans emigrate to Africa. In the 1857 Dred Scott Supreme Court decision, Chief Justice Roger B. Taney declared that black men were inferior and unfit to associate with the white race socially or politically. Indeed, they were so inferior that they had no rights; in effect, African Americans did not have to be treated as citizens of the United States. Several years before the Dred Scott decision, Delany anticipated Taney's ruling when Delany described African Americans as constituting a "nation within a nation." Delany argued that African Americans would not be free until they were an essential part of the nation's governance. He did not believe political participation possible until slavery was abolished.

Paul Cuffe, like Delany, advocated emigration to Africa. The son of a free slave and Indian mother, Cuffe was born near New Bedford, Massachusetts, in 1759. He earned a small fortune as a ship captain and purchased a farm in **Westport, Massachusetts**. Cuffe and his brother, John, in 1780, refused to pay taxes until they were allowed to vote. He was concerned about the condition of former slaves in the United States and took thirty-eight emigrants to Sierra Leone in 1815. He died two years later, after formation of the American Colonization Society, which settled former slaves in Liberia beginning in 1821. Most free African Americans opposed the American Colonization Society, maintaining that it was a white-dominated organization that sought to perpetuate slavery by removing all freed slaves from the United States. The outbreak of the Civil War also dampened support for emigration abroad to achieve racial equality.

THE CIVIL WAR PERIOD

When the Civil War started on April 12, 1861, with the Confederate attack on Fort Sumter in Charleston harbor, Frederick Douglass immediately recognized that slavery lay at the heart of the conflict. Although President Abraham Lincoln justified the war as a means to preserve the Union, Douglass championed the battle as a way to free the slaves. He prodded Lincoln to enlist black men in the Union Army and to deprive the South of an important asset, its slaves. Lincoln was in a difficult position as he had to maintain northern support for the war effort while keeping the border states (Delaware, Maryland, Kentucky, and Missouri) in the Union. Each of those states defended slavery. While the North in general was antislavery, it was not necessarily pro-black. In 1860, black men could vote on an equal basis with whites only in Massachusetts, Maine, New Hampshire, Vermont, and Rhode Island. Illinois, Indiana, Iowa, and Oregon between 1850 and 1857 prohibited the further settlement of African Americans within their borders. By law or custom, African Americans in the North faced segregation in public transportation and accommodations, education, housing, religious service, hospitals, prisons, and cemeteries.

Lincoln, therefore, moved with caution in freeing the slaves. The Emancipation Proclamation, which took effect on January 1, 1863, freed only those slaves in states that remained in rebellion against the Union. Its most immediate and dramatic effect was provision for the enlistment of black soldiers. Approximately 180,000 black men fought in the Union Army and 30,000 in the Navy during the Civil War. About one in five black males over the age of fifteen joined the Union forces. They acquitted themselves well in combat, with sixteen of them winning the Congressional Medal of Honor. Unlike black soldiers in the Revolutionary War, they served in all-black units under the command of white officers. Initially, black soldiers received $6.50 less a month than white troops. The famed Fifty-fourth Massachusetts Regiment, immortalized by the sculptor Augustus Saint-Gaudens in a memorial on the Commons in **Boston** and featured in the 1989 Academy Award-winning film *Glory,* refused any pay until the War Department began paying black men as much as whites. The Fifty-fourth went for a full year without pay in protest against discriminatory wages before their demands were met in 1864.

Robert Smalls of South Carolina was the only black man to hold the rank of captain in the Union Navy. Born a slave in 1790, Smalls became an expert coastal pilot and worked on the Confederate steamer *The Planter* when the war started. With his wife, two children, and five others, he successfully piloted the ship through Confederate lines and gave it to the Union Navy in May, 1862. The ship was assigned to transport duty with Smalls as its pilot. He was promoted to captain in 1863 when the vessel was refitted as a gunboat. After the war, he was elected to Congress from South Carolina. He served five terms, the longest tenure of any black Congressman during Reconstruction. His home in **Beaufort, South Carolina** is a National Historical Landmark. John Lawson, at the battle of Mobile Bay in 1864, was the first black man in the Navy to receive the Congressional Medal of Honor for manning his gun while wounded until help arrived for his ship.

THE RECONSTRUCTION PERIOD

The valor displayed by black men in fighting for their freedom helped to gain support for their civil and political rights after the war. The states ratified the Thirteenth Amendment ending slavery in 1865 and the Fourteenth Amendment affirming the citizenship of former slaves in 1868. The Fifteenth Amendment in 1870 acknowledged the right of black men to vote. Congress in 1875 passed a civil rights act that prohibited discrimination in public transportation and accommodations, as well as in jury selection.

African Americans made great strides after the war. Black soldiers from the Sixty-second and Sixty-fifth U.S. Colored Infantry funded establishment of a school for former slaves in Jefferson City, Missouri, named **Lincoln University**. The Freedman's Bureau started **Howard University** in Washington, D.C., in 1867. Several church groups, black and white, founded colleges throughout the South. **Hampton Institute** in Virginia had its beginnings under an oak tree, where Mary Peake, a free black woman, held classes for children of fugitive slaves during the war. About sixty church-sponsored schools were established in the South. Southern states created about thirty-five public colleges and universities for African Americans, primarily as a result of the Second Morrill Act, which Congress enacted in 1890, authorizing the creation of black land-grant colleges.

The black church, known as the "invisible institution" during slavery, became highly visible in the South after emancipation. The Baptist, African Methodist Episcopal, and African Methodist Episcopal Zion churches organized congregations throughout the South. The Colored (now Christian) Methodist Episcopal Church broke away from the Methodist Episcopal Church South which supported the Confederacy during the war. Although African Americans joined other denominations, they were attracted primarily to the Baptist and Methodist churches which did not require literacy for church membership and were more evangelical in worship. The church became the most important institution among African Americans, nurturing leadership, providing a social outlet, and offering a haven in a society that remained racist.

For a time during the Reconstruction Era, 1867-77, black men were able to participate in politics in the South and to hold elective office. They enjoyed greatest political influence in South Carolina, where they made up a majority of the population and the registered voters. Black men (women could not vote until ratification of the

Nineteenth Amendment in 1920), were a majority of the registered voters in Florida, Louisiana, and South Carolina until 1877. From 1869 to 1901, two African Americans served in the Senate and twenty in the House of Representatives. Blanche K. Bruce, from Mississippi, was the first African American elected to a full term in the U.S. Senate (1875-81). Hiram R. Revels, also from Mississippi, served in the Senate before Bruce but only for a year, filling the unexpired term of Jefferson Davis, former president of the Confederacy. The **Blanche K. Bruce Home** in Washington, D.C., is a National Historic Landmark.

AFRICAN AMERICANS IN THE WEST

In a compromise to win control of the White House in the closely contested election of 1876, the Republican Rutherford B. Hayes agreed to pull federal troops out of the South. That action brought Reconstruction to a close and allowed reactionaries to regain control of the South. Through violence, threats, and intimidation, southern white supremacists disenfranchised black voters. De facto segregation nullified the civil rights gains made during Reconstruction. To escape violence, disenfranchisement, and segregation in the South, approximately 60,000 African Americans migrated to Kansas between 1875 and 1881. Thousands more moved to other parts of the West where they established black towns, such as **Nicodemus** in Kansas, **Allenworth** in California, and **Boley** and **Langston** in Oklahoma.

Black soldiers, organized into the Ninth and Tenth cavalry and the Twenty-fourth and Twenty-fifth infantry, were stationed in the West after the Civil War. Twelve soldiers from those units won Congressional Medals of Honor during the Indian Wars. The "Buffalo Soldiers," as the Indians called these troops, saw action in Arizona, Colorado, Montana, New Mexico, South Dakota, and Texas. The first black graduate of West Point, Henry O. Flipper, joined the Tenth cavalry in 1878.

Black cowboys were also an important presence in the West, as they constituted almost twenty-five percent of the crews driving cattle along the trails from the southwestern ranges to midwestern pens. Nat Love, better known as "Deadwood Dick," drove cattle along the Chisholm trail north from Texas. He was born a slave in Tennessee in 1854, but moved west in 1869. Love was a contemporary of such well known cowboys as Bat Masterson, the James Brothers (Frank and Jesse), and Billy the Kid. The nickname "Deadwood Dick" came from his exploits at a rodeo in Deadwood City, Dakota Territory, in which he won the roping and shooting contests. John Swain, a cowhand and expert rider in Tombstone, Arizona, is buried in its infamous **Boot Hill Cemetery.** One of the most famous black cowboys was Bill Pickett, who is credited with inventing the rodeo sport of bulldogging, where a cowboy leaps from his horse, grasps a steer by the horns, wrestles it to the ground, and ties its hooves with a rope. He was the star of the **101 Ranch** Wild West Show that toured the country. Two of Pickett's early assistants were Tom Mix and Will Rogers. The **Great Plains Black Museum** in Omaha, Nebraska exhibits the history of black pioneers and settlers in the Dakotas, Montana, Nebraska, and Wyoming, while Denver's **Black American West Museum and Heritage Center** highlights the role of the black cowboy on the frontier.

INSTITUTIONALIZED SEGREGATION

By the 1890s, the door to opportunity that had opened for African Americans during Reconstruction closed shut. The courts supported the rise of Jim Crow laws, or racial segregation, by nullifying civil rights legislation. The crowning blow came in 1896, when the U.S. Supreme Court ruled in Plessy v. Ferguson that "separate but equal" facilities could be provided for African Americans. With the courts on their side, white supremacists removed the remaining black voters through devices such as the grandfather clause, poll taxes, white primary, and understanding clauses. De jure segregation reinforced de facto segregation as southern state statutes separated the races in practically every area of life. White segregationists used indiscriminate violence to keep black people in their place. From 1889 to 1903, almost 113 African Americans a year were lynched in the South.

The black population was divided in its response to this racial oppression. In his 1895 Atlanta Exposition Address, Booker T. Washington, founder of **Tuskegee Institute** in Alabama and the most influential black leader after Frederick Douglass's death, first uttered his now famous words, "In all things that are purely social we can be as separate as the fingers, yet one as the hand in all things essential to mutual progress." He counseled African Americans to "cast down your bucket where you are," or, to make the most of their situation in the South. Washington advocated economic development as the means to achieve racial equality. He was willing to forgo political participation and protest against racial oppression. Once African Americans acquired important skills and provided essential services, Washington maintained that the southern states, indeed the nation, would accord them the rights and privileges of first-class citizenship.

W. E. B. Du Bois, who in 1895 became the first black recipient of a doctoral degree in history from Harvard University, initially thought that Washington's program of racial solidarity and self-help might improve the status and condition of African Americans. As their plight deteriorated and Washington sought to muffle dissent against his program, Du Bois openly criticized Washington's conciliatory and accommodationist position in his now classic book *The Souls of Black Folk*, published in 1903. Du Bois argued that no people advanced by voluntarily conceding their fundamental rights. He believed that "manly" agitation was necessary for African Americans to achieve and to defend racial equality.

MIGRATION AND URBANIZATION

Although most African Americans regarded Washington very highly, a large portion of them voted with their feet in migrating from rural to urban areas of the South and to urban areas of the

North and to some extent the West. In 1890, ninety percent of the black population lived in the South, with eighty percent in rural areas. By 1940, less than seventy-five percent resided in the South, and almost fifty percent now lived in urban areas. The urbanization of African Americans had consequences in practically every area of black life and culture. As African Americans moved from the country to the city, they encountered a different life-style. The black population also became more concentrated, especially in urban ghettoes. Similar to the post-Revolutionary War era when African Americans became more separated from the broader society of the new nation, so too during the late nineteenth and early twentieth centuries, the gulf between the races widened, economically, socially, and politically. Just as African Americans were forced by racial segregation to form their own institutions during the early national period in American history, they had to establish their own professional organizations during the so-called "progressive era" of the early twentieth century.

Black dentists, doctors, lawyers, nurses, teachers, and businessmen formed their own associations. Black women organized the National Association of Colored Women in 1896 to counter the stereotypical images of black women as ignorant, lewd, and licentious. The organization provided a voice for black women who sought to improve conditions for themselves and the race. On September 9, 1915, Carter G. Woodson and four other black men started the **Association for the Study of Negro** (now Afro-American) **Life and History** in Chicago. (He later incorporated the group in Washington, D.C., where he operated it out of his home.) A year later, Woodson, who became known as the "Father of Negro History," began publishing the *Journal of Negro History;* subsequently he created Associated Publishers in 1921, initiated the observance of Negro History Week in 1926, and founded the *Negro History Bulletin* in 1936. Although he did not graduate from high school until he was twenty-one years old because he had to work in the coal mines to assist his family, Woodson in 1912 became the second African American to earn a Ph.D. in history from Harvard University. During his lifetime, he wrote a dozen books and edited eight volumes to inform the nation about black contributions to American society and to inspire African Americans, especially black youth, to greater achievement.

As racial segregation, discrimination, and violence grew more pronounced during the early twentieth century, W. E. B. Du Bois, William Monroe Trotter, and other African Americans formed the Niagara Movement in 1905 to protest racial oppression, to gain the ballot, and to improve educational opportunity. The Niagara Movement led the way to the National Association for the Advancement of Colored People (NAACP) in 1910, when liberal whites joined with African Americans to stop racial violence (especially lynching), to end forced segregation, to acquire the right to vote, to achieve equal education for black and white youth, and to define the citizenship rights of African Americans by law. Du Bois became the director of publicity and research for the NAACP, whereby he published the magazine *The Crisis* as a record of the darker race. A year after the NAACP, the National Urban League was established to help black migrants to the cities in employment, housing, and general welfare.

The growing concentration of African Americans in the cities, particularly in the North, helped them to organize more effectively for social, economic, and political advancement. No one was better at organizing the black masses than Marcus Garvey, whose Universal Negro Improvement Association (UNIA) became the largest black organization in the U.S., with branches throughout the world. Greatly influenced by Booker T. Washington's philosophy of racial solidarity and self-help, Garvey added the dream of a great black nation in Africa to protect the interests of people of African ancestry everywhere. The feud between Du Bois and Washington, who died in 1915, continued between Du Bois and Garvey. Du Bois accused Garvey, among other things, of abandoning the struggle for racial equality in America for an unlikely utopia in Africa. Meanwhile, Garvey castigated Du Bois, the NAACP, and others for cooperating with whites and seeking to become part of a racist society.

THE HARLEM RENAISSANCE AND THE JAZZ AGE

This debate took place primarily in New York City, which by the 1920s had become the cultural capital of black America. It was home to the "Harlem Renaissance," a flowering of black art, dance, drama, music, and literature between 1919 and 1930. During this period, new and established black writers published more fiction and poetry than ever before, the first influential black literary periodicals were established, and black authors, artists, and musicians received their first widespread recognition and serious critical appraisal.

During the 1920s, often characterized as the "Jazz Age," African-American music had an unprecedented influence on American society. Other than native Americans, African Americans created this country's only indigenous music. Blues and jazz lie at the heart of American popular music and have affected musical styles throughout the world. The story of black music's development in the United States is well-preserved from the **Delta Blues Museum** in Clarksdale, Mississippi to the **Cab Calloway Jazz Institute** at Coppin State College in Baltimore, Maryland. The **Storyville** section of New Orleans spawned the beginnings of jazz and one of its legends, Louis Armstrong. A park named after him sits today near Storyville and encompasses Congo Square, a place where slaves were permitted to congregate on Sunday afternoons to play their music and to dance.

From the Delta, blues migrated up the Mississippi River to Memphis, where W. C. Handy became known as the "Father of the Blues" for collecting, transcribing, and composing blues songs. Memphis's **Beale Street,** which today features a statue of Handy, was once the heart of the city's black community. Top musicians performed in its clubs and theaters, merging blues with the new jazz sound. In **Florence, Alabama,** Handy's birthplace, a Museum and Library are devoted to him. In St. Louis, Scott Joplin innovated the syncopated sound of ragtime. Across the state in Kansas City, the

Mutual Musicians Association Hall, now a National Historic Landmark, was home to the black musicians' union. It was frequented by Herschel Evans, Charlie Parker, and Lester Young, all of whom hailed from Kansas City, as well as Count Basie, who organized his band in the city.

THE CIVIL RIGHTS MOVEMENT

After the onset of the Depression, black migration to the cities slowed, to be revived by labor shortages during World War II. While black men fought in each of the country's wars, African Americans resolved during World War II, unlike World War I, to press for a "double victory" at home and abroad. During World War I, black leaders had advised African Americans to put their grievances temporarily behind them, to support the war effort, and to look forward to better opportunities after the war. In many respects, conditions got worse, as evidenced by the race riots of 1919, which led to the loss of many black lives and the destruction of their homes and property. In 1941 the famous black labor leader A. Philip Randolph proposed a massive march on Washington, D.C., to dramatize racial discrimination in the armed forces and defense industries. To forestall the potentially disruptive demonstration, President Franklin D. Roosevelt issued Executive Order #8802, providing for nondiscriminatory employment in defense industries and establishing a Fair Employment Practices Committee to monitor compliance.

During World War II, the black population in urban areas exceeded the black population in rural areas for the first time, a stage the white population had reached a generation earlier. But as African Americans moved in greater numbers to the cities, whites began an exodus to the suburbs. Whereas the black middle class grew significantly in the post-World War II years, that growth slowed considerably by the mid-1970s, as America entered a post-industrial economy and many job opportunities followed "white flight" from the cities. One salutary effect of black migration North and West was the increasing significance of the black vote, which provided the margin of victory in several local, state, and national elections. The black vote, together with cold war tensions between the U.S. and the Soviet Union, set the stage for vast changes and improvements in civil rights. In its rivalry with the Soviet Union for the support of other nations, particularly the emerging nations of Asia, the Caribbean, and Africa, the U.S. could not claim itself as the defender of freedom and democracy abroad while it practiced racial segregation and discrimination at home.

The NAACP, among other fronts, pressed to end the dual education systems in the South which separated students by race and spent often four times as much annually for white schools as for black schools. Its legal drive culminated in 1954 with the momentous Supreme Court decision in Brown v. Board of Education which overturned the doctrine of "separate but equal." That decision was one of the first major victories in the battle against Jim Crow. Along

the way, other organizations joined the fight, such as the Congress of
Racial Equality (CORE), which was organized in Chicago in 1942 and
initially fought segregation in public accommodations in the North;
the Southern Christian Leadership Conference (SCLC), which in
1957 grew out of the southern bus boycotts; and the Student Non-
Violent Coordinating Committee (SNCC), which emerged in 1960
from the student sit-in movement.

The road to the 1964 Civil Rights Act and the Voting Rights Act of
1965 sound like military campaigns, beginning with Montgomery in
1955. In **Montgomery, Alabama,** African Americans waged a
successful bus boycott that brought to prominence a little-known
minister named Martin Luther King, Jr. After Montgomery, the
battles for desegregation took place at **Central High School** in Little
Rock, Arkansas in 1957; at lunch counters in **Greensboro, North
Carolina** in 1960; bus terminals throughout the South with CORE's
"freedom rides" in 1961; public facilities and department stores in
Birmingham with SCLC's assault in 1963; SNCC's Mississippi Freedom Summer in 1964; the court house in Selma in 1965. Each of
those campaigns carried much pain and suffering as demonstrators
were beaten, homes were bombed, and churches were burned. The
Civil Rights Memorial in Montgomery, Alabama, designed by Maya
Lin who planned the Vietnam Veterans Memorial in Washington,
D.C., immortalizes the names of forty martyrs, black and white, in the
cause for civil rights from May, 1955 to the assassination of Dr. King
in April, 1968. The memorial, a circular black granite table with a
curved black granite wall, records the names of the martyrs and
chronicles the history of the civil rights movement. Water flows across
the table's top over the inscriptions and down the face of the wall,
which displays Dr. King's quotation from the Bible: "We will not be
satisfied *until justice rolls down like waters and righteousness like a mighty
stream.*" Cities and towns throughout the South have erected
monuments to individuals and places of significance to the civil rights
movement. That struggle, perhaps more than any other event in the
nation's history with the exception of the Civil War, forced the
country to confront the question of what type of society it would be.
The civil rights movement, as historian Vincent Harding has stated,
was like a 'wedge" that opened American society to all of its citizens
and pioneered struggles for equality on many fronts.

Although the civil rights movement made impressive gains in
securing legislation against racial discrimination in public accommodations, transportation, and housing, and in winning the right to vote,
it also made stark the contrast between reality and the goal of racial
equality. In the North, Malcolm X eloquently identified the contra-
diction between America's principles and her practices. While African
Americans in the South dismantled segregation and appeared to be
making remarkable improvements in their lives, African Americans in
the North faced deteriorating ghettoes, police brutality, inadequate
recreational facilities, poor housing, few public services, and rising
unemployment. Northern inner cities exploded into riots in the mid-
1960s, with the most serious rebellions in the loss of lives and
property taking place in Harlem, 1964; Watts, 1965; Newark, 1967;

and Detroit, 1967. From 1964 to 1968, there were about 329 riots in 257 cities across the country. Legal segregation was on the wane but problems of drugs, crime, unemployment, underemployment, housing, and family instability confronted a sizeable segment of the black population.

The civil rights struggle in large measure has been transformed into a drive for political empowerment and use of the political process for change and improvement in the lives of African Americans. In 1970, five years after passage of the voting rights act, there were 1,469 black elected officials. By 1985, there were 6,056 black elected officials throughout the nation, with most of the increase taking place in the South. Jesse Jackson in the presidential primaries of 1984 and 1988 electrified Black America and the nation with the possibility of a black person holding the highest elective office in the land. In 1990 L. Douglas Wilder brought that possibility closer to reality with his election as governor of Virginia, the first black man ever elected to such an office. Today, African Americans hold the mayor's office in most of the country's major cities, North and South.

CONCLUSION

Although problems persist, African Americans have made tremendous strides over the past three hundred and seventy years. From a people valued among whites exclusively for their labor and ostracized as an inferior race, African Americans have become an integral part of American society. As W. E. B. Du Bois once stated, America would not be America without her black folk. The art, dance, drama, folklore, literature, and music of African Americans have enriched the nation and given it its special character. The labor of black men and women, in slavery and freedom, has contributed to the nation's prosperity. And black men and women have served with valor in the military to secure and to defend America's liberty. The civil rights movement made equal opportunity a greater reality for all Americans. From the mathematical genius of Benjamin Banneker, who helped to design the nation's capital city, to the inventions of Elijah McCoy (automatic lubrication for machines), Jan E. Matzeliger (shoe last machine), Granville T. Woods (automatic air brakes), Garrett A. Morgan (the stoplight), and Lewis H. Latimer (light bulb carbon filament), and the discoveries of George Washington Carver, (numerous products from the peanut and soybean), Daniel Hale Williams (open heart surgery), Charles Drew (blood plasma), and Percy L. Julian (cortisone), African Americans have been essential to the nation's development and have left an indelible imprint on the land, its character, and its culture. Time spent perusing this guide and visiting some of its sites will bring inestimable insight into the African American, indeed the American, past.

Historic Landmarks
of Black America

1

The Midwest

Illinois

•

Indiana

•

Iowa

•

Michigan

•

Minnesota

•

Ohio

•

Wisconsin

The Midwest

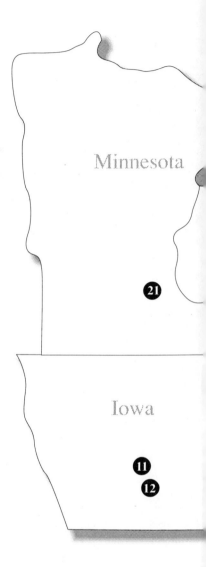

ILLINOIS

1. Du Sable Marker, Du Sable Cabin Replica, Du Sable Museum of African-American History and Art, *Chicago*
2. Johnson Publishing Corporation, *Chicago*
3. Milton Olive Park, *Chicago*
4. Provident Hospital, *Chicago*
5. Victory Monument, *Chicago*
6. Fr. Augustine Tolton Monument, *Quincy*

INDIANA

7. Levi Coffin House, *Fountain City*
8. Freetown Village of the Indiana State Museum, *Indianapolis*
9. Madame Walker Urban Life Center, *Indianapolis*
10. Union Literary Institute, *Spartanburg*

IOWA

11. Fort Des Moines, *Des Moines*
12. Simpson College, *Indianola*

MICHIGAN

13. Sojourner Truth Memorial, *Battle Creek*
14. Dr. Ossian Sweet House, *Detroit*
15. Joe Louis Memorials, *Detroit*
16. Motown Museum, *Detroit*
17. Museum of African American History, *Detroit*
18. National Museum of the Tuskegee Airmen, *Detroit*
19. Famed Black Resort, *Idlewild*
20. Crosswhite Boulder, *Marshall*

MINNESOTA

21. Fort Snelling State Historical Park, *Minneapolis-St. Paul*

OHIO

22. Sojourner Truth Monument, *Akron*
23. Stowe House, *Cincinnati*
24. Taft Museum, *Cincinnati*
25. African American Museum, *Cleveland*
26. Karamu House, *Cleveland*
27. Paul Laurence Dunbar House, *Dayton*
28. Emancipation Festival, *Gallipolis*
29. John M. Langston House, *Oberlin*
30. Rankin House, *Ripley*
31. Wyandotte Indian Missionary Church, *Upper Sandusky*
32. Benjamin Hanby Home, *Westerville*
33. National Afro-American Museum and Cultural Center, Wilberforce University, Col. Charles Young House, *Wilberforce*
34. "Blue Jacket," *Xenia*

WISCONSIN

35. Tallman Restorations, Milton House, *Janesville-Milton*
36. Wisconsin Historical Society, *Madison*

I N D I A N A

Fountain City

Levi Coffin House

"They must have an underground railroad running hereabouts," muttered a frustrated slavehunter from Kentucky, "and Levi Coffin must be the president of it."

That, by one tradition, was the origin of the phrase that described the system by which abolitionists and their allies spirited escaping slaves off to safety in the North and Canada. And while there were other lines through the East, it was Coffin's midwestern operation in Indiana that became known as the Underground Railroad's "grand central station."

Coffin was a Quaker, as were most of the other inhabitants of Fountain City, which was then called Newport. Many of them settled there specifically because of their opposition to slavery and desire to help fight it. Coffin arrived from North Carolina in 1827, and from his home on the town's main street he helped an estimated two thousand black slaves get away over the next twenty years. His boast was that he never lost one of them.

He was an extraordinary administrator, setting up the mechanics of his surreptitious network while knowing that one mistake could mean jail, or even death at the hands of night-riders. Three different routes to the North converged in Fountain City, coming from the critical Ohio River crossings at Cincinnati, Madison, Indiana, and Louisville. The road that is now U.S. 27 was the main avenue to freedom, and Coffin's house sat beside that road, offering shelter.

In 1847, Coffin moved to Cincinnati and is credited with aiding another one thousand slaves out of the dry goods store he ran downtown. Another Cincinnati resident, Harriet Beecher Stowe, was one of his admirers, and Coffin appears in *Uncle Tom's Cabin* as Simeon Halliday, a Quaker who works with the Underground Railroad.

> **Location:** Fountain City is 6 miles north of I-70, from the northbound U.S. 27 exit, and 9 miles north of Richmond. The Coffin House is on N. Main St., near the center of town.

13

Levi Coffin, engineer of the Underground Railroad

Exhibits: The house was restored in 1970 to its appearance during the years Coffin was active there. The furnishings are meant to reflect that era.
Hours: Tuesday to Sunday, 1-5, June through mid September; weekends only, through October.
Admission charge: $1.50
Telephone: (317) 847-2432.

Indianapolis

Freetown Village of the Indiana State Museum

This permanent exhibit tries to recreate what daily life was like for black settlers in a rural Indiana village immediately after the Civil War. Staffers enact the roles of historical figures, using their actual words as recovered through letters and diaries. Others perform typical activities that black settlers would have engaged in at that time in such a setting.

Location: The museum is in downtown Indianapolis one block north of Market Square Arena, at 202 N. Alabama St.
Exhibits: Besides Freetown Village, the museum contains a wealth of material on the state's history and people, from prehistoric times to the present.
Hours: Monday to Saturday, 9-4:45; Sunday, 12-4:45.
Admission charge: None.
Telephone: (317) 232-1637.

Madame Walker Urban Life Center

One of the surest paths to financial success for blacks in the late nineteenth century was hair. Some of the first black fortunes accumulated in the South had their start in a barbershop, because this was one of the few trades slaves were allowed to learn which could be applied in private business with minimal start-up capital.

The first black woman millionaire in the country, Madame C. J. Walker, followed this route. Born Sarah McWilliams to former slaves in Louisiana four years after the Civil War, she grew up in poverty, married as a teenager, and was a widowed mother by the time she was twenty. She moved to St. Louis and worked as a laundress, eventually marrying Charles J. Walker. About that time she had her great idea: beauty products for black women, especially hair-styling formulas. She may have been the first entrepreneur to identify this distinct and growing market.

Walker moved to Indianapolis in 1910 and made it her base for distributing an entire line of cosmetics and establishing a national system of beauty shops, aimed at the emerging black middle class in the northern cities. She is believed to have been the wealthiest black woman in the country at the time of her death in 1919.

Five years later her daughter, A'Lelia, put up the Walker Building on Indiana Avenue, the main artery of the city's black community. It housed offices of the various Walker enterprises and a theater, built in an African-Egyptian style, which became a major stop on the black entertainment circuit through the 1940s.

As the area started to decline in the early fifties, the theater closed and the building started to deteriorate. In 1979 it was purchased by the Madame Walker Urban Life Center, Inc., which restored the structure and turned it into a cultural center for the black community. The project was topped off by the reopening of the Walker Theater in 1988, on the sixty-first anniversary of its original opening night.

Location: Indiana Ave. runs northwest from downtown Indianapolis and was historically the main business street of the black community. The Madame Walker Urban Life Center is at 617 Indiana.
Exhibits: Displays on local black history, an ongoing program of cultural events and theatrical productions.

Hours: Business hours, Monday to Saturday, with tours arranged by appointment.
Admission charge: $2 for tours.
Telephone: (317) 236-2099.

Spartanburg

Union Literary Institute

In the years before the Civil War, Indiana, like many other northern states, had laws prohibiting black children from attending public schools. A few communities tried to deal with this deprivation by establishing schools for black children. The only surviving school building put up at that time in the state is the Union Literary Institute in rural Randolph County.

Opened in 1846, the school provided the rudiments of an elementary school education, with advanced students taking classes in chemistry, algebra, or Latin. Parents who could afford it paid an annual fee, while other students repaid their tuition through manual labor for the school, a common arrangement in the Midwest at the time. A two-story red brick building was erected in 1860 and stands today. The school was not then completely segregated. Records from 1850 indicate that out of a total of 131 students, ninety-seven were black. The rest were white children from nearby farm families.

After the Civil War, Indiana began providing public education for blacks on a segregated basis, and the Institute closed in 1874, reopening the next year as a public school for blacks. It continued in that capacity until 1910.

Location: Spartanburg is located just north of U.S. 36, near the Ohio border, about 11 miles northeast of Fountain City (see entry on Levi Coffin House above). The institute (which was also known as Greenfork Township School) is two miles northeast on a county road—ask directions in town. The building is not open to the public.

I O W A

Des Moines

Fort Des Moines

This was a deactivated cavalry post when it was chosen by Congress in 1917 as a base for training black officers to lead the segregated units being formed to fight in World War I. Between June and December of that year, hundreds of junior officers were trained at the facility, while Camp Dodge, a few miles away, became a massive training base for white troops. One of the officers trained at Fort Des Moines, Charles Houston, who later became dean of Howard University Law School, was disgusted by pervasive military segregation. He wrote: "There is no sense dying in a world ruled by them. German prisoners were kinder than our white American comrades."

After the war, the fort was turned into a hospital facility and then the base for an armored division. The grounds are now a city park.

> **Location:** A historical marker has been placed on the site of Fort Des Moines, just south of the Raccoon River bridge on S.W. 9th St., immediately south of downtown.

Indianola

Simpson College

For a black man to get a higher education in the 1890s was no minor accomplishment. Only a few schools in the Northeast and Midwest, and the black colleges in the segregated South, admitted black students. George Washington Carver had known frustration in his attempts to seek higher education. He moved to Kansas after a childhood in Missouri in order to enter high school, but was refused admittance to one college in Kansas that had accepted him on his academic credentials, when school officials learned his race.

At the age of twenty-six, Carver clung to the idea of becoming a painter. He was fascinated by the prairie, but studied it with the eye of an artist rather than a scientist. Finding college closed to him, he drifted into a series of odd jobs and found himself in Iowa. There he was told that tiny Simpson College might accept a black student. Unconvinced but willing to try, he walked twenty-five miles to Indianola, and to his astonishment was permitted to enter classes.

Simpson at that time was a thirty-year-old school run by the Methodist Episcopal Church. Indianola itself was an upright community, known in Iowa as the Holy City. It was the steadfast dedication to religious principles in Indianola that opened the door to Carver.

He managed to raise money to live on by doing laundry for other students. But the course of his life changed when he began taking science classes. He abandoned his artistic ambitions, convinced he had found his calling. After a year he was accepted at Iowa Agricultural College (now Iowa State) and began the career in science that would lead him to international fame.

Simpson still recalls its most famous alumnus in the name of its science building, which has a plaque and memorial inscription to Carver in its entrance hall.

For information on Carver's subsequent career see the entry on the Tuskegee Institute, Tuskegee, Alabama.

> **Location:** Indianola is 17 miles south of Des Moines, on U.S. 65 and 69.
> **Hours:** Open during daylight hours.
> **Telephone:** (515) 961-6251.

M I C H I G A N

Battle Creek

Sojourner Truth Memorial

The stories about her have the ring of legend. She was born a slave, Isabella Baumfree, in New York's Hudson Valley and grew to a strapping six feet tall. New York emancipated its slaves in 1827 when she was thirty years old, but her owner did not tell her. Then he gave her son to his own daughter when she married and moved to Alabama.

Isabella was eventually freed, but when she learned how she had been betrayed by her owner she prayed to God for vengeance. Shortly afterwards, according to the story, she learned that her former owner's daughter had been killed by her new husband in a drunken rage. Eventually, the courts returned her son, but she was conscience-stricken at how her prayer was answered. She decided that if God was on her side, she would dedicate her life to doing God's work.

"When I left the house of bondage," she said later, "I left everything behind. Wasn't going to keep nothing of Egypt on me. So I went to the Lord and asked him to give me a new name. And the Lord gave me Sojourner for a name, because I was to travel up and down the land, showing people their sins and being a sign unto them."

She later added the surname of Truth as a token of the validity of her message. True to her word, she became a wanderer, speaking out against slavery wherever she was given a forum, from shacks to great halls. She was illiterate but became a powerful speaker, her imposing physical presence backed up with an innate command of language and the rhythm of the spoken word. Her message was usually couched in religious terms. Some contemporary observers said that she had a distinct Dutch accent, having grown up on a Dutch-owned farm.

The stories of her wit abound. Giving an antislavery speech she was heckled from the crowd. "Old woman, do you think your talk about slavery does any good?" she was asked. "I don't care any more about it than I do for the bite of a flea."

"Maybe not," she answered. "But the Lord willing, I'll keep you scratching."

19

Sojourner Truth's tombstone

Another abolitionist was denouncing the cowardice of the churches on the slavery issue when a burst of thunder rattled the hall. A minister leaped to his feet and declared that God's judgement was about to strike them down for such blasphemy. "Don't be scared," shouted Sojourner. "You ain't going to be hurt. I don't expect God ever heard of you."

Once she was listening to a Frederick Douglass address, in which the black abolitionist spoke in despair of the hopelessness of the struggle. When he sat down, Sojourner rose to her feet and, looking directly at Douglass, demanded: "Frederick, is God dead?" The question is inscribed on her tombstone.

She eventually settled in the Battle Creek area. Western Michigan was an especially active center of antislavery sentiment, and one of her daughters had moved there. Stations on the Underground Railroad were abundant in the vicinity, and Sojourner actively assisted escaping slaves in reaching safety in nearby Canada. She was invited to the White House and met with Abraham Lincoln in 1864, and a portrait of her reading the Bible with the President hung in Battle Creek until it was destroyed by fire in 1898. She died in Battle Creek in 1883, and forty-six years later a memorial was erected to her at the site of her grave.

> **Location:** The Sojourner Truth Memorial is in Oakhill Cemetery, immediately south of the business district by way of South St., then left on Oakhill Dr. From I-94, take I-194 north to Exit 3, eastbound Dickman St., then an immediate right on South St. and left on Oakhill Dr. The cemetery is open during daylight hours.
>
> **Additional attractions:** There is a legend that one of the figures on the Soldiers and Sailors Monument in downtown Detroit was modelled after Sojourner Truth. The heroic sculptures were funded by public subscription and unveiled in 1867. She was a frequent visitor to Detroit in those times and a well-known figure in the state, but there is no proof that she actually sat for sculptor Randolph Rogers. Nevertheless, a civil rights march dedicated to her memory, which was held in 1942, ended in a wreath-laying ceremony at the statue. The monument is located at Cadillac Square and Woodward Ave., in the heart of downtown Detroit.

Detroit

Dr. Ossian Sweet House

Late in the summer of 1925, a black physician, Dr. Ossian Sweet, and his family moved into a house on Garland Street, in an all-white area on the east side of Detroit. Detroit was a booming city. The automotive industry was at the height of its prosperity, and people

Dr. Ossian Sweet

from all over the country and the world were pouring into Detroit to get rich. The black community was restricted to an area on the near east side. Few dared or were permitted to buy a home outside the area. But Dr. Sweet, with a thriving practice, decided to make the move. Word of the move swept through the neighborhood, and an angry mob gathered in front of the Sweet house.

Then several shots were fired from an upstairs window. One struck a man standing on his front porch across the street. He died on the way to the hospital. Police stormed the house. Sweet, his wife, and nine other black adults were arrested and charged with either first-degree murder or conspiracy. According to the police report, the shooting was unprovoked.

The city was outraged and public opinion was against the Sweets. The NAACP hired Clarence Darrow, then the country's top criminal attorney, to defend them. It became one of the landmark cases of his long career. As the trial began in late October, the city's mayoral campaign was entering its final days. The Ku Klux Klan was openly backing one of the candidates (the eventual loser) and using the Sweet case to stir emotions in its campaign.

But Darrow slowly and surely broke down the police version of the events before the all-white jury. Finally, Dr. Sweet took the stand and was asked about his feelings on the night of the shooting. "When I opened the door and saw the mob, I realized I was facing the same mob that had hounded my people through its entire history," he said. "I was filled with a peculiar fear, the kind no one could feel unless they had known the history of our race. I knew what mobs had done to my people before."

After forty-six hours of deliberation, the trial ended in a hung jury. The prosecution immediately made a motion for a retrial, but charges against everyone except Dr. Sweet's brother, Henry, were dropped. In the seven-hour closing argument of this second trial, Darrow drew all the strands of the case together: "They took guns there that in case of need they might fight, fight even to the death for their home, and for each other, for their people, for their race, for their rights under the Constitution and the laws under which all of us live; and unless men and women will do that, we will soon be a race of slaves, whether we are black or white."

Presiding Judge Frank Murphy, later the state's governor and a U.S. Supreme Court Justice, said afterward that he was in tears at the end of Darrow's argument, as were many members of the jury. Sweet was acquitted. The case is regarded as a civil rights landmark in establishing the principle that a man has a right to defend his home no matter what his color. It also led to the permanent establishment of the NAACP Legal Defense Fund.

Dr. Sweet lived on Garland Street until 1944. Sixteen years later, with his wife dead and his practice in decline, he committed suicide.

> **Location:** The Sweet house is located at 2905 Garland St. at the corner of Charlevoix St., about three miles east of downtown Detroit by way of East Jefferson Ave. The house is private and there is no admittance. A memorial plaque to the Sweet case, described as the first memorial to a Michigan legal milestone, was unveiled in 1986 in the Frank Murphy Hall of Justice, the Detroit criminal court building named for the judge in the two trials. The Hall is located at the corner of Gratiot and St. Antoine, at the eastern edge of downtown Detroit.

Joe Louis Memorials

On the nights of his fights, in the 1930s and 1940s, it is said you could walk up any street in Detroit's black neighborhood, Paradise Valley, and not miss a single round. Every radio was tuned in, every household clustered around it, and the sounds poured through the open windows into the streets. Then came the inevitable eruption of elation, as the champ, Joe Louis, won another one.

He was Detroit's own hero, the most popular black fighter in the history of the sport. Almost thirty years before Louis won the heavyweight title in 1937, another black fighter, Jack Johnson, had been champion. The country recoiled in horror and for the next seven years cheered on a succession of "great white hopes" to wrest

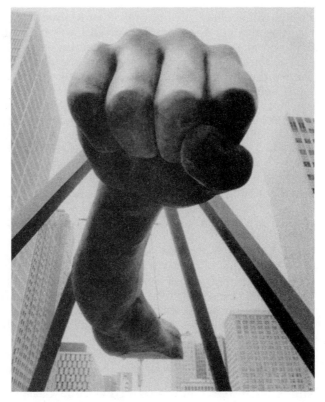

The big fist (a memorial to Joe Louis)

the title from him. Finally, wearied by legal harassment, Johnson lost the title in 1915 to Jess Willard in a fight that many ring historians are convinced he lost deliberately.

Almost none of that racial hatred attached itself to Louis. Born Joseph Louis Barrow in Alabama, he came to Detroit as a child and grew up in poor black neighborhoods on the east side. His quickness and devastating power sent him on a quick rise through the ranks of the heavyweights, and on June 22, 1937, he knocked out Jim Braddock in eight rounds to win the title.

Exactly one year later he was matched against the only man who had ever beaten him during his professional career, Max Schmeling of Germany. Schmeling had been adopted by the Nazis as the perfect example of the Aryan superman. Although Schmeling himself was a decent man, his match against Louis was seen as a clash between good and evil, democracy and dictatorship. When Louis destroyed him in one round, the entire country went mad with joy and the fighter from Detroit became the first black national sports hero.

He held the crown for ten more years, defending it a record twenty-six times and retiring as champion. He also served his country with honor during World War II. He attempted a comeback in 1950 only to be defeated by the new champion, Ezzard Charles, and, after a subsequent knockout by Rocky Marciano, he retired. Afterwards, through financial problems and declining health, he remained one of the country's most popular sports figures. He died in 1981.

As a young man in Detroit, Coleman A. Young was a devoted fan of the fighter. After becoming mayor of the city, Young determined to honor his former hero by naming Detroit's newest sports facility for him. Joe Louis Arena now hosts hockey's Detroit Red Wings, as well as various concerts and civic gatherings.

Young wanted a more artistic commemoration as well. So when the magazine *Sports Illustrated* gave the city a $350,000 gift for the 100th birthday of the Detroit Institute of Arts, the funds were used for a Louis sculpture. The result was unveiled in 1986 and became the city's most controversial piece of art. Sculptor Robert Graham produced a twenty-four-foot-long sculpture of a powerful arm with a clenched fist. As symbolic art, *The Fist* met with acclaim among those who felt it represented the essence of the fighter's power and skill. Others, however, felt it was an unnecessarily violent image for a city that had seen more than its share of violence, and that it led to inevitable comparisons with the Black Power salute.

A more traditional tribute to Louis was put in place the following year in the atrium of the city's Cobo Convention Center. Commissioned by a civic committee, this twelve-foot-high statue, by Louisville sculptor Ed Hamilton, shows Louis in a typical boxing stance.

Hamilton expressed relief that the Graham sculpture had gone up first and taken the heat off his work. "The committee specified a sculpture the community can identify with," he said, "one that looks like the Brown Bomber."

> **Location:** The Graham sculpture, *The Fist*, is mounted at the foot of Detroit's main street, Woodward Ave., at the corner of Jefferson Ave. The Hamilton sculpture is inside Cobo Convention Center, three blocks west on Jefferson Ave.

Motown Museum

He started off as a songwriter. But when he received his first royalty check and found that it amounted to the grand total of $3.40, Berry Gordy, Jr., decided there had to be a better way. He found it, too. Moving into an old house on what was once Detroit's most fashionable thoroughfare, West Grand Boulevard, he started his own record label.

For a black businessman in the late 1950s to enter the record business was unheard of. There was no shortage of black singing stars. Rock and roll ruled the charts, and with its success a whole array of black artists, whose records had never previously been sold to white buyers, had become popular. But the men behind the scenes, who made the decisions and controlled the financing, were white executives in large corporations. Trying to break through the control they exercised and penetrate their distribution networks was regarded as

Motown Museum

an almost impossible task for a seat-of-the-pants operation in an out-of-the-way place like Detroit. But Gordy, a former auto assembly line worker, felt he could do it.

What he imagined was a fresh, black, urban sound. A pounding beat, much like the rhythm of the factories in which he'd worked. Lyrics that reflected real life in the black neighborhoods of the northern cities in the words that people used. Gordy's move also coincided with revelations of "payola" scandals, bribes paid by the major labels to disc jockeys to play certain records on the air. The threat of legal action made many stations far more receptive to playing songs on smaller labels, which never would have received a hearing previously.

An old Detroit friend offered Gordy some songs he had written. Gordy looked through the music, about one hundred songs in all, and politely rejected every one. But he encouraged his friend to keep trying. And Smokey Robinson did. In 1961 Robinson recorded one of his own numbers, "Shop Around," for Gordy's Tamla label. It shot up to number two on the national charts, the first big hit for the company. A few months later, a group of young Detroiters, The Marvelettes, made the breakthrough to number one with "Please, Mr. Postman." Suddenly the sign that Gordy had hung outside the old house proclaiming it to be "Hitsville, U.S.A." didn't seem farfetched at all.

He brought out a new label, Motown, named after the black nickname for Detroit, and throughout the sixties it churned out one hit after another. The Motown Sound and the Beatles defined popular music in this decade, and the only group that rivalled the British quartet in popularity was the Supremes. This trio of young women who started hanging out at the Motown studios, looking for a chance to record, became the label's biggest stars.

Part of the Motown phenomenon was the homegrown talent that turned up at its doors, kids from Detroit neighborhoods who could write and sing with the best of the pros: the Four Tops, the Temptations, Martha and the Vandellas, Mary Wells. Soon the label began to attract talent from other cities. Marvin Gaye came from Washington, D.C., and Stevie Wonder from Flint. By the early seventies, a group of brothers from Gary, Indiana, the Jackson Five, had joined the Motown roster.

And then it ended. Gordy's enterprise had simply outgrown the opportunities available to him in Detroit. He dreamed of expanding into motion pictures and television, and he was a man who believed in the power of dreams. The only logical place for him to be was Los Angeles. So Motown left the Motor City in 1971, leaving behind a whiff of magic, memories, and an old house with a sign out front that reads "Hitsville, U.S.A."

> **Location:** The former headquarters of Motown Records is about 3 miles north of Detroit's central business district. Take the Lodge Fwy. (U.S. 10) to the W. Grand Blvd. exit, then turn left. The museum is at 2648 W. Grand Blvd.
> **Exhibits:** Many of the studios have been restored to the way they looked when the country's biggest hits were recorded there. The museum also contains mementoes of Motown's biggest stars, many of whom continue to live in the Detroit area and record for other labels.
> **Hours:** Monday to Saturday, 10-5; Sunday, 2-5.
> **Admission charge:** Adults, $3; Children, $2.
> **Telephone:** (313) 875-2264.

Museum of African American History

The handsome facility in Detroit's midtown Cultural Center is a tribute to the vision and stubborness of one man. Dr. Charles Wright was an obstetrician. He was troubled that as new generations of black children were being born, there was a danger that the story of previous generations was being forgotten. "Distortions and ignorance may undo us all," he said.

After joining Dr. Martin Luther King, Jr., in the Selma to Montgomery voting rights march in 1965, he returned home determined to preserve the historical record. Within a few months, he had opened a small historical exhibit in his former home and office on the city's west side. He added to it for the next twenty years, wheedling and cajoling funds from the city's black community and its corporations.

"What I'm doing at the museum is an extension of my practice as an obstetrician," he said. "It is how I view the human condition and how I try to intervene on its behalf."

He said that he was inspired by a museum he saw in Denmark, in which the Danes commemorated their resistance to the Nazi occupation. "I thought, if the Danes can do this over four years of repression, we ought to be able to do it for three hundred years."

In 1987 Dr. Wright's dream was realized when the current $3.5 million building opened. Its major ongoing exhibit relates the story of the Underground Railroad and Michigan's role in it. Detroit, with its position on the Canadian border, was one of the primary escape routes for black fugitives. Another section graphically displays the horror of the middle passage, as slaves crossed the Atlantic in the cramped holds of ships.

> **Location:** The museum is located about 2 miles north of downtown Detroit. The best way to reach it is by taking the Chrysler Fwy. (I-75) north to the Warren Ave. exit, left to Brush St. The museum is 2 blocks up on the left. The address is a bit of historical coincidence. The street it faces was formerly known as Frederick St. When the museum opened it was simply changed to Frederick Douglass St.
> **Hours:** Wednesday to Sunday, 10-5.
> **Admission charge:** None.
> **Telephone:** (313) 833-9800.

National Museum of the Tuskegee Airmen

This all-black unit of World War II fighter pilots, who trained at Alabama's Tuskegee Institute, achieved admirable records both in combat with the enemy and against racial discrimination at home in the various military bases at which they were stationed. (See also Tuskegee Institute National Historic Site, Tuskegee, Alabama.) A national group composed of these veterans was formed in 1972 with twenty-two chapters across the country. Many of its members went on to prominence, including Detroit's Mayor Coleman A. Young, in whose hometown the museum of its achievements was placed. It is housed in Fort Wayne, a historic nineteenth-century military post on the Detroit River.

> **Location:** The museum is 3 miles southwest of downtown Detroit and can be reached by taking the Livernois exit of I-75 (Fisher Fwy). Fort Wayne is at the foot of Livernois and W. Jefferson Ave.
> **Exhibits:** Memorabilia of the airmen, displays of their training and combat history, exhibits on their current concerns about minority rights in aviation.

Hours: Wednesday to Sunday, 9:30-5, May-August.
Admission: None.
Telephone: (313) 297-9360.

Idlewild

Famed Black Resort

In the early years of the twentieth century, a black middle class began to develop in the booming midwestern cities of Chicago and Detroit. Outside the cities, though, segregation was still the rule when it came to vacation travel. It was impossible for a black person to book a room at most resorts or to buy property in a private development. In 1912 a group of white developers, sensing a new market, purchased twenty-seven hundred acres of forest land in Lake County, and hired black salesmen to peddle the lots in the cities.

W. E. B. Du Bois bought a lot and his endorsement insured the success of the Idlewild development. Among the other early buyers was the famous Chicago surgeon Dr. Daniel H. Williams (see the entry on Provident Hospital, Chicago, Illinois). His property is now a park.

Idlewild's glory years were from the 1920s to the 1950s. Its Paradise Club was among the top stops on the summer entertainment circuit for black performers. Della Reese and Sarah Vaughn, among others, got their starts there, and the biggest names in show business played the room. One Idlewild resident compared it to New York's famed Catskills.

With the end of segregation and the enforcement of federal equal accommodations laws in the 1960s, Idlewild lost much of its appeal. Many of the homes were sold, some were torn down. But there are still many year-round residents who have been property owners since the old days and fondly recall the resort that used to be.

> **Location:** Idlewild is located about 80 miles north of Grand Rapids by way of U.S. 131 and westbound U.S. 10, in the midst of the Manistee National Forest. The Paridise Club was torn down several years ago, but the residents of the community welcome visitors.

Marshall

Crosswhite Boulder

The southern part of Michigan was settled by New Englanders who brought with them a burning hatred of slavery. Slaves escaping from Kentucky often settled in these communities. One such family was that of Adam Crosswhite. They became residents of the properous town of Marshall, a commercial center on the Detroit-Chicago Trail.

In 1846, a band of slavehunters arrived in the town and demanded that the Crosswhites be turned over as fugitives. When they tried to seize the family, town officials arrested the Kentucky slavers instead and charged them with attempted kidnapping. The Crosswhites were spirited out of town and taken to safety in Canada and then the Kentuckians were released.

The arrest of the slavehunters caused a national sensation. The former owner of the Crosswhites filed a suit for damages against several Marshall officials. The first trial ended in a hung jury. Meanwhile a second group of slavehunters was arrested in nearby Cass County and again the blacks they were seeking were permitted to escape.

Henry Clay and other southerners denounced Michigan on the floor of Congress, demanding punishment for the "Michigan rioters." The controversy was also hurting the presidential bid of Michigan native Lewis Cass, who was seeking the Democratic nomination for 1848. Political pressure was brought to bear on the second trial and the Kentuckian was awarded damages of $1,925, less than half of what he had sought.

The Crosswhite case led directly to southern demands for protection of their property and in 1850 the notorious Fugitive Slave Law was passed by Congress, giving slavehunters the right to retrieve escaped blacks anywhere in the United States.

Location: The Crosswhite Boulder marks the place at which the Kentucky slave hunters were arrested. It is located in Triangle Park, near the business district, at the corner of Michigan Ave. (Business I-94) and Mansion St. Marshall is located southeast of the intersection of I-94 and I-69.

M I N N E S O T A

Minneapolis–St. Paul

Fort Snelling State Historical Park

This limestone citadel, set high on a bluff overlooking the junction of the Mississippi and Minnesota rivers, was once known as the Gibraltar of the West. The lands beyond were unknown and unmapped, the northwestern frontier of the Louisiana Purchase. It was the outpost from which the federal government tried to impose control and some degree of order on its new territories.

Named for Col. Josiah Snelling, its first commander, the fort was completed in 1825. Eleven years later, the new post surgeon, Dr. John Emerson, arrived from St. Louis and brought with him a black slave, Dred Scott.

The two men lived here only two years. But it was on the basis of this residence in territory in which slavery had been outlawed by the Northwest Ordinance that Scott would sue for his freedom ten years later.

There were a handful of black slaves at Fort Snelling at this time. One of them, James Thompson, who owned a business near the fort, was given his freedom when residents of Wisconsin Territory raised funds on his behalf. More significantly, in 1836, a slave girl named Rachel won her freedom in a St. Louis court on the basis of having lived at Fort Snelling. It was this precedent that Scott's attorneys would cite in his own case.

Also living at the fort was Harriet Robinson, a slave owned by a federal Indian agent, Lawrence Taliaferro. In the summer of 1837, she and Scott were married and she was given her freedom. The following spring, as the Scotts were returning to St. Louis by boat, she gave birth to a daughter, born north of the Missouri Compromise line and legally not a slave. This, too, would figure in the historic trials to come (see the entry on the Old Courthouse, St. Louis, Missouri).

> **Location:** Fort Snelling is located south of the Twin Cities. From Minneapolis, take southbound I-35W to eastbound Minnesota 62 and Minnesota 55 to the Fort Snelling exit. From downtown St. Paul, take southbound I-35E to westbound Minnesota 110 and Minnesota 55 to the fort.

Drills at Fort Snelling are carried out by troops costumed as they appeared when Dred Scott lived there

Exhibits: Fort Snelling has been restored to its frontier era appearance. There are seventeen buildings on the grounds and costumed guides play the roles of residents going about their daily jobs. There are also displays of military drill and musketry.
Hours: Daily, 10-5, May through October.
Admission charge: Adults, $2.50.
Telephone: (612) 726-1171.

Akron

Sojourner Truth Monument

The campaigns against slavery and in support of votes for women were natural allies in the mid-nineteenth century. One figure who became a major presence in both camps was Sojourner Truth. She is best known for her impassioned abolitionist oratory and for guiding escaping slaves through the northern portion of the Underground

Sojourner Truth

Railroad (see the entry on the Sojourner Truth Memorial, Battle Creek, Michigan). But she was also an active feminist.

An outstanding speaker, she traveled the country throughout the years of slavery, speaking wherever she found a forum. In 1852, she turned up in Akron to attend the second National Woman Suffrage Convention. W. E. B. Du Bois, in his book *The Gift of Black Folk*, described the scene at the meeting. There was some reluctance to let her speak. The suffragettes were predominantly women of wealth and education and a six-foot-tall black woman was not quite the spokesperson the movement welcomed. Nonetheless, when Sojourner Truth wanted to speak it was rather difficult to deny her.

The speakers, many of them men, had stressed the helplessness of women and their need for the assistance of men to win their program. It was at this point that she rose to speak.

"That man over there says that women have to be helped into carriages and lifted over ditches and to have the best places everywhere. Nobody ever helped me into carriages or over mud puddles or gave me any best place. And ain't I a woman?

"Look at me! Look at my arm! (And Du Bois says she bared her muscular arm to her shoulder and drew herself to her full height at this point.) I have plowed and planted and gathered into barns and no man could beat me—and ain't I a woman? I could work as much and eat as much as a man, when I could get it, and bear the lash as well—and ain't I woman?

"I have borne thirteen children and seen most of them sold off into slavery and when I cried out with a mother's grief none but Jesus heard—and ain't I a woman?"

Mrs. Frances Gage, presiding officer of the convention, wrote that when she had finished speaking, the crowd rushed to her to shake her hands and offer their respect and congratulations. "I have never in my life seen anything like the magical influence that subdued the mobbish spirit of the day and turned the jibes and sneers of an excited crowd into notes of respect and admiration," wrote Mrs. Gage.

The speech is regarded as a landmark in the history of both the abolitionist and feminist movements.

> **Location:** The site of Sojourner Truth's speech is now occupied by the Donner Press Building, at 37 N. High St., in the heart of downtown Akron. A stone monument marks the location.

Cincinnati

Stowe House

Born in New England, Harriet Beecher Stowe came to Cincinnati as a young woman of twenty when her father, Rev. Lyman Beecher, was appointed to head Lane Theological Seminary. During the years

Stowe House, Cincinnati

she spent here she would acquire a firsthand knowledge of slavery that would find its way into her landmark novel a few years later.

Rev. Beecher was an ardent abolitionist but felt it necessary to prohibit any discussion of the slavery issue at the seminary. Cincinnati was an emotional tinderbox in the 1830s. Some of his students had outraged local citizens by walking down city streets with blacks. With the slaveholding state of Kentucky just across the Ohio River, he was afraid of violent confrontations, but he found it impossible to keep a lid on the students' outrage. One of his students, Calvin Stowe, married his daughter. It was only after they had moved to Maine and she had a chance to reflect upon her experiences in Cincinnati, however, that she wrote *Uncle Tom's Cabin* (Mrs. Stowe's experiences in the area are also discussed in the entries on the Rankin House, Ripley, Ohio; and on the Old Slave Market, Washington, Kentucky).

> **Location:** The Stowe House is located east of downtown Cincinnati by way of 7th St. Just as it curves toward I-71, the street becomes Gilbert Ave. The house is located at 2950 Gilbert. Although it is named after Mrs. Stowe, this was actually the residence of the Beechers from 1832 to 1836. It is now a museum of the Beecher and Stowe families and their campaign against slavery, and of black achievements.
> **Hours:** Tuesday to Thursday, 10-4.
> **Admission charge:** None.
> **Telephone:** (513) 632-5120.

Taft Museum

When Nicholas Longworth, one of this city's wealthiest men, built his mansion east of downtown in the 1850s, he turned to a fellow Cincinnatian, Robert Duncanson, to paint the murals for his entrance hall. The Longworth home eventually was purchased by an equally prominent local family, the Tafts. It was on the front steps of this house that William Howard Taft accepted the Republican nomination for the presidency in 1908. It has been the Taft Museum since 1932 and the entrance hall still displays the work of Duncanson, the only surviving murals by one of the nineteenth century's greatest black artists.

Duncanson was born in New York and took up residence in Cincinnati as a teenager, sometime in the 1830s. He was sent to study art in Britain for three years by the local Freedman's Aid Society and upon his return made his living as an artist and in daguerreotypy. By the 1850s he was recognized as the foremost portraitist and landscape artist in the city. The portrait of Longworth he did at the time hangs in the Taft Museum. In the 1860s a London journal hailed him as one of the top landscape artists in the world. At the peak of his fame, however, he suffered a mental breakdown and died in a Detroit rest home in 1872.

> **Location:** The museum is located at 316 Pike St., at the eastern edge of downtown Cincinnati.
> **Exhibits:** Besides the Duncanson murals, the Taft Museum also has a fine collection of European art, enameled plaques, Chinese porcelain and jewelry.
> **Hours:** Monday to Saturday, 10-5, and Sunday, 2-5.
> **Admission charge:** None.
> **Telephone:** (513) 241-0343.
> **Handicapped access:** Yes.

Cleveland

African American Museum

One of the stated themes of this facility, which was established in 1956, is to correct errors of omission in black history. For example, displays celebrate the achievements of little-known Cleveland inventor Garrett A. Morgan, who did as much as anyone to reshape American street scenes, giving the world the first automatic traffic light. Before Morgan's device was installed in 1923, traffic control signals were operated manually by a police officer perched above the streets in a tower. Morgan's invention made a smooth traffic flow possible (theoretically, at least) over a long stretch of roadway.

Morgan also invented a belt fastener for sewing machines, but the invention he was able to use most dramatically was a smoke mask. He had been awarded a gold medal for the invention in 1914, and two

Garrett Morgan, inventor of the traffic light

years later when an excavating party was trapped by a gas explosion under Lake Erie, Morgan was called in to assist the rescue with his smoke mask. Assisted by his brother, he entered the fume-filled shaft and pulled six workers out. Only two of them survived, and a total of seventeen were killed that day. Morgan was acclaimed as a hero in Cleveland, but he was haunted until the end of his life by what he experienced in that rescue. "When I shut my eyes I can still see the men curled up in that death chamber," he said years later.

Location: From downtown Cleveland, head east on Chester Ave. (U.S. 322). Immediately past E. 82nd St., look for the turnoff on the left to Crawford Rd. The museum is located at 1765 Crawford Rd.
Hours: Monday to Thursday and Saturday, 12-3; Friday, 12-8.
Admission charge: $2.
Telephone: (216) 791-1700.

Karamu House

The word is Swahili for a "center of enjoyment, a place to be entertained." Karamu House has earned a national reputation as a

center of black culture. Its theater presents the works of young
African-American playwrights, classics of black theater and revivals.
In the 1990 season, for example, it mounted the first production of
Paul Laurence Dunbar's *In Dahomey* in seventy-five years.

Karamu House was founded in 1915 by Russell and Rowena Jelliffe
as a multicultural center for Cleveland's ethnically diverse east side.
In the 1960s, however, with growing black cultural awareness, it
became predominantly an African-American facility.

> **Location:** Karamu House is reached from downtown
> Cleveland by heading east on Euclid Ave. (U.S. 20) and
> then right on E. 89th St. It is located at the corner of 89th
> and Quincy Ave.
> **Telephone:** (216) 795-7070.

Dayton

Paul Laurence Dunbar House

In a matter of months, he went from running an elevator in a
Dayton office building to being the most famous young poet in
America. It was a far dizzier ascent than anything he had experienced
on his elevator, and for Paul Laurence Dunbar it began a ten-year
ride that would lead to international acclaim, illness, alcoholism, and
death at the age of 34.

Born in Dayton, Dunbar was the child of former slaves and the only
black in his high-school class. He was editor of the school paper,
president of the literary society, the star of the debating team, and a
member of the honor society. With college out of reach financially,
the only job open to him was running an elevator at $4 a week. He
made use of his time on these vertical trips, though, by reading
voraciously and writing poetry. His first volume, *Oak and Ivy*, was
published by a local church in 1892, when he was twenty-two years
old. Dunbar underwrote part of the cost by selling it to his elevator
passengers. It was written in African-American dialect, which was
regarded as a startling innovation. There had been other African-
American dialect poets, but none with Dunbar's command of the
language: most black poets with his skills chose to write in a more
formal, academic style.

Slowly, his fame spread throughout Ohio and, finally, a volume of
his poetry reached William Dean Howells, the most influential literary
critic in the country. The rave review Howells gave Dunbar in
Harper's Magazine in 1896 made him a major American poet. He was
invited to New York, and Howells enthusiastically wrote the introduction to his next volume of poems, *Lyrics of Lowly Life*. It went through
eleven printings and became one of the best-known volumes of poetry
in those times.

A prolific writer, Dunbar turned out a rapid succession of poems
and articles for the top periodicals. He toured England for a series of

Paul Laurence Dunbar

readings and was lionized by the British. However, his British tour manager had skimmed the profits, leaving Dunbar broke and stranded, and he had to repay the debts he incurred. Financial pressures forced him to publish work that he felt was less then his best. In addition, he was frustrated to find that there was no interest in his work other than that written in black dialect. "I'm tired of dialect but the magazines aren't," he wrote at the time. "Every time I send them something else they write back asking for dialect. A Dunbar just has to be dialect, that's all." '

A frail man, he finally collapsed under the pace and later was diagnosed with tuberculosis. To ease his wracking cough, doctors prescribed whiskey, and Dunbar soon developed a drinking problem. His marriage failed and his health continued to deteriorate. He died in Dayton in 1906. "He was not, perhaps, a great poet, but he was a real one," noted the *Boston Evening Transcript* in his obituary. "He has given value and permanence to the folklore of the race in this country."

Location: The Dunbar House, built with the profits he made from *Lyrics of the Lowly*, is west of Dayton. From I-75, take the westbound 3rd St. exit (Ohio 4) and turn right at

Summit Ave. The house, at 219 N. Summit, is furnished almost as it was at his death.
Hours: Wednesday to Saturday, 9:30-5, Sunday, 12-5, Memorial Day to Labor Day; Saturday and Sunday only, Labor Day to late October.
Admission charge: $1.50.
Telephone: (513) 224-7061.

Gallipolis

Emancipation Festival

On September 22, 1862, buoyed by news of the Union victory at Antietam, President Lincoln issued the Emancipation Proclamation, freeing all slaves in the Confederacy. Ever since, this Ohio River town has observed a two-day celebration on the weekend closest to that date. Ironically, the Proclamation affected only those enslaved in the southern states. Another 800,000 slaves in the border states remained unaffected by it until the end of the war.

> **Location:** Gallipolis is 45 miles north of Huntington, West Virginia, by way of Ohio 7. The celebration is held at the Junior Fairgrounds, on the Jackson Pike.
> **Telephone:** (614) 446-4120.

Oberlin

John M. Langston House

John M. Langston was elected clerk of an Ohio township in 1855. This vote marked the first time a black man had been elected to public office anywhere in the United States.

Langston was a graduate of Oberlin College, which had been formed in 1833 with the expressed purpose of educating a generation of abolitionists. Other schools had allowed black students to enter, but Oberlin was the first to make nondiscriminatory admissions an official policy. By the start of the Civil War, one-third of its student body was black.

Langston, born in Virginia, was freed as a young man and sent to Cincinnati to attend school. He received a degree in theology from Oberlin and later returned to graduate from its law school. He became a recruiting agent for black regiments during the Civil War, the first dean of the Howard University Law School, minister to Haiti, and, in 1888, was elected U.S. Representative from Virginia. But charges of voter fraud kept him out of the seat he had won for all but the last few months of his term, and he was not re-elected in 1890.

John M. Langston

Location: The Langston House, a National Historical Landmark, is located at 207 East College St., just off the Oberlin campus. Oberlin is about 40 miles southwest of Cleveland, by way of Ohio 10.

Ripley

Rankin House

High on a bluff above the Ohio River, the beacon from the Rankin House shone in the night, through the darkness of slaveholding Kentucky across the water, to light the way for escaping slaves. Rev. John Rankin had sought out this site carefully. He deliberately tried to provoke Kentuckians. He dared them to try and stop him. He risked alienating his Presbyterian flock, not all of whom sympathized with his antislavery stand. And after passage of the Fugitive Slave Act of 1850 he risked his own property in carrying on the struggle: anyone caught sheltering slaves could be heavily fined.

The rickety stairway that leads from the Ohio River to the Rankin House

The Rankin House became one of the most important entry points on the Underground Railroad. Between 1825 and the end of the Civil War, the minister and his family are credited with sheltering more than two thousand escaping slaves, as many as a dozen at a time, and helping them head north to Canada. Their proudest claim was that they never lost a passenger to slavehunters. Rankin organized an entire network of allies and developed an assortment of tricks to foil pursuers, including decoy escapes and the spreading of deliberate misinformation.

He was actively preaching against slavery in Tennessee as early as 1815 but decided the most direct involvement would be in Ohio, a state in which slavery had been outlawed by the Northwest Ordinance of 1787. The beacon on the river bluff soon became a goal known to every Kentucky slave seeking freedom.

One of the stories Rankin delighted in retelling was the daring winter escape of a young woman, who crossed the river on ice floes while clutching her children in her arms. The story was later used by Rankin's friend, Harriet Beecher Stowe, for the episode involving the character of Eliza in *Uncle Tom's Cabin*.

Rankin lived to see slavery abolished and died at the age of ninety-three. The house became a state memorial in 1938 and is run on a nonprofit basis by Ripley Heritage, Inc. and the Ohio Historical Society.

> **Location:** Ripley is on U.S. 52, about 55 miles southeast of Cincinnati. The Rankin house is at the western edge of town and is reached by a blacktop road ascending Liberty Hill. Guided tours by local history enthusiasts, dressed in mid-nineteenth-century costume, enliven the visit. Many items belonging to the Rankin family are found throughout the house.
>
> **Hours:** Wednesday to Sunday, 12-5, Memorial Day to Labor Day.
>
> **Admission charge:** $1.
>
> **Telephone:** (513) 392-1627.
>
> **Other attractions:** A memorial to John Rankin and his wife, Jean, saluting them as "freedom's Heroes," can be found in Maplewood Cemetery, off U.S. 52, in the eastern end of town.

Upper Sandusky

Wyandotte Indian Missionary Church

John Stewart was a dyer, a former alcoholic who found the strength to put aside drink when he became a Methodist. Early histories describe him as being disabled in early life by illness, but there is no description of how severe his disability was. His father was a black

Virginia freedman who claimed to be descended from Indians. But there is no way of knowing this for a fact, either.

In 1814 Stewart was living in the growing frontier town of Marietta, Ohio, and was taken ill. He promised to dedicate his life to church service if he recovered. Going out into the fields, he wrote later, he heard a voice saying "You must declare my counsel faithfully." The voice seemed to come from the northwest, so Stewart, a simple and uneducated man, struck out in that direction. He came to land inhabited by Christianized native Americans, the Delaware, and was told of another tribe living further to the northwest, the Wyandotte, who had not been converted. Stewart concluded that this was where he was meant to go.

He arrived in the settlement of Upper Sandusky in 1816 and after telling his story to impressed settlers was directed to another black man, Jonathan Pointer. A former slave, Pointer had been carried off by Indians on a raid into Kentucky and was raised among the Wyandotte. Using Pointer as an interpreter, Stewart began to preach. He had a fine singing voice and from all accounts it was his songs that delighted the Wyandotte and enticed them to listen to the religious message. He stayed on until his death seven years later and left a converted community behind.

The church that stands in Upper Sandusky was built in 1824, the year after his death. When the Wyandotte were removed to Kansas by the federal government in 1843, one of their stipulations was that the mission remain under the auspices of the Methodist Church. It has been designated a shrine by that church.

> **Location:** Upper Sandusky is located in north central Ohio, about 70 miles north of Columbus by way of U.S. 23. Take the westbound U.S. 30 exit into town, then turn north on Ohio 53 to Church St. The mission is 1 block to the right. There is a memorial marker to Stewart at the entrance to the mission cemetery and his grave is near the church.
> **Hours:** Irregular; call in advance.
> **Telephone:** (419) 294-4841.

While you walk through the old cemetery, by the way, notice the tombstone near the path on which the date of death is given as February 31.

Westerville

Benjamin Hanby Home

As antislavery ferment swept the northern states in the 1850s, it wasn't only the written word that stirred emotions. One of the most powerful abolitionist arguments was contained in a song.

"Darling Nelly Gray" was published in 1856 and in the years prior to the Civil War it helped, to use a contemporary phrase, raise consciousness about the human toll of slavery. The ballad is sung by Nelly's lover, who is separated from her forever when she is sold by their Kentucky plantation-owner in Georgia. The chorus laments:

O my poor Nelly Gray, they have taken you away.
And I'll never see my darling anymore.
I'm sitting by the river, and I'm weeping all the day.
For you've gone from the old Kentucky shore.

The composer of the song was Benjamin Hanby, a young theological student and schoolteacher. According to several sources, he was moved to write the ballad by a gravestone he saw in his boyhood home of Rushville, Ohio. It marked the grave of Joe Selby, an escaped slave, who, according to abolitionists in the town, related on his deathbed the story that Hanby turned into "Nelly Gray." In 1933, on the centennial of Hanby's birth, several of his former students recalled him writing the words to the song on the blackboard as a classroom singing exercise. Hanby's family had moved to Westerville by this time and it is believed that he actually composed the song in that home.

Despite the national popularity of the song, Hanby received no royalties. The publishing company told him that the fame he received was reward enough, indicating the absence of a lawyer in the proceedings. Hanby went on to write several other politically-inspired songs and died at the age of thirty-four in 1867. Interest in Hanby was revived at his centennial, and his home here was dedicated as a state memorial in 1937.

Location: Westerville is just northeast of Columbus, by way of the northbound Ohio 3 exit from I-270, the beltway that encircles the city. The Hanby House is at 160 W. Main St. Also a stop on Ohio's Underground Railroad network, it contains many of Hanby's personal belongings.
Hours: Saturday, 10-4, and Sunday, 1-5, May to September.
Admission charge: $1.
Telephone: (614) 891-6289.

Wilberforce

National Afro-American Museum and Cultural Center, Wilberforce University, Col. Charles Young House

Walk into this museum and you return to the America of 1955, a country at the pivotal point of its civil rights history. Funded by a 1971 act of Congress, the museum takes a unique approach to the era it covers. It places the civil rights revolution in its historical setting by

National Afro-American Museum on the campus of Wilberforce University

examining not only the great issues of the times, but the minutiae of daily life. So there are galleries dealing with typical businesses, churches and homes in the African-American community of the fifties. There is an examination of how music influenced this community, and of how the northern migration and the consequences of World War II shaped the civil rights movement.

This approach humanizes history and makes the setting intelligible for those too young to remember the times firsthand and for those whose ideas of fifties nostalgia extends only to white America.

Included in the museum is an art gallery, with a permanent collection and changing exhibits of contemporary African-American painting and sculpture. The striking thirty-five thousand square foot facility is expandable and the final plan calls for it to grow to about seven times its present size and house a research and conference center.

The museum is located on the original campus of Wilberforce University, the oldest black-run institution of higher learning in the country. It grew from a seminary established in 1856 by the African Methodist Episcopal Church, which combined, seven years later, with another church-run school and was renamed Wilberforce, in honor of a British abolitionist. Wilberforce was the first school to experiment with the work-study program. This became a national model according to which poor black students obtained their education by working for the schools they attended. The Ohio legislature formed a state-run normal and industrial school for blacks in 1888 which was run on the same campus but with a different board of trustees. This unusual arrangement lasted until 1947, when Central State University became a separate institution. Wilberforce has moved to a new campus nearby and the historic campus is now part of the museum conference center.

> **Location:** Wilberforce is located about 20 miles east of Dayton. From I-75, take the eastbound U.S. 35 exit at West Lancaster to Xenia, then north on U.S. 42. The museum is on Brush Row Rd., which runs north from U.S. 42. The road passes the campus of Central State before reaching the museum and the old Wilberforce Campus. The Carnegie Library now houses museum administrative staff, and historic Emery Hall, a former dormitory, will become a conference center.
> **Hours:** Tuesday to Saturday, 9-5, and Sunday, 1-5.
> **Admission charge:** $1.
> **Telephone:** (513) 376-4944.
> **Handicapped access:** Yes.
> **Other attractions:** The present Wilberforce campus is on the south side of U.S. 42. On the highway nearby, the Omega Psi Phi fraternity house is the onetime home of Col. Charles Young, a former instructor of military history at Central State and the highest ranking black officer in the U.S. Army during World War I.
> **Telephone:** (513) 376-6011.

Xenia

"Blue Jacket"

The historical epic, complete with special effects and an outdoor setting, has become a staple of summertime America. *Blue Jacket*, performed in Caesar's Ford Park near Xenia, is one of the few to tell the story of the westward expansion from the viewpoint of native Americans. Its story revolves around the attempts by Ohio's Indians to hold off the tide of white settlement.

Drawn from both historical sources and legend, the Xenia production is the story of a white Shawnee chief and his ally, a black warrior named Caesar, who try to defend their lands in the Ohio of the late eighteenth century. The production features fifty actors, as well as antique firearms and flaming arrows dramatically shot into the sky. Caesar's Creek runs through the tract on which the amphitheater is set.

> **Location:** Caesar's Ford Park is located southeast of Xenia. From the center of town, take Jasper Rd. from its junction with U.S. 35.
> **Hours:** Tuesday to Sunday, early June to Labor Day, at 8:30 p.m.
> **Admission charge:** Adults, $10; children under 13, $6.
> **Telephone:** (513) 376-4318.

W I S C O N S I N

Janesville-Milton

Tallman Restorations, Milton House

This part of south-central Wisconsin was a major transfer point on the Underground Railroad. Wisconsin was among the most liberal of northern states, many of its settlers arriving here in the 1840s as refugees from failed revolutionary movements in Europe. They reacted strongly against slavery and enthusiastically enlisted in the work of sheltering fugitives and helping them on their way to safety. The Janesville area contains two of the most unique structures employed in this fashion.

William M. Tallman was a wealthy attorney and outspoken abolitionist when he moved here from New York. The Italianate mansion he built in Janesville, completed in 1857, was regarded as a marvel of the northwestern frontier. It featured running water, central heating, plumbing, and other conveniences known only to the great cities of the East. It also contained space in its twenty-six rooms for hiding slaves. Surely one of the most lavish stops on the Underground Railroad, the house also welcomed Abraham Lincoln as an overnight guest in 1859, the year before his election precipitated the Civil War.

Joseph Goodrich was also a New Yorker. He arrived in the area eleven years before Tallman to run a stagecoach inn in Milton, which was then a focus for overland travel in Wisconsin. The Inn's basement was connected by a tunnel to an adjacent log cabin and it was here that Goodrich hid slaves who passed through the area. The Milton House is also known as the first structure made of poured concrete in the United States.

> **Location:** The Tallman Restorations are just north of Janesville's business district, on U.S. 14, at 440 N. Jackson St. Milton is located 6 miles to the northeast by way of Wisconsin 26. The Milton House is near the intersection of that road with Wisconsin 59, near the center of town, at 18 S. Janesville St.
>
> **Exhibits:** The Tallman Restoration is regarded as one of the country's most significant Civil War era homes. It is furnished with articles accurately reflecting the domestic

The Tallman House

style of the upper middle class. The Stone House, also on the property, was built in 1842 and is designed to show the life of those with lesser means. The Milton House has also been restored and a country store and livery are on the grounds.

Hours: Tallman Restoration, Tuesday to Sunday, 11-4, June to August; weekends only in May, September, and the first three weekends in October. Milton House, daily, 11-4, June to Labor Day; weekends only in May and from Labor Day to mid-October.

Admission charge: $3 to each.

Telephone: Tallman Restorations, (608) 752-4519; Milton House, (608) 868-7772.

Handicapped access: Tallman Restorations, no; Milton House, yes.

Madison

Wisconsin Historical Society

One of the largest archives of material relating to the civil rights movement is being assembled here. It contains material going back to the founding of the National Association for the Advancement of Colored People (NAACP), but it concentrates especially on the 1950s through the 1970s.

Included in its collection are the complete papers of the Congress on Racial Equality and the histories of many of the small Mississippi organizations that struggled to wrest political control from the state's regular Democratic party. The Historical Society mounts occasional exhibits drawn from the archive materials, but it is primarily a research facility.

> **Location:** The Wisconsin Historical Society is at 816 State St.
> **Hours:** Monday to Friday, 8-5, and Saturday, 9-4.
> **Admission charge:** none.
> **Telephone:** (608) 262-3266.
> **Handicapped access:** Yes.

2

The Northeast

Connecticut
•
Delaware
•
Maine
•
Maryland
•
Massachusetts
•
New Hampshire
•
New Jersey
•
New York
•
Pennsylvania
•
Rhode Island
•
Vermont

The Northeast

CONNECTICUT

1. First Church of Christ, The Amistad Trials
Farmington
2. Fort Griswold State Park, *Groton*
3. United Church-on-the-Green, *New Haven*

DELAWARE

4. Richard Allen Marker, *Dover*
5. Asbury Methodist Episcopal Church, *Wilmington*

MAINE

6. First Parish Church, Stowe House, Peary-McMillan Arctic Museum, *Brunswick*

MARYLAND

7. Banneker-Douglass Museum, *Annapolis*
8. Matthew Henson Memorial, *Annapolis*
9. Cab Calloway Jazz Institute at Coppin State College, *Baltimore*
10. Eubie Blake Cultural Center, *Baltimore*
11. Great Blacks in Wax Museum, *Baltimore*
12. Morgan State University, *Baltimore*
13. Harriet Tubman Birthplace, *Cambridge*
14. Antietam National Battlefield, *Sharpsburg*

MASSACHUSETTS

15. African Meeting House, Abiel Smith School, *Boston*
16. Boston Massacre Site, Granary Burying Ground, Crispus Attucks Monument, *Boston*
17. Robert Gould Shaw and Fifty-fourth Regiment Memorial, *Boston*
18. W. E. B. Du Bois Memorial, *Great Barrington*
19. Jan Ernst Matzeliger Statue, *Lynn*
20. African Baptist Church, *Nantucket*
21. Whaling Museum, *New Bedford*
22. Witch House, *Salem*
23. Paul Cuffe Memorial and Farm, *Westport*

NEW HAMPSHIRE

24. Amos Fortune's Legacy, *Jaffrey*

NEW JERSEY

25. Afro-American Historical Museum, *Jersey City*
26. *Lawnside*
27. Paul Robeson Center of Rutgers University at Newark, *Newark*
28. Grave of First Black Voter, *Perth Amboy*
29. T. Thomas Fortune House, *Red Bank*

NEW YORK

30. Harriet Tubman House, *Auburn*
31. Madame Walker Home, *Irvington*
32. Fraunces Tavern, *New York City*
33. Louis Armstrong House, *New York City*
34. St. George's Episcopal Church, *New York City*
35. Abyssinian Baptist Church, *New York City: Harlem*
36. Apollo Theatre, Hotel Theresa, *New York City: Harlem*
37. Black Fashion Museum, *New York City: Harlem*
38. Shomburg Center for Research in Black Culture, *New York City: Harlem*
39. Strivers' Row, Historic Homes of West 135th Street, *New York City: Harlem*
40. Studio Museum of Harlem, *New York City: Harlem*
41. Frederick Douglass Memorial and Grave, Susan B. Anthony House, *Rochester*

PENNSYLVANIA

42. James Bland Grave, *Bala Cynwyd*
43. Thaddeus Stevens Tomb, *Lancaster*
44. Lincoln University, *Oxford*
45. Afro-American Historical and Cultural Museum, *Philadelphia*
46. All-Wars Memorial to Black Soldiers, *Philadelphia*
47. Frances Ellen Watkins Harper House, *Philadelphia*
48. Henry O. Tanner House, *Philadelphia*
49. Johnson House, *Philadelphia*
50. Mother Bethel AME Church, *Philadelphia*
51. St. George's Methodist Church, *Philadelphia*

RHODE ISLAND

52. Black Regiment Memorial of the Battle of Rhode Island, *Portsmouth*
53. Rhode Island Black Heritage Society, *Providence*

VERMONT

54. Garrison Marker, Bennington Museum, *Bennington*
55. Constitution House, *Windsor*

Pennsylvania

C O N N E C T I C U T

Farmington

First Church of Christ, The Amistad Trials

In the last week of August, 1839, the U.S. Navy brig *Washington*, engaged in a coastal survey near Montauk Point, Long Island, came upon a ship that seemed to have sailed out of a legend. Manned by Africans who spoke no English, the slave ship *Amistad* would soon become the focus of the growing abolitionist movement and pit two U.S. presidents against each other.

It had left Havana almost two months before on a routine delivery of slaves to plantations along the Cuban coast. But among its human cargo was a natural leader, a persuasive orator, called Cinque. Brutalized to the point of desperation, the recently kidnapped slaves mutinied under Cinque's direction. Most of the crew was killed in the first rush on deck. Two Cuban planters who had purchased the blacks were kept alive on condition that they sail the ship back to Sierra Leone, on Africa's west coast.

While the Cubans sailed east by day under Cinque's watchful eye, they doubled back at night to the northwest. After six weeks of this zig-zag journey they found themselves off Montauk Point. When sailors from the *Washington* boarded the *Amistad* (Spanish for friendship), the Cubans greeted them as rescuers. They demanded to be returned with their slaves to Cuba. But when the ship landed at New London, Connecticut, the press picked up the story and abolitionists demanded protection for the slaves.

President Martin Van Buren's administration backed the Cubans. Despite the fact that a nineteen-year-old treaty with Great Britain outlawed the slave trade in Spain's colonies in the West Indies, the Attorney General held that the slaves should be returned. A federal attorney was appointed to represent the Cubans in a trial.

The court in New Haven ruled in favor of the slaves and ordered them transported back to Africa. But the government appealed, and the case advanced to the U.S. Supreme Court in February 1841. This time the slaves were represented by one of the most illustrious men in New England, former president John Quincy Adams. Now a Congressman, Adams was outraged at Van Buren's handling of the matter. In a withering, four-and-a-half hour speech, Adams ridiculed

The slave ship "Amistad"

the president and tore apart the contention that the slaves were Cuban natives, not covered by the provisions of the treaty with Britain. He also produced secret correspondence which indicated that had the slaves lost the original trial, arrangements had been made to return them immediately to Cuba with no right of appeal. The Court ruled that the slaves be set free.

While awaiting the outcome of these trials, the *Amistad* insurrectionists were taken to Farmington, a town with strong abolitionist sympathies. They were given schooling and religious instruction, while funds were raised for their defense and return to Africa. The First Church of Christ was their center of community life during the stay.

Their return to Africa was not a happy one. Cinque and many others found that their families had been sold into slavery during their absence. A mission was established there and called Mendi, the native name for the region. Descendants of the *Amistad* slaves lived there through the 1880s. The *Amistad* incident had a more beneficial aftermath in America. In 1846 several groups that had worked on behalf of the mutineers formed the American Missionary Association, which was instrumental in founding many of the leading black universities of the nineteenth century.

> **Location:** Farmington is 9 miles west of Hartford, by way of Farmington Rd. (Connecticut 4). The Congregational Church is at 75 Main St. It is a National Historic Landmark and is also recognized as a fine example of Georgian architecture. In nearby Farmington Cemetery is

a memorial to a member of the *Amistad* group, Foone, who accidentally drowned while in Farmington.
Hours: Monday to Friday, 8-4.
Telephone: (203) 677-2601.

Groton

Fort Griswold State Park

One month before the final battle of the Revolutionary War, one of that conflict's least glorious and most treacherous chapters was written here. The British had no love for the Connecticut towns on Long Island Sound. Vessels from these ports had raided British shipping throughout the war, inflicting costly losses in supplies and vessels. In September 1781, under the direction of the turncoat Benedict Arnold, the British launched a retaliatory strike on the most troublesome of these towns.

A rebel force at Groton provided unexpected resistance. Holding the hilltop Fort Griswold, they stalled the British attack for hours and inflicted heavy casualties. Finally overcome by sheer weight of numbers, the American commander, Col. William Ledyard, offered his sword as a token of surrender.

The British were infuriated, however, because a black orderly, Jordan Freeman, had cut down one of their officers in the battle. The officer who took the sword ran Ledyard through with it, killing him. Immediately, another black orderly, Lambert Latham, attacked the British officer and was cut down by bayonets. This touched off a wholesale slaughter and eighty-four Americans, most of whom had already surrendered, were massacred. Among the dead was Freeman.

> **Location:** Groton is directly east of New London, across the Thames River. Fort Griswold is south of town, off U.S. 1.
> **Exhibits:** A 135-foot high monument near the site of the fort contains a tablet listing the victims of the massacre. Monument House nearby has relics of the battle.
> **Hours:** The monument and museum are open daily, 9-5, Memorial Day to Labor Day; weekends only, until Columbus Day.
> **Admission charge:** None.
> **Telephone:** None.

New Haven

United Church-on-the-Green

The city was named for a port in England, but through its history it was indeed a haven. First it protected Puritans who fled the

Jordan Freeman

vengeance of the Royalists after the Stuarts were restored to the British throne in 1660. Then, two hundred years later, its citizens provided a haven for countless black slaves escaping to Canada. New Haven was a hotbed of abolitionists and its churches, especially the three prominent congregations on The Green, led the way.

While all were active in the struggle against slavery, the most fervent was the United Church, which was then known as North Church. In a famous sermon delivered in 1855 by Rev. Henry Ward Beecher, the Brooklyn clergymen who was the brother of Harriet Beecher Stowe, funds for eighty Bibles and eighty rifles were raised for a company of men setting out to fight pro-slavery forces in Kansas. Both items were regarded as necessities.

> **Location:** The Green is in the heart of the city, adjoining Yale University. United Church is at the corner of Temple and Elm Streets.
>
> **Exhibits:** Besides its abolitionist associations, the church, built in 1815, is regarded as an outstanding example of New England architecture.
>
> **Hours:** Tuesday to Thursday, 9:30-4:30.
>
> **Telephone:** (203) 787-4195.

D E L A W A R E

Dover

Richard Allen Marker

The founder of the African Methodist Episcopal Church was a gifted orator and a man of inspirational presence. His early years as a slave in Delaware gave an indication of that. Among the first converts he made was his owner, who had permitted Allen to study religion. Allen purchased his freedom shortly after this religious awakening

Rev. Richard Allen

59

and went on to Philadelphia, where he played a leading role in both the religious and political history of black Americans in the early years of the nineteenth century (see also the entries for the Mother Bethel AME Church and St. George's Methodist Church, Philadelphia, Pennsylvania).

> **Location:** The historical marker, which was unveiled in 1990 on the 230th anniversary of Allen's birth, is at Lockerman and Federal Streets, just north of The Green and the State Capitol.

Wilmington

Asbury Methodist Episcopal Church

It wasn't only political revolution that swept America in the late eighteenth century. A parallel revolution was going on in religious life, too. The Great Awakening spread a spirit of theological democracy throughout the colonies and newly formed churches began challenging the Episcopal establishment.

One of the most widely accepted of the new religious doctrines was Methodism. Francis Asbury was its most eloquent American spokesman, and in 1773, as revolutionary discontent swept the British colonies, he presided over its first conference in the colonies. In 1784, three years after the Revolution was won, his church formally broke with the Episcopalians and Asbury became its first bishop.

In its early years, the new church welcomed blacks in the spirit of democracy. The Wilmington church, dedicated by Asbury in 1789, had several black parishioners. Asbury's gifts as a speaker were such that many Established Church members, who did not deign to enter his building, would instead gather nearby to hear him preach. According to a local tradition, Asbury sometimes asked one of the church's black members, who was known as Harry, to deliver the sermon in his place. The crowd outside, under the impression that they were listening to the renowned bishop, went away completely satisfied. By 1805, however, the church was insisting that black parishioners be restricted to the upper galleries. At that point, those members split off to form their own congregation.

> **Location:** The church is at 3d St. and Walnut St., in the southeastern corner of Wilmington's central business district. It is now a mission to feed the hungry and is called Emmanuel Dining Room. Call ahead for an appointment to see the interior.
> **Telephone:** (302) 652-2577.

M A I N E

Brunswick

First Parish Church, Stowe House, Peary-McMillan Arctic Museum

In this lovely college town, all the experiences of her years in faraway Ohio, on the borders of slavery, crystallized for Harriet Beecher Stowe. This is where she wrote *Uncle Tom's Cabin*. Actually, she said later, God dictated and she just took it down.

It was while listening to her husband, Dr. Calvin Stowe, preaching an antislavery sermon, as she sat in the twenty-third pew of the church, that she was inspired. The church, built in 1846, has a long activist tradition, and Dr. Martin Luther King, Jr., also delivered a sermon from its pulpit. The Stowe home in which the book was actually written is a few blocks away, on Federal Street.

The Stowes were part of Bowdoin College, a school which graduated some of New England's most famous nineteenth-century writers. It also was a home base for Arctic exploration. Admiral Robert E. Peary was a Bowdoin man, and the college supported his repeated quests for the North Pole. Exhibits on Peary and his black aide, Matthew Henson (see the entry under Annapolis, Maryland), who was with him on his race for the Pole in 1909, are a major part of the displays in the Peary-McMillan Arctic Museum, in the center of campus.

> **Location:** Brunswick is about 25 miles northeast of Portland, by way of U.S. 1. First Parish Church is at the head of Maine St., the broad main thoroughfare of the town. The Bowdoin campus begins directly behind the church and the Arctic Museum is housed on the ground floor of Hubbard Hall, the library. The Stowe House, which is now a restaurant, is just to the east, at 63 Federal St.
>
> **Hours:** The Arctic Museum is open Tuesday to Saturday, 10-4, and Sunday, 2-5. The Church is open by appointment.
>
> **Telephone:** Museum, (207) 725-3000; Church, (207) 729-7331.

M A R Y L A N D

Annapolis

Banneker-Douglass Museum

This museum of African-American life and history was dedicated to the memory of two famed black Marylanders: the colonial era scientist and surveyor Benjamin Banneker and the fiery abolitionist Frederick Douglass. (See also the entries for the Frederick A. Douglass House in Washington, D.C., and the Benjamin Banneker Boundary Stone in Arlington, Virginia.) Located in the historic district of the state's charming capital, the museum features changing exhibits relating to black culture in Maryland.

> **Location:** The museum is at 84 Franklin St., a block from Church Circle.
> **Hours:** Tuesday to Friday, 10-3, and Saturday, 12-4.
> **Admission charge:** None.
> **Telephone:** (301) 974-3955.

Matthew Henson Memorial

On a windy April morning in 1988, Matthew Henson finally won the last measure of appreciation for his role in one of the great adventures of the century. His remains were reinterred next to those of his old companion, Admiral Robert E. Peary, in Arlington National Cemetery, with recognition as co-discoverer of the North Pole. It was seventy-nine years to the day that the two men had reached their goal at the top of the world.

Actually, Henson claimed until his death in 1955 that he had reached the Pole first. The final dash covered 133 miles in two days, a distance that Peary's badly frozen toes would not permit him to walk. So he was pulled in a sledge by four Eskimos, while Henson walked in front blazing the trail across the ice.

"I was in the lead that final morning," he said in a newspaper interview in 1934, "and when Peary took his sights we found out that we had overshot the mark a couple of miles. We went back then and I could see that my footprints were the first at the spot."

It was also Henson who planted the American flag at the Pole, since Peary was too weak to get up from his sledge. Henson was born on a

Matthew Henson

Maryland farm in 1866 and ran away to sea at the age of thirteen. He apparently met Peary, then a young Naval officer, at this time and agreed to accompany him on an expedition to chart possible canal routes in Nicaragua. Peary was impressed by his stamina and intelligence, and Henson became his permanent assistant in the series of Arctic voyages that culminated in the race to the Pole in 1909.

The journey was surrounded by controversy immediately. A rival claimant to the achievement already had returned from the Arctic and been hailed in the press. A study by the National Geographic Society, based on data compiled by the two parties, concluded that Peary had actually won the race. But a re-examination of that data in 1989 by the Society once more clouded Peary's claim.

Henson never doubted the validity of what he had achieved. But while other Arctic explorers returned to honors, Henson spent the thirty years after his polar trip working quietly as a clerk in the federal customs house in New York. Only in the last years of his life was his role officially acknowledged. In 1945, years after Peary's death, Congress voted him a silver medal, the duplicate of one awarded to the admiral. But he was buried in a shared grave in New York because his estate could not afford a separate plot.

Bandleader Cab Calloway

Harvard history professor Dr. S. Allen Counter petitioned for years to have Henson's remains moved to Arlington. He delivered the eulogy on that day. "A tragic wrong has been righted," he said. "Welcome home, Matthew Henson, to a new day in America. May your presence here inspire generations of explorers."

Location: The Henson Memorial, unveiled in 1961, is on the grounds of the Maryland State House.

Baltimore

Cab Calloway Jazz Institute at Coppin State College

One of the top nightclub performers and big band leaders of the 1930s, Calloway assumed the persona of the smooth-talking, sharp-dressing hipster, the essence of urban sophistication. His sing-along version of "Minnie, the Moocher," in which the audience was implored to repeat a series of increasingly complex scat phrases, was still being heard in venues as varied as baseball parks and concert halls half a century later. Calloway was one of the first black performers to be featured in Hollywood musicals and also scored successes as Sportin' Life in the postwar revival of *Porgy and Bess* and playing opposite Pearl Bailey in the all-black version of *Hello, Dolly!* He delivered the eulogy at Bailey's funeral in 1990.

> **Location:** Coppin State College is located in midtown Baltimore, at 2500 W. North Ave. Founded in 1900, it was named for Fannie Jackson Coppin, believed to be the first black woman in America to earn a college degree. The Calloway exhibits are located in the Parlett Moore Library.
> **Exhibits:** Personal effects and memorabilia of Calloway's long career in show business.
> **Hours:** Monday to Friday, 8-5.
> **Admission charge:** None.
> **Telephone:** (301) 333-7427.
> **Handicapped access:** Yes.

Eubie Blake Cultural Center

When Eubie Blake died in 1983, five days past his 100th birthday, it snapped the last link to the beginnings of American popular music. Performing enthusiastically almost to the end, Blake delighted in introducing a song called the "Charleston Rag," and hearing the audience gasp when he told them that he had written it in 1898.

Rediscovered in the early 1970s after decades of obscurity, Blake was regarded as a living treasure in his last years by musicologists and serious composers. The revival of ragtime had renewed interest in composer Scott Joplin (see the entry for the Scott Joplin House in St. Louis, Missouri). Blake not only knew Joplin but was his friend and associate. He had made his mark, though, not in ragtime but on the Broadway stage. His 1921 review *Shuffle Along* was the first to be written and produced by blacks, and also the first to incorporate jazz compositions in its score. One of its big numbers, "I'm Just Wild About Harry," would resurface twenty-seven years later as the presidential campaign theme for Harry S Truman. Blake and his collaborator, Noble Sissle, were major figures of the jazz age. Their shows launched the careers of many top black performers, including Josephine Baker, and they turned out jazz-based material for Sophie Tucker and even Noel Coward.

"I came to New York as a buck dancer in 1902 and we played the Academy of Music," he recalled in a 1972 interview with the *New York Times*. "But I never saw 14th Street. Every night they backed a wagon right up to the stage door on 13th Street and carted us down to Bleecker Street. In those days, the colored artists had to stay in the crumb joints. We couldn't even go to the door of a good hotel, let alone stay there.

"What makes me so damn mad is these young guys who call us handkerchief heads and Toms. We made the way. In order for a Negro to get on the Keith (vaudeville) Circuit he was better than anyone doing his line. The best of us played for the Goulds and the

Eubie Blake (seated) and his partner Noble Sissle in 1919

Carnegies and the rest of 'em in their homes. But we didn't play for the Fords or the Rockefellers—you know why? Because they weren't bluebloods. They couldn't even get in there."

For years, Blake pretended he couldn't read music, "because blacks were supposed to write naturally." But he was an accomplished musician who delighted in composing mathematically in his head.

Born in Baltimore, Blake always considered the city his home and wanted a showcase for his memorabilia there. He liked to recall his first trip back after making a success in New York and how he took his mother, an ex-slave, to his show. She regarded the theater as sinful but told him at intermission: "It's wonderful, son. Now if they were just doing this for Jesus." To which Blake responded: "That would be fine, mama, but Jesus don't pay nothin'."

Location: The Eubie Blake Cultural Center is at 409 N. Charles St., a few blocks north of downtown.
Exhibits: A museum houses belongings and musical items relating to the composer.
Hours: Monday to Friday, 12-6.
Admission charge: None.
Telephone: (301) 396-1300.

Great Blacks in Wax Museum

It bills itself as the country's first and only wax museum of African-American culture and history, saluting Eubie Blake, Billie Holiday, and other famous blacks from Maryland and the rest of the country.

> **Location:** The museum is at 1601 E. North Ave., about 2 miles northeast of downtown.
> **Exhibits:** There are about 100 figures immortalized in wax.
> **Hours:** Tuesday to Saturday, 10-6, and Sunday, 12-6.
> **Admission charge:** $4.50
> **Telephone:** (301) 563-3404.

Morgan State University

Established in 1867, during the era in which many of the country's historically black schools were organized, Morgan State became a state institution in 1939. Near the center of campus is a twelve-foot statue of abolitionist Frederick Douglass, completed in 1956 by black sculptor James Lewis. In the Beulah M. Davis Special Collections Room in Soper Library are artifacts associated with a number of famous black Marylanders, including Douglass, Matthew Henson, and Benjamin Banneker. The Murphy Fine Arts Gallery schedules changing exhibits featuring the works of black artists.

> **Location:** Morgan State is in the northeastern part of the city, at Hillen Rd. and Cold Spring Ln. From downtown, take Charles St. north to 33d St., then east to northbound Hillen Rd.
> **Hours:** The Murphy Galley and Soper Library are open Monday to Friday during normal class hours; other times by appointment.
> **Admission charge:** None.
> **Telephone:** (301) 444-3333.
> **Handicapped access:** Yes.

Cambridge

Harriet Tubman Birthplace

They compared her to Moses, this short, stout woman who wore a turban and spoke of the visions and premonitions that came to her. In fact, "Go Down, Moses" was one of the spirituals she sang to communicate with field hands she intended to take north to freedom on the Underground Railroad. And like the biblical figure, she experienced her moment of awakening when she interposed herself between an overseer and a slave he was trying to kill.

Harriet Tubman

Harriet Tubman was born in Maryland's Eastern Shore, and it was to this tobacco-growing area that she returned repeatedly to rescue three hundred slaves, including most of her own family. She had become a legendary figure in her own lifetime, a phantom singing in the night to signify the way to freedom.

Born in 1820, she grew up on a plantation south of Cambridge. As a teenager, watching an overseer pursue an escaping slave, she threw herself between them and was struck in the head by a two-pound weight. It left her with a crease in her skull and recurring seizures, during which she saw visions and heard voices. One such voice kept urging her "Arise, flee for your life." Finally, in 1849, she left her husband and children and made her way to the north.

Upon reaching safety, however, she decided her own freedom was worthless if others remained in bondage. So, beginning in 1850, she returned south nineteen times to take out as many slaves as she could, including her children, brothers, and parents. Her husband, John Tubman, had opposed her flight, and when she left he married another woman.

Traveling by night and resorting to disguises when she had to go out in the day, she was never caught and never lost a passenger on the Railroad. John Brown referred to her as General Tubman, and she was a keen supporter of the abolitionist's plan to seize the arsenal at Harpers Ferry. During the Civil War, she was used as a spy and scout because her forays into the south had made her intimately familiar with the countryside.

She settled in Auburn, New York (see also the entry for the Harriet Tubman House in Auburn), where she lived out her days on a small government pension until 1913.

> **Location:** A historical marker marks the site of the plantation on which she was born, near Bucktown, 8 miles south of Cambridge on Maryland 397.
> **Exhibits:** The Harriet Tubman Association in Cambridge has outlined tours of places associated with her in the area and also presents a slide show about her in the Dorchester County Library.
> **Telephone:** (301) 228-0401.

Sharpsburg

Antietam National Battlefield

This was the bloodiest battle of the Civil War, a horrible day of carnage in which twenty-three thousand men were killed or wounded, and it changed the war completely.

Before Antietam, it had been a war to preserve the Union. Afterwards, it was a war both to preserve the Union and to end slavery. President Abraham Lincoln was waiting for a Union victory that would enable him to issue an Emancipation Proclamation, ending slavery in the breakaway southern states. Five days after the battle, on September 22, 1862, he made the announcement. It took effect on January 1, 1863, but it wasn't for another two years that Congress approved the Thirteenth Amendment to the Constitution, which prohibited slavery throughout the United States.

> **Location:** Sharpsburg is about 65 miles northwest of Washington, D.C., by way of Interstates 270 and 70 and Maryland 34. The battlefield adjoins the town on the east.
> **Exhibits:** A self-guided tour circles the battleground, which is dotted with memorials to the participating military units. A museum in the Visitor Center gives an overview of the engagement and explains its significance.
> **Hours:** Daily, 8:30-5.
> **Admission charge:** None.
> **Telephone:** (301) 432-5124.

MASSACHUSETTS

Boston

African Meeting House, Abiel Smith School

The northern slope of Beacon Hill contains the nation's largest collection of historical sites associated with a pre-Civil War black community. Massachusetts outlawed slavery in 1783, and newly freed blacks flocked to Boston, choosing this area of the city in which to settle. Many of the sites are in the process of being stitched together to form the African American National Historic Site.

The focus of the area was the corner of Joy Street and Smith Court. This is where the city's first school for black children was built in 1834, a building which now houses the Museum of Afro-American History. The school was named for Abiel Smith, a white merchant whose bequest to the city went specifically for the education of black children. Within a decade, the school was boycotted by black parents protesting segregation. In a distant forerunner of the lawsuit that would end segregated schools nationwide, Benjamin Roberts sued the City of Boston in 1848 because his daughter was forced to attend Smith School and denied entrance to one closer to her home. He lost in court, but Boston became the first major city to end segregated school facilities in 1855. (Ironically, more than a century later, Boston would become the site of the most bitter racial conflict in its history over the issue of desegregating neighborhood schools.)

Around the corner, on Smith Court, are several residences built in the nineteenth century for the black middle class. Some were rental properties owned by wealthy professionals who lived elsewhere. Number 3 was the home of William C. Nell, an attorney and leading abolitionist, who refused to take the oath admitting him to the bar because he didn't want to swear to defend a Constitution that permitted slavery. Nell published one of the first histories of black Americans to be written by an African American and is also believed to be the first black man appointed to a federal position, with the U.S. Postal Service, in 1860.

In the middle of this block is the African Meeting House, the center of the community and the oldest black church building in the United States. Built in 1806 and constructed by blacks, it was a center of political activity in the years before the Civil War. It was known as the

70

African Meeting House (left) in Boston's Beacon Hill district

Black Faneuil Hall, because the meetings held here corresponded in significance to those in Boston that preceded the American Revolution. Most of the leaders of the abolitionist movement, both black and white, spoke from its pulpit. Declared a National Historic Site in 1974, the building was recently restored and reopened to visitors.

> **Location:** Joy St. is 1 block west of the State House in the heart of Boston.
> **Exhibits:** A longer walking tour, which includes 14 locations related to black history, is called the Black Heritage Trail. Maps and information about this walk can be obtained at either the Afro-American Museum, at 46 Joy St., or the National Park Service booth at 30 State St.
> **Hours:** Monday to Friday, 9-5.
> **Admission charge:** None.
> **Telephone:** (617) 742-1854. Information on the Black Heritage Trail is available at (617) 742-5415.

Boston Massacre Site, Granary Burying Ground, Crispus Attucks Monument

As massacres go, it didn't amount to much: five shot dead by British troops in front of the Old State House. But those five bodies were all the colonial firebrands needed to further inflame popular sentiment against the British. It would be five more years before hostilities actually broke out, but John Adams would later write: "On that night the foundation of American independence was laid."

Crispus Attucks Monument

No one is sure how Crispus Attucks happened to be with the mob that marched on the British garrison the night of March 5, 1770. Boston had been seething for weeks over these troops, sent there to enforce the Townsend Acts. The British Parliament had decided three years before that colonists should help pay the costs of military protection in North America, so a series of import duties were approved to be collected at major ports. The duties had been defied or ignored for years and now Parliament had sent troops to show it meant business. Boston became an occupied city. The poor and unemployed of the city were most susceptible to mob action, eager for a fight and egged on by merchants who had to pay the duties.

Attucks was a runaway slave from Framingham, Massachusetts, and he was near the front of the crowd that surrounded the detail of soldiers on State Street. He was the first to fall. Some historians have interpreted this to mean that he was leading the mob, but that is unproven. From contemporary accounts, we know that a thrown chunk of ice hit one of the soldiers, who lost his footing. As he recovered his balance, against orders, he fired, and his companions did likewise. Attucks and two others were dead at the scene, two more died later, and six were wounded.

The soldiers were tried, with Adams defending their commander, and all but two were acquitted. The others were found guilty of manslaughter, branded and released. The issues raised by the Massacre, however, refused to go away and called into question the entire matter of legitimacy of British rule in America. The Townsend Acts were repealed within weeks, except for the duty on tea. That would, eventually, provide another issue on which Britain could be defied.

Attucks was buried with the other Massacre victims in the Granary Burial Ground. The Crispus Attucks Monument, commemorating the victims of the Massacre, was dedicated on Boston Common in 1888.

> **Location:** All three sites are located within blocks of each other in downtown Boston. A cobblestone circle on the State St. side of the Old State House marks the spot of the Massacre. The Granary Burial Ground is on Tremont St., 2 blocks west. The Common is directly south on Tremont from the Burial Ground.
> **Exhibits:** These sites are part of the Freedom Trail, a walking tour of major historical places in central Boston. Information and maps can be obtained at the kiosk on Tremont St. at the Common, or at the National Park Service office at 15 State St.
> **Hours:** Dawn to dusk.
> **Admission charge:** None.

Robert Gould Shaw and Fifty-fourth Regiment Memorial

The story of this all-black unit and its commander was told in the 1989 Academy Award–winning film *Glory*. This was the first black

Oscar winner Denzel Washington (center) in a scene from the 1989 film "Glory"

regiment raised in the North, although the First Kansas predated it and saw action before the Fifty-fourth went into battle. Colonel Shaw was killed in 1863 in the attack on Battery Wagner, South Carolina, a battle which also resulted in the first Congressional Medal of Honor awarded to a black soldier. The monument by sculptor Augustus Saint-Gaudens was dedicated in 1897. (See also the entries on Fort Shaw in Fort Shaw, Montana, and on Battery Wagner on Morris Island, South Carolina.)

> **Location:** The memorial is at the entrance to Boston Common in front of the State House, at Beacon St. and Park St.

Great Barrington

W. E. B. Du Bois Memorial

Born in this lovely resort town in the Berkshires three years after the end of the Civil War, W. E. B. Du Bois became a seminal figure in the intellectual history of the twentieth century, an architect of black protest. A sociologist, writer, historian, lecturer, teacher, and activist, Du Bois was near the center of every significant movement involving African Americans. He went to Africa, at the age of ninety-three, to help edit an African encyclopedia in Ghana.

He established himself as an opposing force to Booker T. Washington's policy of living within the framework of segregation. Like many

W. E. B. Du Bois

other black intellectuals, he was disturbed by the implications of Washington's Atlanta Compromise, formulated in 1895. To Du Bois, the policy seemed like surrender, a permanent acceptance of inferior status within an established racist order. His answer was *The Souls of Black Folk*, published in 1903, in which he stated "The problem of the twentieth century is the problem of the color line." He criticized Washington for acquiescing to injustice and turning away from the concept of "higher training and ambition of our brighter minds. So far as he, the South, or the nation, does this—we must unceasingly and firmly oppose them."

With Washington accepted by the overwhelming majority of white Americans as the leading black spokesman, Du Bois consigned himself to the role of dissenter. The split was also sharp within the black community. His friend and associate, James Weldon Johnson, wrote later that "one cannot imagine the bitterness of antagonism between these two wings."

He became a leading force in the founding of the NAACP in 1909 and served the organization as a writer and molder of policy for the next twenty-five years. Calling for an end to segregated facilities, the right to vote, equal education, and freedom from violence, Du Bois's program appears unexceptional to a reader at the end of the century.

Jan Matzeliger

But at its beginning, it was regarded as dangerous and its author a man of radical ideas. Permeating all his writings was Du Bois's consistent belief that black people must be true to their own cultural values while striving for an equal place in American life. He died in Ghana in 1963, shortly after making his final gesture of protest by joining the Communist Party.

> **Location:** Great Barrington is 18 miles south of Pittsfield, on U.S. 7. The memorial is on the site of the Du Bois home, east of town, on Massachusetts 23.

Lynn

Jan Ernst Matzeliger Statue

There were shoemakers in this town as early as 1635. By the end of the colonial period, Lynn had assumed its position as the industry's North American center, and by the Civil War the town was dominated by the shoe industry.

It was natural then that Jan Matzeliger would make his way here. After emigrating from the Dutch East Indies, he found work in a Philadelphia shoe factory. Although production was highly mechanized, there was no machine that could "last" a shoe, automatically fitting leather over the sole. But Matzeliger, who had worked in machine shops since he was ten, observed the process and thought he could develop an idea to make it work. So he moved to Lynn to be near the heart of the industry. By 1883 he had patented the first such machine, and in the next eight years added four more patents as he perfected it. His invention was the basis of the U.S. Shoe Company, which became the industry leader. Matzeliger, however, died in 1889 before the enormous profits his invention earned began rolling in.

Ironically, the automatic lasting machine also contributed to the death of the industry in Lynn. With the process thoroughly mechanized, there was no longer any need for skilled craftsmen. After the turn of the century, the shoe manufacturers began moving into other parts of country with lower labor costs.

> **Location:** Lynn is about 10 miles northeast of Boston by way of Massachusetts 1A. A small monument has been placed on Matzeliger's grave in Pine Grove Cemetery. There is also a portrait of him in the First Church, on Lynnfield St. (Massachusetts 129), west of downtown.

Nantucket

African Baptist Church

During the great days of the whalers, this island off Cape Cod attracted a fair-sized population of black men who made their living on the sea. The African Baptist Church, built in 1830 by shipbuilders from the island, is believed to be the second oldest black church structure in the country. It is now owned by Boston's Afro-American Museum and is being restored.

> **Location:** The church is at the corner of York St. and Pleasant St.
> **Hours:** For information on visiting hours, call the Boston Afro-American Museum at (617) 742-1854.

New Bedford

Whaling Museum

Some of the first and best-known black characters in American fiction appear as shipmates on the *Pequod*, the whaling vessel in Herman Melville's classic novel *Moby Dick*. Melville worked on a whaler out of New Bedford, and many of the characters he created

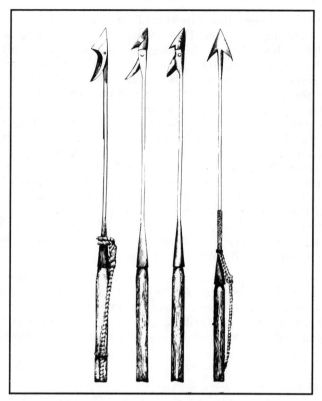

The toggle harpoon, invented by black whaler Lewis Temple

are based on actual figures he encountered at sea. The museum at this greatest of all New England whaling ports pays tribute to the blacks who went down to the sea in ships.

Location: The Museum is on Johnny Cake Hill, just south of U.S. 6 at the eastern entrance to the town.
Exhibits: This is the most complete collection of whaling memorabilia and artifacts in existence, including the harpoon invented by Lewis Temple, an African-American blacksmith.
Hours: Monday to Saturday, 9-5, and Sunday, 1-5.
Admission charge: Adults, $3.50; children 6-14, $2.50; children under 6, free.
Telephone: (508) 997-0046.

Salem

Witch House

Three centuries have passed since the good folk of Salem put twenty people to death upon their conviction for witchcraft. The

The Witch House, Salem

episode has become one of the most enduring chapters in American history, a parable of what can happen to a community when hysteria is wed to power. In the midst of the Joseph McCarthy era in the 1950s, playwright Arthur Miller turned to Salem to draw a parallel to his own times in his play *The Crucible*.

Appearing in Miller's play is the character of Tituba, a West Indian slave. According to most accounts of the witch hunts, she was an actual resident of Salem and the outbreak originated with voodoo tales that she told some teenaged girls. Afterwards, they shivered and screamed whenever she approached and claimed to have been bewitched by her. Tituba and two old women were hanged, the first victims of the hysteria, which raged for a year and only ended when the wives of high officials were accused.

> **Location:** Salem is 15 miles northeast of Boston. The Witch House is at 310 1/2 Essex St., just east of Massachusetts 107.
> **Exhibits:** Built in 1642, this was the home of one of the judges in the trials and the site of some of the early examinations, presumably including Tituba's.
> **Hours:** Monday to Friday, 10-4, and weekends, 10-5, March through November.
> **Admission charge:** $2.50.
> **Telephone:** (508) 744-0180.

Westport

Paul Cuffe Memorial and Farm

He was one of the wealthiest black men in early America, building a fortune in overseas trade. Paul Cuffe used his power and position to try to find answers to the dilemma of race in America, but with varying success.

Born in 1759, the son of a freed slave, Cuffe was a Quaker and dedicated to expanding civil rights. On one occasion, he refused to pay property taxes on the grounds that he was denied full rights as a Massachusetts citizen. In a state in which a claim of taxation without representation still resonated, the courts agreed with Cuffe and granted him full legal rights, making him the first black man to be given civil equality in Massachusetts.

In his later years, he was an enthusiastic supporter of African colonies for freed slaves. He made one journey to Sierra Leone to establish such a venture, but became disillusioned when he found that backers from the southern states supported his plan as a way of getting freedmen out of America. He died in 1817, a few years before elements of his scheme did come to fruition with the founding of Liberia.

Paul Cuffe, New England trader

Location: Westport is on U.S. 6, adjoining Fall River on
the east. The Cuffe Memorial is on the grounds of the
Friends Church, in the Central Village area of town, at 938
Main Rd. Nearby, at 1504 Drift Rd., is the site of Cuffe's
farm, which is designated a National Historic Landmark.
Both can be reached by way of Massachusetts 177 and
southbound Drift Rd.

NEW HAMPSHIRE

Jaffrey

Amos Fortune's Legacy

He gained his freedom at an age when most men are reaching the end of their careers. But for Amos Fortune, his sixtieth year was only the beginning. After a lifetime of servitude, it was time to start life anew.

He moved to this New Hampshire village, in the shadow of Mt. Monadnock, in 1781, established a tanning business, and in the twenty years of life left to him became one of Jaffrey's leading citizens.

He founded a library, trained both black and white apprentices, represented other blacks in legal matters. And when he died in 1801 he left a fund to be used to support the local school.

The school closed down in 1927, but the legacy did not die. It was, instead, used to found the Amos Fortune Forum, still a summertime institution here. A series of speakers are brought in each Friday evening in July and August to give educational talks in the Old Meeting House.

Fortune and his third wife are buried in back of the Meeting House. The epitaph on his stone notes that he "lived reputably and died hopefully."

> **Location:** Jaffrey is 40 miles west of Manchester, by way of New Hampshire 101 and U.S. 202. The Old Meeting House is on Meeting House Rd.
> **Exhibits:** The Jaffrey Public Library, at 111 Main St., has reference material on Fortune.
> **Telephone:** (603) 532-7301.

N E W   J E R S E Y

Jersey City

Afro-American Historical Museum

This facility concentrates on the lives of prominent African-American residents of New Jersey and contains an exhibit showing a typical black household in the state in the 1920s.

> **Location:** 1841 Kennedy Memorial Blvd. Take the southbound exit of the boulevard from U.S. 1 and 9 or from the Holland Tunnel.
> **Hours:** Monday to Saturday, 10-5.
> **Admission charge:** Donation requested.
> **Telephone:** (201) 547-5262.

Lawnside

The name sounds like just another suburban station on the rail line to Philadelphia. But it was originally called Free Haven, which gives you a greater insight into its history.

It was established by Quakers, and a black presence in the area has been traced back to 1792 when integrated religious services were held here. But within twenty years, white members had withdrawn to form their own church, and the remaining blacks affiliated themselves with the African Methodist Episcopal Church. The current Mount Pisgah AME church, built in 1912, is the third on the site.

It became a primary Underground Railroad stop, and William G. Still, a black journalist whose meticulous records are the best surviving eyewitness account of the era, based himself here. After the Civil War, the community developed as a favored location for former slaves. When the railroad arrived in the 1880s, the name was changed to Lawnside. It remains a predominantly black town.

> **Location:** Lawnside is about 7 miles east of Camden, north of U.S. 30 and just east of the Interstate 295 intersection. Mt. Pisgah Church is on Warwick Rd. (Camden County

William G. Still, who wrote an account of the Underground Railroad

Hwy 669) and Mouldy Rd. Black veterans of American wars, dating back to the War of 1812, are buried in its churchyard. Call ahead to see the interior.
Telephone: (609) 547-9895.

Newark

Paul Robeson Center of Rutgers University at Newark

His life was the stuff of tragedy. He excelled in every endeavor, from the classroom to the football field to the stage to the concert hall. But his political views and the racial climate of the day eventually destroyed his career and made Paul Robeson's life the All-American might-have-been.

He was born in Princeton in 1898, the son of a minister, and became the third black student to be admitted to Rutgers, then a private school. He was a Phi Beta Kappa and an All American selection in 1918 as an end, then went on to gain a law degree at Columbia. He practiced for one year with a silk stocking firm, saying

Paul Robeson at a union rally in Detroit in 1941

afterwards that he felt he could not overcome the pervasive racial prejudice in the legal profession. He turned instead to the stage, joining playwright Eugene O'Neill's company, and scored a sensation in *The Emperor Jones*. Finding roles scarce for black actors, he was persuaded to give a concert at the Greenwich Village Theatre, and his 1925 debut saw him acclaimed as the greatest living interpreter of black folk music. He went on to repeat his stage roles in Hollywood, worked overseas, and was feted by the British royal family. A 1934 biographical sketch confidently asserted that "his genius has hurdled the barriers of race prejudice."

Shortly afterwards, on a tour of the Soviet Union, Robeson found himself strongly attracted to the Communist system. It was seemingly so free of racial prejudice and imbued with the spirit of equality that he became an enthusiastic advocate. "It is the one place in the world today where one can live as a human being without prejudice entering the scene at all. In Russia, you feel the vitality of a people who are building a new world; in comparison, other countries are dead."

In the 1930s, statements like this were common enough. Many liberals embraced Russia both as a model of a progressive society and as an enemy of Nazi Germany. But in ten years, those statements would destroy him. He was called before the House Un-American Activities Committee, defied the questioners, and was branded a Communist. A concert in Peekskill, New York, was broken up by right wing rioters in 1949, and Eleanor Roosevelt, bowing to pressure, cancelled his appearance on her radio show. In 1950, at the height of the McCarthy era, his passport was suspended, and he could not leave the country. Robeson denied later that he was ever a Communist, and that his uncompromising fight against racism simply coincided with the position of the Communist party. But he was blacklisted, his records removed from sale, all personal appearances halted. When his travel privileges were restored in 1958, he was given a hero's welcome in Moscow for his sixtieth birthday and settled in England to live.

He died in 1976. Only in recent years has a new generation begun to understand the range of his talents and his contributions to American life. A touring show based on his career aided that process, although it was opposed in an earlier version by his son, who felt the script "sugar coated" his father's life. Even after his death there seemed to be no separating Robeson from controversy.

Location: The Rutgers campus in Newark is part of the city's midtown educational complex, located on Central Ave. near Broad St.

Exhibits: The school administration hopes to obtain some of Robeson's personal memorabilia to display at the Center.

Hours: Open during regular classroom hours.

Telephone: (201) 648-1766.

Perth Amboy

Grave of First Black Voter

The Fifteenth Amendment to the United States Constitution, which barred race as a qualification for voting, went into effect on March 30, 1870. On March 31, Thomas M. Peterson cast his ballot. It came in an election to revise the city charter of Perth Amboy, and he was recognized as the first black to exercise his franchise under the new amendment. Blacks had voted before, of course, but in many states race was still a barrier to the polls (as it remained through most of the South until passage of the Voting Rights Act of 1965).

Peterson, a school custodian, went on to serve on the charter commission he voted for and was named a delegate to the county's Republican convention. The town gave him a gold medal in 1884, and he remained an honored figure in local history for years. In 1959, some fifty-five years after his death, he was honored with a memorial at his burial place, at St. Peter's Church.

> **Location:** Perth Amboy is just across the Arthur Kill from Staten Island, by way of the Outer Bridge, New Jersey 440. The church is located in the center of this heavily industrialized city, at 183 Rector St. Phone ahead for admission.
> **Telephone:** (908) 826-1594.

Red Bank

T. Thomas Fortune House

An influential black journalist of the late nineteenth century, Fortune founded the *New York Age*. In its pages, he campaigned ceaselessly for integrated public schools and attacked politicians who waffled on civil rights issues. Fortune was a combative man, and one who could change directions with bewildering speed. He was, for example, one of the early supporters of the Niagara Movement of black protest but also worked closely with Booker T. Washington, whom the Movement bitterly opposed. His formidable writing talents made him one of the first black editorial staffers hired by the *New York Sun*. At his death, fifty years later, he was still an active force in New York journalism.

> **Location:** Red Bank is about 40 miles southeast of Newark by way of the Garden State Pkwy. The Fortune House, on the National Historical Register since 1976, is at 94 W. Bergen Pl. He lived here from 1901 to 1915. The house is not open to the public.

N E W   Y O R K

Auburn

Harriet Tubman House

The house was once a way station on the Underground Railroad, on the line from the East Coast to sanctuary in Canada. Harriet Tubman knew the route well. She came this way more than a dozen times, along the road that is now U.S. 20, through New York's Finger Lakes and across the international bridge at Niagara Falls. (For more information on Tubman, see the entry on the Harriet Tubman Birthplace in Cambridge, Maryland.)

During the years that the Fugitive Slave Act was in force, she lived in St. Catharines, Ontario. After the Civil War she moved back to this house and, for the next forty-eight years it was her home, the base for a variety of humanitarian pursuits. A few years before she died, in

Harriet Tubman, far left

1913, she turned it into a home for the aged. The house was restored in 1953.

> **Location:** Auburn is about 25 miles southwest of Syracuse. The Harriet Tubman House is just south of the business district, on New York 34, at 180 South St.
> **Exhibits:** The house has been restored to its appearance in Tubman's time and contains some of her possessions.
> **Hours:** By appointment.
> **Admission charge:** Donation requested.
> **Telephone:** (315) 252-2081.

Irvington

Madame Walker Home

The Hudson Valley north of New York City was the favored locale for America's rich in the early years of the twentieth century. The Carnegies and Rockefellers and Vanderbilts built their estates near the old Dutch towns along the eastern bank of the river. So did Madame C. J. Walker, who had made a fortune selling beauty aids to black women out of her Indianapolis offices. She was regarded as the first black woman millionaire in the country. (See also the entry on the Madame Walker Urban Life Center in Indianapolis,Indiana.) Her home here, Villa Lewaro, was designed by black architect Vertner Woodson Tandy.

> **Location:** Irvington is about 25 miles north of midtown Manhattan, by way of U.S. 9. The Villa Lewaro, a National Historic Landmark since 1976, is identified by a marker on North Broadway. The house is not open to the public.

New York City

Fraunces Tavern

On December 4, 1783, the revolution won and the peace treaty signed, Gen. George Washington entered this restaurant, which was old even then, to say goodbye to his officers. That gathering has given the Fraunces Tavern, a landmark in the Wall Street area, a niche as both a restaurant and a museum.

Washington chose this place because it was owned by Samuel Fraunces, a stalwart supporter of the colonial cause. Fraunces, a black of West Indian descent, had opened the tavern in 1762 as the Queen's Head. He purchased it from the aristocratic De Lancey family. It was built in 1719 as a residence and had been turned into a warehouse and store in 1757. Despite the royal title Fraunces gave the place, it was a favored rendezvous of the rebellious Sons of

Fraunces Tavern in 1854

Liberty in the 1770s, and Washington himself is said to have come here then.

The relationship between the two men continued through the war, despite the occupation of New York City by the British for most of its duration. So the renamed Fraunces Tavern was a logical choice for the farewell dinner. According to contemporary accounts, the buffet meal was a melancholy affair, with no one quite knowing what to say and emotions running very close to the surface. Washington looked old and his hands shook when he accepted a glass of wine. Raising the glass he said: "With a heart full of love and gratitude I now take my leave of you. I most devoutly wish that your latter days may be as prosperous and happy as your former ones have been glorious and honorable."

No one could have guessed that in little more than five years he would return to New York as the first president of the United States. Washington didn't forget his old friend Fraunces. The tavern owner was named Steward of the Household and supervised the staff of the Executive Mansion in New York.

Location: The Tavern stands at the corner of Pearl St. and Broad St., just steps from the New York Stock Exchange, at the southern tip of Manhattan.

Exhibits: The Long Room, in which the farewell banquet was held, has been restored to its appearance of that time. A museum contains memorabilia of the Revolutionary era and the history of New York.

Hours: The museum and restaurant are open Monday to Friday, 10-4. Reservations are necessary for lunch at the restaurant.
Admission charge: Donation requested.
Telephone: (212) 269-0144.

Louis Armstrong House

This was home to the famed New Orleans–born jazz artist for longer than any other in his life. He bought it in 1943 and lived here until his death in 1971. After the death of his wife, in 1983, the house became an archive and museum of Armstrong's career. (For a more complete discussion of Armstrong's achievements, see the entry on Louis Armstrong Park, Preservation Hall, and the Old Mint Museum in New Orleans, Louisiana.)

Location: The home is in the Corona area, at 3456 107th St. From Manhattan, take the Queens Midtown Tunnel and Long Island Expy. (I-495) to the 108th St. exit and turn north.
Exhibits: Armstrong's personal memorabilia and music collections are kept here just as he left them.
Hours: The house is open by appointment only.
Telephone: (718) 478-8274.

St. George's Episcopal Church

It was among the most aristocratic of Manhattan's silk-stocking churches. J. P. Morgan was a parishioner, as were Seth Low and Henry Bacon, men of enormous wealth and power in the early years of the twentieth century. And the featured baritone soloist at St. George's, a position he held for fifty-three years, was Harry T. Burleigh, a black man who was the son of slaves.

Burleigh, more than any other individual, is credited with popularizing the black spiritual and adapting the music to the concert stage. He also composed more than three hundred songs, the most notable being "Deep River." He studied with Edward MacDowell, who personally sponsored his admission to the National Conservatory of Music. Later, he worked with the Czech composer Antonin Dvorak and helped him adapt traditional black melodies into his *New World Symphony*.

Burleigh was encouraged by his mother to apply for the job at St. George's in 1894 to earn funds needed to supplement his scholarship at the Conservatory. He thought the errand was pointless but was given an interview by the rector and to his shock was awarded the job. Whatever misgivings the parishioners had at the appointment were quickly set aside. Morgan, in fact, left specific instructions about what songs he wanted Burleigh to sing at his funeral.

Besides his Sunday duties at St. George's, Burleigh was also the featured soloist for Saturday services at Temple Emanu-El, on Fifth Avenue at 65th Street, mastering the ancient Hebrew melodies he was called upon to sing there. His concert tours were attended by members of the British Royal Family and he received the 1917 Springarn Medal from the NAACP for excellence in creative music.

The spirtual, he said in an interview on his thirtieth anniversary at St. George's, in 1924, "should be taken as the Negro's greatest contribution to artistic possessions. In them we show a spiritual security as old as the ages. These songs always denote a personal relationship. It is 'my saviour' and 'my sorrow.' America's only original and distinctive style of music is destined to be appreciated more and more."

The thirtieth anniversary was celebrated with great ceremony, but Burleigh continued at the church for fully another generation, until two years before his death in 1949.

> **Location:** The church is located on Stuyvesant Square, at 209 E. 16th St.
> **Hours:** Call in advance for visiting hours.
> **Telephone:** (212) 475-0830.

New York City: Harlem

The most famous black community in the world, Harlem is in itself an attraction. It stretches across the upper portion of Manhattan Island, from 90th Street to 178th Street and from the Hudson to the East and Harlem Rivers. It has been the home of some of the greatest American artists, politicians, entertainers, clergymen, and writers of the twentieth century. Subject of poems, novels, songs, plays, and dreams, Harlem functions as much in the realm of myth as in reality. In the 1920s, the creative energies of the Harlem Renaissance sent a thrill through America's black community. It became a beacon for talented young African Americans. As the poet Langston Hughes, who came here at that time, said: "I stood there, dropped my bags, took a deep breath, and felt happy again."

Harlem began as a Dutch farming community in the seventeenth century and thrived for two hundred years as a rural retreat, until it was swallowed by the city. By the late nineteenth century, it was a fashionable German neighborhood, noted for its rows of aristocratic brownstones. As rail lines expanded and the area was built up, the wealthy decamped for greener fields in Westchester County. Harlem became a middle-class area and attracted its first black residents after 1910. New subways made access to the area easier and a few black churches, especially St. Phillip's Episcopal, encouraged their congregations to move uptown. St. Phillip's is still one of the largest landowners in Harlem.

By 1920, Harlem had become a predominantly black, middle-class community. Small businesses flourished on 125th Street and the intersection with Seventh Avenue became its focus. There had never been such a commingling of black talent. Claude McKay and Countee Cullen, Duke Ellington and Lena Horne, Langston Hughes and James Weldon Johnson, Marcus Garvey and W. E. B. Du Bois. Working, performing, creating, all within the same few square miles of New York City real estate.

Many elements of that Harlem can still be discerned, although the area has never really come out of a long commercial decline that began in the 1950s. During the civil rights era, it was once again the center of intellectual ferment in the writings of Malcolm X, James Baldwin, and Imamu Amiri Baraka. Community leaders insist the cultural institutions and sense of black pride instilled by this legacy make Harlem a viable place today. When Nelson Mandela spoke here in the summer of 1990 his platform was set at the corner of 125th Street and Seventh Avenue (now renamed Adam Clayton Powell Boulevard), still the heart of Harlem.

> **Tours:** Harlem's historical attractions would fill a guide-book in themselves. Several companies offer tours of Harlem's highlights and that is probably the best way to be introduced. The Harlem Tourism Association—(212) 427-7201—has a listing of accredited operators. Many of them offer Sunday morning gospel tours and evening restaurant and night club tours. The two largest, commu-nity-based companies are Harlem, Your Way!, Tours Unlimited, Inc., at 129 W. 130th St., (212) 690-1687, and Harlem Renaissance Tours, 18 E. 105th St., (212) 722-9534.

Abyssinian Baptist Church

There have been few figures in the history of American politics or religion or civil rights as controversial or contradictory as the Rev. Adam Clayton Powell, Jr. He was a pioneer in the tough battles for civil rights in the North. He was the first black member of the New York City Council and the first black Congressman from an eastern state. He and his father built their church into the largest black congregation in the country. His flamboyant life style infuriated many of his contemporaries and delighted others. He was stripped of his committee chairmanship in the House of Representatives on charges of misconduct and was repudiated at the polls. After his death, however, one of the main thoroughfares of Harlem was renamed in his honor.

Powell arrived in New York as a twelve-year-old when his father assumed the pastorate of the Abyssinian Baptist Church. The senior Powell had risen from poverty in Virginia to a degree at Yale, but the church he took over was small and debt-ridden. Within a few years, he had made it one of the largest Protestant congregations in the world.

The Abyssinian Baptist Church

The younger Powell became assistant minister after graduating from Colgate University in 1930. His return to the church coincided with the onset of the Depression. He assumed leadership of the church's free meal program and within months was coordinating relief efforts throughout Harlem. This work evolved into a series of community protests, demanding that white businessmen hire black labor. A dynamic speaker, a man of magnetic charm and keen intellect, he is credited with winning jobs for blacks in some of New York's biggest companies, including the giant public utilities. "He mobilized inarticulate sections of the Harlem population during the dark and seemingly pathless days of the Great Depression," said NAACP Executive Director Roy Wilkins in a 1967 interview. "He taught them how to ask and work for what they needed, and what, it may be added, was due them."

Through the late 1930s, Powell kept up the pressure, winning highly publicized hiring concessions from the transit companies and the World's Fair. Running as an independent, he was elected to the city council in 1941 and three years later was elected to Congress. He hit Washington like a whirlwind, attacking Jim Crow practices in the capital, integrating the press galleries and restaurants in the Capitol Building, advocating desegregation of the armed forces. He also

berated Washington's black leadership as "the black bourgeoi-
sie... still wrapped up in antebellum dreams of a mulatto society,"
and castigated black religious leaders as "Uncle Tomming clergymen
with Harvard accents."

His romantic dalliances, trips to Europe, and expensive tastes in
restaurants and cars won him notoriety. Finally, in a 1960 radio
interview, Powell's cavalier approach caught up with him when he
referred to a New York woman as "a bag woman for the police
department." She sued and won. Powell refused to pay and was
slapped with a contempt of court citation. He ignored it, trying to use
Congressional immunity as a shield. Congress responded by stripping
him of his seniority and refusing to seat him, on the grounds that he
had misused his position and public funds. The decision to exclude
him was reversed by the U.S. Supreme Court. By this time, however,
Powell had angrily endorsed the Black Power agenda and declared
that non-violence had failed as a workable policy. He spent most of
the remainder of his term at his retreat in the Bahamas and was
narrowly defeated for a fourteenth consecutive term by Charles
Rangel in the 1970 election. He died two years later, leaving a legacy
of achievement in the fields of civil rights and social legislation and
the image of a defiant and independent black man, who lived his life
to please himself. The course of Seventh Avenue running through
Harlem was renamed in his honor to Adam Clayton Powell, Jr.,
Boulevard.

> **Location:** The Abyssinian Baptist Church, built by the
> senior Powell in 1923 and the base of his son's political
> power, is located at 132 W. 138th St.
> **Exhibits:** The church houses a museum of Powell memora-
> bilia, besides being an impressive edifice in its own right.
> **Hours:** Monday to Friday, 9-5.
> **Telephone:** (212) 862-7474.

Apollo Theater, Hotel Theresa

When the color line kept blacks out of most American theaters and
hotels, Harlem established two landmarks of its own. The Apollo
became the summit of the black show business circuit. From the
1920s to the 1960s, no act was really considered a star unless it played
the Apollo. From vaudeville hoofers to the big bands to rhythm and
blues to rock, they all wanted to be booked here. Eventually, the
changing economics of show business closed it up, but the Apollo
reopened in 1989 after a multimillion dollar renovation and is once
again showcasing the biggest names in black show business.

At the same corner is the Theresa Towers. Built in 1913 as a
luxury hotel, it eventually became the preferred stopping place for
visitors to Harlem. Most of the acts that played the Apollo signed the
guest register at the Theresa. Its most notorious guest, however, was
Cuban Premier Fidel Castro, who stayed there in 1960 on his visit to
New York and greeted admirers and television cameras from the

Harlem's legendary Apollo Theater

balcony of his room. The hotel closed a few years afterwards, and it is now an office building.

> **Location:** Both the Apollo and the Theresa are located at W. 125th St. and Adam Clayton Powell, Jr., Blvd.
> **Hours:** The Theresa Towers is open during regular business hours. For hours and attractions at the Apollo call (212) 749-5838.

Black Fashion Museum

Established in 1979, this unique facility displays the history of clothing worn by African Americans, from the late seventeenth century to contemporary Broadway shows and couturiers.

> **Location:** The museum is at 155 W. 126th St., between Lenox Ave. and Adam Clayton Powell, Jr., Blvd.
> **Hours:** Monday to Friday, 12-8.
> **Admission charge:** Donation requested.
> **Telephone:** (212) 666-1320.

Schomburg Center for Research in Black Culture

The most complete research facility in the world for studies of black life and culture, this branch of the New York Public Library system began as a private collection. Arthur A. Schomburg was a Puerto Rican of African descent. A historian and bibliophile, he began to assemble rare material on the African diaspora early in this century.

In 1926, the collection was purchased by the Carnegie Foundation and presented to the library, which built a special branch for it in Harlem. Its material furnished a spark for the Harlem Renaissance. Writers and scholars pored through its contents to draw inspiration from the new perspectives it cast on the black experience. The original collection contained five thousand volumes, three thousand manuscripts, and two thousand etchings. It has now grown to more than five million items and contains information on every significant grouping of black population in the world.

> **Location:** The Center is located at 135th St. and Lenox Ave.
> **Holdings:** The material ranges from books to audio-visual presentations. None of it circulates.
> **Hours:** Monday to Saturday, 10-5:45.
> **Admission charge:** None.
> **Telephone:** (212) 491-2200.

The Schomburg Center

James Weldon Johnson, who lived on West 135th Street from 1925 to 1938

Strivers' Row, Historic Homes of West 135th Street

Harlem contains several reminders of its aristocratic past, but none so impressive as the St. Nicholas Historical District. This development, from 137th to 139th Streets between Adam Clayton Powell, Jr., Boulevard and Frederick Douglass Boulevard (Seventh to Eighth Avenues) was completed in 1891. It remains one of the finest surviving examples of Victorian era townhouses in Manhattan. Composers Eubie Blake, Noble Sissle, and W. C. Handy lived here in the 1920s. Will Marion Cook, an almost forgotten composer who was a major influence on the work of Duke Ellington (who called him "the master of all masters of our people") also lived here. The nickname "Strivers' Row" was given to the area as a tribute to its residents' work ethic, which later generations would call goal-oriented.

Just a few blocks away, on a short stretch of W. 135th Street, is another area associated with some of Harlem's shining names. At 180 W. 135th Street is the home of Claude McKay, regarded as the father of the Harlem Renaissance. His novel *Home to Harlem*, published in 1928, was hailed as a landmark in black literature and his poem "If We Must Die" was chosen as a reading by Winston Churchill when he

addressed Congress to seek funds for British defense during World
War II.

The house at 187 W. 135th Street was occupied by James Weldon
Johnson from 1925 until his death in 1938. It was here that he wrote
his famous book of sermons in verse, *God's Trombones*, and his
autobiography, *Along This Way*. He was also a key executive of the
NAACP during this period, serving as its executive secretary.

The house at 220 W. 135th Street was the home of Florence Mills,
one of the brightest black musical performers of the 1920s. She
starred in Blake and Sissle's landmark revue, *Shuffle Along*, in 1920
and later triumphed in London and Paris with her *Blackbirds Revue*.

All three houses were named National Historic Sites in 1976. None
are open to the public.

Studio Museum of Harlem

It began in 1969 as a hangout for artists who needed working
space, a studio above a liquor store. But within a few years it had
become the black cultural center of New York, a place for established
artists and newcomers alike to show their work and to discuss art-
related issues. It expanded to become a concert hall, a lecture hall, an
assembly hall. Finally, in 1980 it expanded right out of its original
quarters and into enlarged facilities in an old office building on W.
125th Street. It is now recognized as the most important repository of
contemporary black art and African-Caribbean folk art in the
country.

> **Location:** The museum is at 144 W. 125th St., between
> Lenox Ave. and Adam Clayton Powell, Jr., Blvd.
> **Exhibits:** New shows are mixed in with the museum's
> permanent collection throughout the year.
> **Hours:** Wednesday to Friday, 10-5, and weekends, 1-6.
> **Admission charge:** Adults, $2; children, $1; senior citizens
> admitted free on Wednesdays.
> **Telephone:** (212) 865-2420.
> **Handicapped access:** Yes.

Rochester

Frederick Douglass Memorial and Grave, Susan B. Anthony House

Upstate New York provided a haven for many of the great social
movements of the nineteenth century. The area was settled by New
Englanders, whose yearning for a better life first impelled them to
pick up and move west. Once arrived here, this same spirit seemed to
translate itself into social activism. Many of the historic landmarks of
the abolitionist and feminist movements, which were closely allied,

Harlem's Studio Museum

are concentrated here. In Rochester, especially, they coincided. It was home to both Frederick Douglass, the most outspoken of the black abolitionist leaders, and Susan B. Anthony, who led the women's suffrage movement for many years. The two were close allies, and Douglass attended many strategic sessions for both causes at her house.

Douglass edited his newspaper, *The Northern Star,* in Rochester for seventeen years, starting in 1847, although he had to flee to Canada briefly when he was accused of complicity in John Brown's Harpers Ferry raid of 1859. Most of his later years life was spent in Washington, D.C. (see the entry on the Frederick A. Douglass House in Washington, D.C.) but he regarded Rochester as his home, and it was here that he was returned for burial.

> **Location:** The Douglass Memorial, at Central Ave. and St. Paul St., is in the heart of downtown Rochester. It was dedicated by Theodore Roosevelt, who was then Governor of New York, in 1899, four years after Douglass's death. He is buried in Mt. Hope Cemetery, south of downtown by way of Mt. Hope Ave. (New York 15). Also buried there is his old comrade in arms, Susan B. Anthony. The Anthony Home is just west of downtown, at 17 Madison St.

Exhibits: There are memorabilia of Anthony's long career, including her association with Douglass, in her home.
Hours: Mt. Hope Cemetery is open daily, dawn to dusk. The Anthony House is open Wednesday to Saturday, 1-4.
Admission charge: The cemetery is free. There is a $2 charge at the Anthony House.
Telephone: Mt. Hope, (716) 473-2755; The Anthony House, (716) 235-6124 or 381-6202.

PENNSYLVANIA

Bala Cynwyd

James Bland Grave

The man who gave Virginia its state song was born in New York, grew up in the District of Columbia, and enjoyed his greatest success in England. One place he never lived was Virginia. He was the most popular black minstrel of the nineteenth century, but the location of his grave was lost for twenty-eight years. And although his most famous song carried the entreaty to "Carry me back to old Virginny," James Bland rests for eternity in this suburb of Philadelphia.

Minstrel shows today have a negative connotation for perpetuating black stereotypes. They were, nonetheless, an exceptionally popular form of entertainment in the years after the Civil War. Purporting to be authentic southern style, most of the music was imitative, written by whites and based on black themes. The performers almost always were whites in blackface.

Bland wanted to change that. A liberal arts graduate of Howard University, his love was composing music and performing. He had been a page in the U.S. House of Representatives and while working there had been asked to perform at private gatherings for some of the country's top politicians. But the stage was closed to him. Finally, in 1875, he won a job with a newly formed, all-black minstrel troupe and toured the country. "Virginny" was introduced three years later and became a national sensation, followed the next year by "Oh, Dem Golden Slippers."

Touring England in 1881, he gave a command performance for Queen Victoria and was acclaimed as "Prince of Negro Songwriters." His annual income was an estimated $10,000, which was, indeed, a princely figure in those years. But when his popularity faded, he had to rely on the charity of friends to make his way back to America, and he died impoverished in 1911. His burial place was located by the American Society of Composers and Performers (ASCAP) in 1939, and a headstone crediting him with writing six hundred songs was erected.

Location: Bala Cynwyd is on the western edge of Philadelphia. Bland's grave is in Merion Cemetery, north on Pennsylvania 23.
Telephone: (215) 664-6699.

103

James Bland

P E N N S Y L V A N I A

Bala Cynwyd

James Bland Grave

The man who gave Virginia its state song was born in New York, grew up in the District of Columbia, and enjoyed his greatest success in England. One place he never lived was Virginia. He was the most popular black minstrel of the nineteenth century, but the location of his grave was lost for twenty-eight years. And although his most famous song carried the entreaty to "Carry me back to old Virginny," James Bland rests for eternity in this suburb of Philadelphia.

Minstrel shows today have a negative connotation for perpetuating black stereotypes. They were, nonetheless, an exceptionally popular form of entertainment in the years after the Civil War. Purporting to be authentic southern style, most of the music was imitative, written by whites and based on black themes. The performers almost always were whites in blackface.

Bland wanted to change that. A liberal arts graduate of Howard University, his love was composing music and performing. He had been a page in the U.S. House of Representatives and while working there had been asked to perform at private gatherings for some of the country's top politicians. But the stage was closed to him. Finally, in 1875, he won a job with a newly formed, all-black minstrel troupe and toured the country. "Virginny" was introduced three years later and became a national sensation, followed the next year by "Oh, Dem Golden Slippers."

Touring England in 1881, he gave a command performance for Queen Victoria and was acclaimed as "Prince of Negro Songwriters." His annual income was an estimated $10,000, which was, indeed, a princely figure in those years. But when his popularity faded, he had to rely on the charity of friends to make his way back to America, and he died impoverished in 1911. His burial place was located by the American Society of Composers and Performers (ASCAP) in 1939, and a headstone crediting him with writing six hundred songs was erected.

> **Location:** Bala Cynwyd is on the western edge of Philadelphia. Bland's grave is in Merion Cemetery, north on Pennsylvania 23.
> **Telephone:** (215) 664-6699.

James Bland

Thaddeus Stevens

Lancaster

Thaddeus Stevens Tomb

The Civil War era politician who was held in highest esteem by his black contemporaries was Senator Thaddeus Stevens, of Pennsylvania A leader of the Radical Republicans, his voice was the most urgent in asking President Lincoln to turn the basis of the conflict into a war against slavery. He sponsored legislation emancipating slaves in the District of Columbia, restraining Union commanders from returning runaway slaves, and enabling the President to enlist black troops in the U.S. Army. After the war, when the inclination of many in Washington was to return to business as usual, Stevens would have none of it. He was one of the architects of the Reconstruction policies that tried to ensure political equality for southern blacks. He engineered the Fourteenth Amendment to the Constitution through Congress, extending the civil rights guaranteed under federal law to the states. He was also a leader in the move to impeach President Andrew Johnson, whom he suspected of trying to impede the Reconstruction plans. His effort fell one vote short in the Senate, and Stevens died a few weeks afterwards, in August, 1868. According to his instructions, five of his pallbearers were black and part of his honor guard was drawn from the black Fifty-fourth Massachusetts Regiment. He stipulated, finally, that he be buried in the only Lancaster cemetery that permitted black interments. "I have chosen this" he wrote, "that I might illustrate in my death the principles which I advocated through a long life, Equality of Man before his Creator."

> **Location:** The Stevens Tomb is in Shreiner's Cemetery, at Chestnut St. and Mulberry St., located just northwest of downtown Lancaster.
> **Hours:** Daily during daylight hours.

Oxford

Lincoln University

There are many claimants to the distinction of being the country's oldest black university. Wilberforce, in Ohio, is the oldest black-operated school. Oberlin, also in Ohio, was the first to admit black students as university policy. But Lincoln University, in the tiny southeastern Pennsylvania town of Oxford, was the first expressly set up for black students, dating back to 1854.

The U.S. Supreme Court Justice Thurgood Marshall was a graduate, as was the poet Langston Hughes and the first president of Ghana, Kwame Nkrumah. The school's ties to Africa are historically strong. It was first named Ashmun Institute, for the first president of Liberia. At one time, it was credited with educating more African students than any other institution in the country. Its entire three-man first graduating class went to Africa as missionaries, and in 1897 a Zulu choir, touring the country, enrolled in the school en masse.

It was molded in the strong intellectual tradition of Princeton University by one of its early presidents, Isaac N. Rendall, who made a policy of hiring only that school's alumni on the faculty. No black professors taught here, though, until 1932.

> **Location:** Oxford is about 55 miles west of Philadelphia by way of U.S. 1.
> **Exhibits:** Campus landmark is Ashmun Hall, built two years after the school opened. At the time it housed all the school's facilities.
> **Telephone:** (215) 932-8300.

Philadelphia

Afro-American Historical and Cultural Museum

One of the first of the modern museums of black culture, this facility was established in 1976, during the Bicentennial celebration, and attracted one million visitors in its first decade. There are art exhibits, multi-media presentations, and a permanent historical collection outlining the directions of black culture in North America.

> **Location:** The Museum is at 7th St. and Arch St., 1 block west of Independence National Historical Park.
> **Hours:** Tuesday to Sunday, 10-5.
> **Admission charge:** Adults, $3.50; children, students, and senior citizens, $1.75
> **Telephone:** (215) 574-0380.

All-Wars Memorial to Black Soldiers

The monument with its group of twelve military figures was unveiled in 1934 and pays tribute to black Pennsylvanians who fought in the nation's wars. The Quaker influence made the state an early haven for blacks, especially after a 1780 law was passed stipulating that no child born in Pennsylvania would be a slave. By 1814, Bishop Richard Allen was able to raise a force of 2,500 freedmen to defend the city from a threatened British attack during the War of 1812.

> **Location:** The monument is on Landsdowne Dr., at the western edge of Fairmount Park.

Frances Ellen Watkins Harper House

A poet and crusader for the rights of blacks and women, Harper published her first book of poetry as a teenager. She went on to enjoy her greatest success with *Poems on Miscellaneous Subjects,* published while she lived here in 1854. She remained active as a writer for half a century and was noted for her attempts to recreate the speech of southern blacks in her works without using dialect. The home was declared a National Historical Site in 1976.

> **Location:** The Harper house is at 1006 Bainbridge St., about 6 blocks to the south and west of Independence National Historical Park. It is not open to the public.

Henry O. Tanner House

The son of a minister, Tanner decided to make art his career and studied at the Pennsylvania Academy of Fine Arts. He was the first black elected to the National Academy of Design. His early work concentrated on black themes, and he looked for subject matter in the

Henry O. Tanner

South. Tanner was regarded as the finest black artist of his generation. But in 1891, he abruptly abandoned this path and moved to Paris. He turned back to his religious upbringing and infused it with mysticism in his paintings of Daniel in the lions' den and Lazarus. He lived in France for the rest of his life, winning a Medal of Honor at the 1900 Paris Exposition.

> **Location:** Tanner's boyhood home, at 2903 W. Diamond St., was made a National Historical Landmark in 1976. It is in the western part of the city, near Fairmount Park. The house is not open to the public.

Johnson House

This home in Germantown was a stop on the Underground Railroad. It was owned by a prominent Quaker, Samuel Johnson, and was also a meeting place for many activists in the abolitionist movement, including Harriet Tubman and the railroad's chronicler, William Still.

Location: The house is on Germantown Ave., in the northwestern part of the city, at Washington Ln.
Exhibits: The house has been preserved as it appeared when it sheltered fugitive slaves in the basement and attic. It is administered by the Mennonite Information Center.
Hours: Tuesday to Saturday, by appointment.
Admission charge: None.
Telephone: (215) 843-0943.

Mother Bethel AME Church

Pennsylvania's largest city was only a few miles north of the Mason-Dixon Line, the boundary that separated the slave states from the free in the years before the Civil War. Freedmen living here were constantly harrassed by slavers, who came north to seize black men at random on the pretext of capturing fugitive slaves. With a payoff to corrupt judges, the slaver would then return south and collect a bounty for his kidnapped prize.

Even Richard Allen, founder of the African Methodist Episcopal Church and its first bishop, was almost snared in this web. A trader, unaware of whom he was taking on, seized Allen on the streets of Philadelphia and swore out an affidavit that he was an escaped slave. At the court hearing, however, dozens of prominent Philadelphians testified indignantly on Allen's behalf and the slave trader was imprisoned for perjury.

Allen once had been a slave in nearby Delaware. His religious devotion and oratorical gifts were so impressive, however, that he converted his owner, who thereupon gave him his freedom. Allen became a minister of the newly organized Methodist Church, traveling as a circuit preacher out of Baltimore. Assigned to Philadelphia by Bishop Francis Asbury, he soon began attracting large crowds of blacks to his services. This outraged white parshioners of the church to which he was assigned, and when they insisted that blacks be confined to the balcony, an infuriated Allen walked out. He formed the Free African Society, which soon developed into the AME Church, a religious organization entirely separate from existing white churches. In 1793, his congregation dedicated a church building of their own, at the corner of Sixth and Lombard Streets. Mother Bethel AME Church is the fourth to stand on the site and represents the oldest piece of property continuously owned by blacks in this country.

Allen went on, in 1830, to preside over the first black convention organized in America, which was held at his church to unify the black community and address antislavery issues. Under his leadership, the convention committed itself to working for freedom in North America and sponsoring new settlements in Canada rather than advocating a return to Africa. Coming just a few years after the establishment of Liberia by freed slaves, the decision represented a turning point in the way blacks perceived their relationship to the lands to which they had been brought. North America was to be

Rev. Absalom Jones

regarded as a permanent home. Allen died early in 1831, and his crypt is in the basement vault of the church.

> **Location:** Mother Bethel AME Church is at 419 S. Sixth St., about five blocks south of Independence Square.
> **Exhibits:** The present church, built in 1859, houses memorabilia of Bishop Allen and his associate, Absalom Jones, a co-founder of the Free African Society.
> **Hours:** Monday to Saturday, 10-3.
> **Telephone:** (215) 925-0616.

St. George's Methodist Church

This colonial landmark, built in 1769, was where Bishop Richard Allen (see above) was sent as the first black preacher in an American Methodist church. Allen and his associate, Absalom Jones, were removed from the church after insisting that blacks who attended services be allowed to sit with the rest of the congregation instead of in the balcony.

> **Location:** The church is part of Independence National Historical Park, at 235 N. Fourth St.

Exhibits: The oldest Methodist church in the country, St. George's also houses the Methodist Historical Center, with artifacts relating to the church's history.
Hours: Daily, 10-4.
Telephone: (215) 925-7788.

RHODE ISLAND

Portsmouth

Black Regiment Memorial of the Battle of Rhode Island

Unlike many subsequent wars engaged in by the United States, in the American Revolution black soldiers were integrated into regular army units. One notable exception was the First Rhode Island Regiment, organized by General Nathanael Greene into a separate fighting force.

Greene was convinced that African Americans were an untapped resource in the struggle against the British. Such ideas were firmly resisted in the southern colonies. Even when Charleston was hopelessly outnumbered by an attacking British force, the South Carolina government refused to allow blacks to fight. In some cases, slaves went over to the British side upon being given promises of freedom.

The Battle of Rhode Island

In Rhode Island, however, the General Assembly approved manumission of any slave enlisting in the Continental Army. There were two hundred such freedmen in Greene's force, as it was ferried across the Sakonnet River to move upon British entrenchments at Newport. But the colonials were not supported by the French fleet and found themselves trapped on the peninsula. Greene's black soldiers were called on to hold the line against the British assault, while the main force extricated itself. Beating off three charges against their position, the unit enabled Greene to organize an orderly retreat and saved the regiment from destruction. This battle, on August 29, 1778, was the only one of the war fought on Rhode Island soil.

Location: The Memorial is west of Portsmouth, on Rhode Island 114, just north of the Rhode Island 24 intersection.

Providence

Rhode Island Black Heritage Society

A museum and cultural center, the society holds periodic displays on local history and also sponsors discovery tours of black roots in Rhode Island.

Location: The society is located at 1 Hilton St., in central Providence.
Hours: Monday to Friday, 9-4:30.
Admission charge: None.
Telephone: (401) 751-3490.

V E R M O N T

Bennington

Garrison Marker, Bennington Museum

William Lloyd Garrison had a talent for clarity and invective that
any journalist can admire. For more than thirty years, his antislavery
publication, *The Liberator,* poured forth an unending stream of abuse
on those who opposed abolitionists, the Constitution ("a covenant
with hell"), slave-owners, and any other target he got in his sights.

William Lloyd Garrison

"I will be as harsh as truth, and as uncompromising as justice. I will not equivocate—I will not excuse—I will not retreat a single inch—AND I WILL BE HEARD," he wrote in his first issue. He was dragged through the streets by a mob, saw his presses smashed and allies desert him. But he functioned as the unrelenting conscience of the nation.

The Liberator was based in Boston but his career began here when he published *The Journal of the Times* in an office near Bennington Common.

> **Location:** The Garrison Marker and Bennington Museum are within a few feet of each other on W. Main St., near the Bennington Battle Monument.
> **Exhibits:** The Museum features copies of Garrison's publications, as well as a portrait of black minister Rev. Lemuel Haynes preaching in the nearby First Congregational Church.
> **Hours:** Daily 9-5, March through December; weekends only, 9-5, January and February.
> **Admission charge:** Adults, $4.50; students and senior citizens, $3.50; children under 12, $3.
> **Telephone:** (802) 447-1571.

Windsor

Constitution House

In the summer of 1777, as British troops overran their borders on the way to crushing defeat at Saratoga, a group of flinty Vermonters gathered in this town on the Connecticut River to put together an extraordinary document. The constitution of the Republic of Vermont was the first in North America to ban slavery and to grant universal suffrage with no property qualification. Slavery would have been an anomaly among Vermont's stony small-holdings, but the constitution did reflect the future state's independence of mind.

Technically, this was not the first antislavery document in the United States, because Vermont did not join the Union until 1791. By then, Massachusetts and Rhode Island already had outlawed slavery. But the action of the Vermonters gave the impetus to the rest of New England.

> **Location:** Windsor is about 13 miles south of the intersection of I-89 and I-91, at White River Junction. Constitution House, the tavern in which the document was written and signed, is at the northern edge of town on U.S. 5.
> **Exhibits:** The building has been restored to the way it looked in 1777, when the constitution was framed.
> **Hours:** Daily 10-5, mid-May to mid-October.
> **Admission charge:** None.
> **Telephone:** None.

Constitution House

The South Central States

Alabama

•

Arkansas

•

Kentucky

•

Louisiana

•

Mississippi

•

Missouri

•

Tennessee

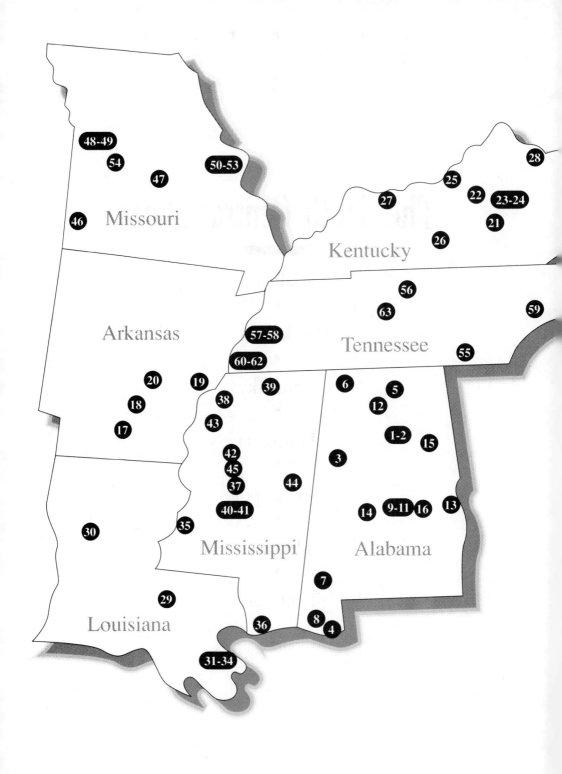

The South Central States

ALABAMA

1. Sixteenth-Street Baptist Church, A. G. Gaston Gardens, Kelly-Ingram Park, *Birmingham*
2. Tuxedo Junction, *Birmingham*
3. Courthouse, *Carrollton*
4. Fort Gaines, *Dauphin Island*
5. Old Courthouse, *Decatur*
6. W. C. Handy Birthplace, Museum, and Library, *Florence*
7. Effigy Cemetery, Mount Nebo Baptist Church, *Jackson*
8. Africa Town, *Mobile*
9. Centennial Hill Historic District, *Montgomery*
10. Civil Rights Memorial, *Montgomery*
11. Dexter Avenue-King Memorial Baptist Church, *Montgomery*
12. Jesse Owens Monument, *Oakville*
13. Horace King Marker, *Phenix City*
14. Edmund Pettis Bridge, Brown AME Chapel, *Selma*
15. Talladega College, *Talladega*
16. Tuskegee Institute National Historic Site, *Tuskegee*

ARKANSAS

17. Red River Campaign, *Camden, New Edinburgh, Sheridan*
18. Hampton Springs Cemetery, *Carthage*
19. Riots of 1919, *Elaine*
20. Central High School, *Little Rock*

KENTUCKY

21. Berea College, *Berea*
22. Kentucky Military History Museum, *Frankfort*
23. Fieldstone Fences, *Lexington*
24. Isaac Murphy Memorial, Kentucky Horse Park, *Lexington*
25. The Kentucky Derby Museum, *Louisville*
26. Mammoth Cave National Park, *Mammoth Cave*
27. Josiah Henson Trial, *Owensboro*
28. Old Slave Market, *Washington*

LOUISIANA

29. Southern University, *Baton Rouge*
30. Melrose Plantation, *Melrose*
31. Amistad Research Center, *New Orleans*
32. Chalmette Battlefield, *New Orleans*
33. Louis Armstrong Park, Preservation Hall, Old Mint Museum, *New Orleans*
34. St. Louis Cemetery Number One, *New Orleans*

MISSISSIPPI

35. Alcorn State University, *Alcorn*
36. St. Augustine Seminary, *Bay St. Louis*
37. Black Confederate Memorial, *Canton*
38. Delta Blues Museum, *Clarksdale*
39. Rust College, Leontyne Price Library, *Holly Springs*
40. Jackson State University, *Jackson*
41. Smith Robertson Museum, *Jackson*
42. Booker-Thomas Museum, *Lexington*
43. Largest black municipality in America, *Mound Bayou*
44. Mt. Zion United Methodist Church, Neshoba County Courthouse, *Philadelphia*
45. Casey Jones Museum, *Vaughan*

MISSOURI

46. George Washington Carver National Monument, *Diamond*
47. Lincoln University, *Jefferson City*
48. The Black Archives of MidAmerica, *Kansas City*
49. Mutual Musicians Association, *Kansas City*
50. Old Courthouse and Dred Scott Case, *St. Louis*
51. Scott Joplin House, *St. Louis*
52. Shelly House, *St. Louis*
53. Vaughn Cultural Center, *St. Louis*
54. Scott Joplin Ragtime Festival, Sedalia Ragtime Archives, *Sedalia*

TENNESSEE

55. Afro-American Museum, *Chattanooga*
56. Fairvue Plantation, *Gallatin*
57. Alex Haley House, *Henning*
58. Fort Pillow State Park, *Henning*
59. Beck Cultural Exchange Center, *Knoxville*
60. Beale Street Historic District, *Memphis*
61. Lorraine Motel, *Memphis*
62. Nashoba, *Memphis*
63. Fisk University, Meharry Medical School, *Nashville*

A L A B A M A

Birmingham

Sixteenth-Street Baptist Church, A. G. Gaston Gardens, Kelly-Ingram Park

The bomb went off at 10:25 on a late summer Sunday morning as church classes were ending and students changed into their choir robes. Thrown from a passing car, the crude dynamite-stick explosive blasted the church basement and in its smoking ruins searchers found the mangled bodies of four little girls: Cynthia Wesley, Carol Robertson, and Addie May Collins who were fourteen; Denise McNair who was eleven.

By the end of a day of rioting and street battles between enraged protesters and the city's all-white police force, two more black teenagers had been killed. Then the city of Birmingham paused in horror and started to come to its senses.

In later years, this day, September 15, 1963, would be regarded as the turning point in the struggle for civil rights in the city. It was a struggle that had become a war, as violence escalated from fire hoses to police dogs to bombs, and finally the most vile act of any committed during the civil rights era of the 1950s and 1960s.

Birmingham was a steel city, with its statue of Vulcan, blacksmith of the gods, in the hills above downtown. "The Pittsburgh of the South" was its proud slogan. But blacks had another name for Birmingham. They called it "The Johannesburg of America." It was part of the new industrial South, noted for the high wages paid for its tough jobs. It lacked the veneer of gentility that covered up the ugliness of racism in many of the region's older, more gracious communities. It was a city, according to the *New York Times* in 1963, in which "every channel of communication, every medium of mutual interest, every reasoned approach, every inch of middle ground had been fragmented by the emotional dynamite of racism, reinforced by the whip, the club, the knife, the mob, the police, and many branches of the state's apparatus."

This was the city targeted by the Southern Christian Leadership Conference for the desegregation of public facilities and jobs in the spring of 1963. The strategy called for an economic boycott of downtown stores and massive street demonstrations. Kelly-Ingram

120

Sixteenth-Street Baptist Church shortly after the bombing and subsequent riot

Park, just to the west of downtown and across the way from the Sixteenth Street Baptist Church, became the gathering point for many of these marches and rallies led by Dr. Martin Luther King, Jr. Police Commissioner Eugene "Bull" Connor closed all city parks rather than open them on an integrated basis. When the demonstrations began, he approved the use of water cannons and police dogs on the marchers. The entire world watched televised images of peaceful marchers blasted off their feet by roaring jets of water and attacked by raging dogs. Support for the demonstrators began to build across the United States.

King was arrested and composed his *Letter from Birmingham Jail,* the most articulate explanation he had yet given of his belief in nonviolent confrontation and civil disobedience. He wrote: "One day the South will know that when these disinherited children of God sat down at lunch counters, they were in reality standing up for what is best in the American dream."

Under tremendous federal pressure, local authorities declared a truce on May 8 and promised fulfillment of basic demands within nine days if the demonstrations stopped. But Gov. George Wallace disavowed the agreement almost immediately and three nights later a bomb went off at the Gaston Motel, the Birmingham headquarters of the protest movement. Under the threat of federalization of the Alabama National Guard, Wallace backed down and a court order for the desegregation of the city was issued.

At the start of the school year, with violence mounting again, President John F. Kennedy federalized state army units. Five days later the bomb went off at the church as Sunday school classes ended a lesson on "The Love That Forgives."

The bombing shook the city to its core. At last Birmingham had had its fill of violence. Except for a few extremists, the white community overwhelmingly accepted the program for desegregating the city, and calm returned to Birmingham.

No arrests were made in the church bombing for eight years. Then the case was reopened with F.B.I. assistance. Finally, in November, 1977, fourteen years after the attack, Robert E. Chambliss, a retired city employee and former member of the Ku Klux Klan, was sentenced to life in prison for the first-degree murder of Denise McNair.

Location: The brick church, with its twin towers and recessed center entrance, is located at 6th Ave. and N. 16th St. From I-20 and I-59, take the 17th St. exit and turn right on 6th Ave. There is a memorial to the four murdered girls in the sanctuary. Inquire at the parsonage, just west of the church, for admittance.
Hours: Open daily.
Telephone: (205) 251-9402.
Other attractions: A. G. Gaston Gardens, formerly the Gaston Motel, is two blocks southwest at 5th Ave. and 15th St. For years the only first-class lodging for blacks in the

Erskine Hawkins

city, it how houses elderly and handicapped tenants. It is not open to visitors. Kelly-Ingram Park is located diagonally across from the church, almost in the shadow of the city's imposing new AT&T Tower. A statue of King, facing the church, occupies the center of the park. An inscription on the base of the monument thanks him for "saving Birmingham from itself."

Tuxedo Junction

The F. N. Nixon Building went up in 1922 at a trolley crossing in the bustling black community of Tuxedo Park on Birmingham's west side. It was just a nondescript office building, but a second-floor dance hall was added and by the start of the big band era it had become a favorite stop for jazz musicians.

One of those who played there was Birmingham-born trumpet man Erskine Hawkins, who fronted his own big band in the thirties. His lightly swinging tribute to the place was named after the trolley stop out front, Tuxedo Junction. Recorded by Glenn Miller, the composition became one of the biggest record hits of 1940.

Location: The building at Tuxedo Junction, now a dental clinic, is located at 1728 20th St., just north of the 20th St. exit from I-20, west of downtown Birmingham. A historic marker attesting to its musical legacy is affixed to the front.

Carrollton Courthouse

In the last weeks of the Civil War, a federal raiding party swept through town and burned down the courthouse. Vengeful residents seized two recently freed slaves and charged them with arson for assisting the troopers. One of them, Louis Wells, escaped, but a few years later he was tracked to the Fairfield area and brought back to Carrollton.

A mob gathered to meet him and the sheriff decided to hustle Wells to the top floor of the new courthouse. As the mob advanced on the building a violent electrical storm hit the area. The lynching was forgotten as townspeople ran for cover. But when the sheriff went to get Wells, he found his prisoner dead at the courthouse window, apparently hit by a lightning bolt as he watched the mob come for him.

Next morning, the story goes, residents of the town were astonished to see the outline of Wells's face clearly etched in the glass of the upper window. Whatever the explanation, the face is still there, one of Alabama's most mysterious bits of folklore.

Location: Carrollton is the seat of Pickens County, west of Tuscaloosa by way of U.S. 82 and southbound Alabama 17. The building is situated on Courthouse Square, in the heart of town.
Hours: Open during business hours, but the face is visible only from the exterior.

Dauphin Island

Fort Gaines

In the summer of 1864, a strong Union fleet, under the command of Admiral David Farragut, moved against the two forts guarding the entrance to Mobile Bay. Shutting down the port of Mobile had become a top priority for the Union army, but Farragut had hesitated offshore for several months. He was concerned about engaging the two heavily armed forts, Gaines and Morgan, and worried even more by the Confederate ironclad, *Tennessee*. Coated with eight feet of iron on its sides, the ship was regarded as invulnerable. Farragut feared it could pick off the fourteen wooden vessels in his fleet at will.

Nonetheless, he began his assault on the morning of August 5. The two lead vessels hit mines, which were then called torpedoes. One sank, the other reeled helplessly, and Farragut's flagship, the

Fort Gaines

Hartford, was left in the lead. It was then that the admiral gave his famous order: "Damn the torpedoes; full speed ahead."

Farragut restored momentum to the assault, and immediately came under attack from the *Tennessee,* aided by three gunboats. "We could direct our fire only on one of them at a time," reported the *Hartford's* captain. "The shots from the others were delivered with great deliberation and consequent effect, a single one having killed ten men and wounded five."

Among those wounded in the bombardment was John Lawson, a black naval volunteer from Pennsylvania. Shot in the leg, he refused medical attention and stayed at his gun for the rest of the engagement, helping to beat off the attack until help could arrive. The *Hartford* survived and led the final attack on the *Tennessee,* which finally struck her colors after continual bombardment from five Union vessels. Lawson was awarded the Congressional Medal of Honor for valor, the first black man to receive this decoration for naval service.

> **Location:** Fort Gaines is located at the southeastern edge of Dauphin Island, on Bienville Blvd., about 30 miles south of Mobile by way of the Dauphin Island Pkwy.
> **Exhibits:** The five-sided structure is essentially the same one that existed during the Battle of Mobile Bay, although some additions were made during the Spanish-American war. The guns fired in the battle are still mounted in position and the anchor and chain from the *Hartford* are displayed near the entrance.
> **Hours:** Daily, 9-5.

Eight of the nine Scottsboro boys

Admission charge: Adults, $2.50; children 6-12, $1; children under 6, free.
Telephone: (205) 861-6992.

Decatur

Old Courthouse

In March, 1931, nine young black men were pulled off an Alabama freight train by police and charged with the rape of two white women. One month later a jury in Scottsboro found eight of them guilty and they were sentenced to death. Within weeks, the fate of the "Scottsboro boys" had become an international cause, adopted especially by the American Communist Party. In November, 1932, the U.S. Supreme Court ruled that they were given inadequate legal assistance in violation of the Constitution and ordered a retrial. This second trial was moved to Decatur, about seventy miles west of Scottsboro, and New York criminal attorney Samuel Leibowitz defended them. He based his defense on a challenge to the systematic exclusion of blacks from jury panels in Alabama. In his examination he also got one of the women to recant her story. She said that she had been told to make the rape charge by police. When the jury returned a verdict of guilty, Judge James F. Horton courageously set it aside and ordered a third trial on the grounds that the evidence did not support the verdict.

But Horton was defeated for reelection to the bench in the Democratic primary and his successor heard the case. Once more the defendants were found guilty and were given the death sentence. But in 1935, the U. S. Supreme Court again reversed the verdict of the state court on Liebowitz's argument that the grand jury returning the original indictments excluded blacks from its panel, denying the defendants "due process of law."

In the fourth trial, also at Decatur, twelve blacks were included in the jury panel, but all were peremptorily challenged by the prosecution and removed. Subsequently, four of the defendants were convicted in 1937, but the death penalties were commuted in every instance. All but one were released from prison within ten years.

The case was a landmark in legal history, the first federal court ruling that blacks could not be excluded from state juries and that all defendants must be given the right to adequate counsel.

> **Location:** The Old Courthouse is located on Court Square, west of I-65 by way of U.S. 72 Alternate.
> **Hours:** Monday to Friday during business hours.

Florence

W. C. Handy Birthplace, Museum, and Library

The Mississippi River cities of Memphis and St. Louis were celebrated forever in his music. But it was the town of Florence, on the Alabama River, that W. C. Handy always regarded as home.

He was born here in a two-room log cabin in 1873, the son and grandson of ministers who expected him to follow their calling. But young William Christopher Handy heard music wherever he turned. The spirituals in his father's church. The chants of the laborers down on the river. Traditional tunes of untold age and unknown origin that seemed to be part of the southern black experience. He was allowed to study music in school. But when he bought a guitar he was told to trade it in for a dictionary. Although music was part of the fiber of the black church, secular music was not encouraged by Reverend Handy.

He was sent off to Huntsville A&M to get a teaching degree. He also managed to obtain a cornet and played with a local brass band. Upon graduation, instead of heading for the classroom he took off for the Chicago World's Fair, only to find that it had been delayed for a year. That started him on thirteen years of wandering around the South, playing his own songs and listening to the music around him.

In 1905, while living in Memphis, he wrote a song for the mayoral campaign of Edward H. Crump. Handy later described it as the first popular composition to employ jazz breaks—natural pauses in the musical line that were to be filled in with improvisational phrases. It was written in a blues form, but it wasn't really a traditional blues. It was something different, a new kind of music that would burst across

W. C. Handy's birthplace

the nation and prepare the way for the coming of jazz. Retitled "Memphis Blues," the song became Handy's first big hit, although he sold all rights to it for $100 and watched in dismay as it earned a fortune for its publisher. Vowing to never make that mistake again, he formed his own publishing company for his next promising song. That was the "St. Louis Blues," and it made Handy a celebrity for the rest of his life, and a wealthy man as well.

Blind during the last twelve years of his life, Handy remained vigorous enough to play at President Dwight D. Eisenhower's inaugural ball in 1953. When he died in 1958, Handy's survivors donated his most prized possessions for a museum to be located in Florence. The composer's cabin birthplace had been moved from its original location and stored in anticipation of such a facility. Funds for the complex were raised through public subscription in Florence.

Location: The W. C. Handy Birthplace, Museum, and Library are situated just west of the city's downtown area, at 620 W. College St., just off U.S. 72.

Exhibits: Memorabilia such as the piano on which he composed the "St. Louis Blues," his cornet, household furnishings, annotated musical scores, tributes from musicians, and other mementos of his long life make up the exhibits. Guides provide commentary on the displays. The library, with material relating to Handy's music and other aspects of black culture, is connected to the museum by a glass-enclosed walkway.

Hours: Tuesday to Saturday, 9-12 and 1-4.

Admission charge: $1.50.

Telephone: (205) 766-7642.

Other attractions: The St. Paul AME Zion Church, in which Handy's forebears were pastors, is located 2 blocks east, on Cherokee St. The building dates from a later period but the stained glass windows were a gift from Handy's father. Inquire at the museum for information about visiting the church. In addition, Florence sponsors the W. C. Handy Music Festival during the first week of every August. The composer's works are highlighted.

Jackson

Effigy Cemetery, Mount Nebo Baptist Church

The making of masks is a cultural motif that runs throughout African art. Placing an effigy mask of the deceased on the burial place has two purposes. It is a way of remaining in the presence of one's ancestors. It is also meant to mislead evil spirits, who might interfere with the passing of the dead into the afterlife, into thinking that the mask was really the living soul of the deceased.

It's rare to find effigy cemeteries in this country, but one of the best-preserved is near this southern Alabama town. The iron masks were cast by a local artisan, Isaac Nettles, and placed on the gravestones in the Mount Nebo Baptist Church cemetery.

> **Location:** The church is located near the village of Carleton, south of Jackson and U.S. 43 by way of Clark County Hwy. 15.

Mobile

Africa Town

The African slave trade was officially ended by an act of Congress in 1807. But for over half a century more, illegal slave ships slipped into hidden landing places throughout the South to unload smuggled human cargo. The last such ship on record was the *Clothilde*, built by Timothy Meaher of Mobile in 1859.

It returned from its first voyage later that year with a cargo of kidnapped inhabitants of the Guinea coast. Alerted to its arrival,

Descendants of those who landed on the last slave ship to America erected this monument in Africa town

federal boats were on patrol in Mississippi Sound. But Capt. William Fowler managed to slip past them into the Mobile River, unloaded his cargo, and burned his ship. With federal authorities all around the area, Meaher and Foster found it impossible to dispose of the intended slaves, and eventually turned them loose.

Many of the freed families banded together to form a community nearby in an area known as Plateau. Their descendants still inhabit the vicinity, four miles north of downtown Mobile, in the shadow of the port city's most industrialized area. The last of the original *Clothilde* passengers, Cudjoe Lewis, died in 1935. A memorial to him, put up by his descendants, now stands at the heart of the Africa Town community, the Union Baptist Church, on Bay Bridge Road. Lewis lived next door to the church until his death and was noted for his prodigious memory; although illiterate, he could quote entire Bible chapters by heart.

> **Location:** Africa Town is reached from central Mobile by taking U.S. 43 north to the Bay Bridge turnoff. The church is 1 block east.
>
> **Exhibits:** The memorial consists of a simple bronze bust bearing Lewis's likeness and a date: 1859. One block away, on a road called Cut Off, is the Plateau Cemetery, containing the grave of Lewis and many others who were aboard on the last voyage of the *Clothilde*.

E. D. Nixon at Alabama State University

Montgomery

Centennial Hill Historic District

When Alabama State University moved to Montgomery in 1887, a middle-class black neighborhood grew up around its location on South Jackson Street. The Centennial Hill area between Jackson and Union, around the intersection of High Street, is now listed in the National Historic Register. The houses, especially those on the three hundred and four hundred blocks of South Jackson, were built by some of the most prominent members of the community. Look for the distinguished home of former state senator John W. Jones, at 341 South Jackson. Dr. Martin Luther King, Jr., lived here in the pastorium of the Dexter Avenue Baptist Church, at 309 South Jackson, during his time in Montgomery. It was here that he saw empty buses running along Jackson Street and realized the boycott was a success, and where his family survived a bomb attack in January, 1956. It is not open to the public.

At the end of South Jackson is Alabama State, founded in Marion in 1874 as a teacher's college for African Americans. In the Levi

Watkins Center are the Dr. E. D. Nixon Archives, the papers and memorabilia of Montgomery's most prominent black leader of the 1950s. It was his decision, for reasons of strategic policy, to shift the spotlight to the unknown Dr. King in the early days of the bus boycott, launching the career of an international figure and selflessly relegating himself to comparative obscurity.

> **Location:** The Centennial Hill area is southwest of downtown Montgomery. Take Madison Ave., U.S. 80 Business, west, then turn right on Jackson St. The homes are not open to the public.
> **Hours:** The E. D. Nixon Archives are open Monday to Saturday, 8-6, and Sunday, 1-6.
> **Telephone:** (205) 293-4100.
> **Admission charge:** None.

Civil Rights Memorial

When the Southern Poverty Law Center sold some downtown property in bustling Montgomery, it found itself with a surprising $750,000 cash surplus. Its response was to commission a memorial to the civil rights era on the plaza in front of its Washington Street headquarters. Architect Maya Lin, who designed the Vietnam War Memorial in Washington, D.C., was given the job.

The result, dedicated late in 1989, is a pair of simple black granite pieces, a circular stone on which the names of forty civil rights martyrs are inscribed, and a wall of rushing water. Carved into the

The Civil Rights Memorial

wall are the words of Dr. Martin Luther King, Jr. taken from the Book of Amos: . . . Until justice rolls down like waters and righteousness like a mighty stream."

Many of the names on the circular stone are those of familiar figures: Dr. King, Medgar Evers, the four girls killed in the Birmingham church bombing (see the entry on Sixteenth-Street Baptist Church, Birmingham, Alabama), the three civil rights workers murdered in Philadelphia, Mississippi (see the entry on Mount Zion United Methodist Church in that section). But others were unknown, forgotten by all but their families, until the Law Center researchers recovered their names and stories from the chronicles. From Rev. George Lee, shot down by nightriders in Belzoni, Mississippi; to Rev. Bruce Klunder, run over by a bulldozer while protesting a segregated school in Cleveland, Ohio, in 1964; to Wharlest Jackson, killed by a car bomb after being promoted to a "white" job in Natchez, Mississippi, in 1967.

"Each name is a history lesson," said Law Center Director Morris Dees at the dedication. "We are saying 'Don't just think of the deaths, but think of a movement of ordinary people who just got tired of injustice'." Dees promoted the idea of such a memorial after addressing an NAACP convention in 1987 and realizing that many of the organization's younger members were unaware of the names of many of the movement's leading historical figures. The Law Center offers legal assistance and education programs, and monitors the activities of racist groups.

> **Location:** The memorial is located 1 block south and 1 block east of the Dexter Avenue–King Memorial Baptist Church, on Washington St. near Hull St.
> **Hours:** Always open.

Dexter Avenue–King Memorial Baptist Church

Among the thousand humiliations and annoyances of segregation, the prohibitions relating to public transportation seemed to come closest to raw nerve. So when Rosa Parks, a tired seamstress on her way home from work, refused to give up her seat to a white man on a Montgomery bus in 1955 and was arrested, her act of defiance struck a chord all across the capital city.

Jim Crow laws had their beginnings in the 1890s by mandating separate cars for black and white rail passengers. It was the challenge to one of these public transportation laws that resulted in the famous Plessy v. Ferguson case, in which the U.S. Supreme Court permitted "separate but equal" facilities, a green light for across-the-board segregation. Over the years, Montgomery had developed an especially onerous system of laws and customs about riding its buses. Blacks had to pay up front, then get off the bus and reboard from the rear. They were permitted to sit anywhere as long as no white passengers had to stand. It was up to the discretion of the driver as to when black passengers were to move back to make room for whites. Most of the

Dexter Avenue Baptist Church

time, the drivers acted like tyrants, abusively demanding that the black riders get in back. There were no black drivers on the buses. Since riding the buses was a necessity for most black people in Montgomery, these conditions had to be faced at least twice every day.

Just a year before, a teenaged girl had been arrested for refusing to yield her seat on a bus. Nothing had come of it. But now there was a sense that something could be done, a quickening of excitement. The Supreme Court had reversed Plessy the previous year in the Brown v. Board of Education case. School desegregation orders had gone out to many southern states and there were plans for integrating the University of Alabama in the spring term. It was in this setting that the city's black leadership met to consider a response to Mrs. Parks's arrest. They hit upon a boycott of the buses and decided that the black churches had to take the lead. For several reasons, they elected Rev. Martin Luther King, Jr., a newcomer in town with no previous leadership experience, to head the boycott committee.

King was called on to address a community meeting on the boycott's first evening. This was a critical period. Many in the community wanted to call it off. They didn't think the boycott could be sustained and felt that if it collapsed the one-day show of black unity would have been wasted. King wrote later that with no chance to prepare, he had to give a speech that would urge confrontation, but on a nonviolent basis. He started off by summarizing the list of grievances that were the lot of blacks in Montgomery.

"But there comes a time," he said, "that people get tired. We are here this evening to say to those who have mistreated us for so long that we are tired—tired of being segregated and humiliated; tired of being kicked about by the brutal feet of oppression. We had no alternative but to protest."

The speech, the first of hundreds that would electrify the country, solidified support for the boycott. King's home was bombed the following month and he made a speech on his front lawn urging nonviolence in response. He rapidly gained a nationwide reputation as a healer. Incredibly, for over a year, Montgomery's blacks refused to ride the buses. They walked and hitched and car-pooled, and in December, 1956, the city removed all restrictions on ridership. For the first time, a sustained black protest had forced the end of a facet of segregation. Mrs. Parks became a national hero of the civil rights movement and Reverend King became its most prominent spokesperson, a position he held until his assassination thirteen years later.

> **Location:** Dexter Ave. is a broad thoroughfare connecting downtown Montgomery to the state capitol, which is situated right across from the church, at 454 Dexter Ave. It was at the western end of this avenue, on Court Sq. in front of the Klein Jewelry Store, that Mrs. Parks boarded the bus for her historic ride.
> **Hours:** Monday to Friday, 9-5.
> **Exhibits:** A large mural, taking up an entire wall in the church office area, recapitulates the landmarks of the civil rights era, beginning with Mrs. Parks's ride. You may also visit the church sanctuary.
> **Telephone:** (205) 263-3970.
> **Handicapped access:** Yes.

Oakville

Jesse Owens Monument

This tiny village near Decatur was the boyhood home of the great Olympic athlete. The son of a sharecropper, Owens said later that he was working in the cotton field by the time was six. His family moved north to Cleveland two years later, in 1921. Owens went on to fame as an athlete at Ohio State University, and most memorably at the Olympic Games in Berlin in 1936.

His gold medals in the one-hundred-meter dash, two-hundred-meter dash, broad jump, and four-hundred-meter relay inspired the entire country and mocked Nazi assertions of racial superiority.

Jesse Owens

Dictator Adolf Hitler left the stadium rather than present Owens with his awards.

After Owens's death in 1980, his hometown decided to honor his memory with a simple granite block, decorated with the five Olympic rings and saluting an athletic performer who "brought hope to his fellow man."

> **Location:** From I-65, south of Decatur, take the Hartselle exit, westbound Alabama 36. Follow it to Morgan County Rd. 61, in the village of Speake, and turn north.
> **Hours:** Always open.

Phenix City

Horace King Marker

Horace King came to this town on the Georgia border in the 1830s as a slave and remained to become a state legislator and an honored architect. His owner, John Godwin, was a contractor and builder, and

King started off as foreman on the first wooden bridge put up across the Chattahoochee River, between Phenix City and Columbus, Georgia.

He and Godwin developed a distinctive lattice style of bridge and King eventually built most of the early bridges that spanned the river, from West Point, Georgia, on the north to Fort Gaines, Georgia, on the south. He was freed by a special act of the Alabama legislature in 1846, and after the Civil War he served in that same body as the representative from Russell County.

When Godwin died, King, by then a well-to-do freedman, provided financial support for his widow for the rest of her life. He also put up a shaft over Godwin's grave, dedicated "in lasting remembrance of the loss and gratitude he felt for his lost friend and former master." The monument still stands in Godwin Cemetery.

Location: The historic marker to King is in downtown Phenix City, off U.S. 80, near the site of his first bridge, at the intersection of Dillingham and Broad.

Selma

Edmund Pettis Bridge, Brown AME Chapel

The final act of the civil rights drama in the South was played out in this town in the Black Belt. Despite passage of the landmark Civil Rights Act of 1964, the black leadership understood that all gains were tenuous until the unchallenged right to vote was secured. This was segregation's ultimate control, exclusion from the ballot box and the democratic process. By literary tests and poll taxes, by outright intimidation and terror, the states of the Deep South had maintained white control of all political offices, from national to local, for seventy years by keeping blacks out of the voting booth. In Alabama and Mississippi, states with the largest black minorities in the country, black registration in the early sixties was less than five percent of total eligible voters.

Campaigns to register black voters in the summer of 1964 were met with unremitting violence. Local police, recognizing that the success of such a campaign threatened the very basis of their power, openly allied themselves with racist organizations to resist. In Selma, a population that was almost half black had less than one percent as registered voters. Sheriff Jim Clark jailed two thousand demonstrators in early 1965 during repeated protest marches to the courthouse. On February 26, Jimmie Lee Jackson was shot to death by a state trooper during a march in nearby Marion.

In was in this atmosphere that civil rights leaders announced a fifty-mile march along U.S. 80, from Selma to Montgomery, to dramatize the situation. It left Selma on Sunday, March 7, over the Pettis Bridge. Waiting on the far side of the Alabama River were state

Dr. Martin Luther King, Jr., leading the civil rights march from Selma to Montgomery in March, 1965

troopers, massed under directions from Gov. George Wallace, who had issued an executive order forbidding the march. The troopers attacked with fury, driving the marchers back into Selma with tear gas and clubs. Again, the nation watched in anger as they saw unarmed demonstrators beaten savagely by police officers. Hundreds of sympathizers, many of them drawn from religious organizations, flocked to Selma to assist. One of them, Rev. James Reed, died as a result of a beating suffered during a March 11 demonstration.

Finally, under federal protection ordered by President Lyndon B. Johnson, the march began again, on March 21, this time led by Dr. Martin Luther King, Jr., and concluded with a demonstration in front of the state capitol five days later. But one final, murderous attack was still to come. As Mrs. Viola Liuzzo, the wife of a Detroit Teamsters Union official, ferried marchers back to Selma that evening, she was killed by shots fired into her car by assailants who were later identified as members of the Ku Klux Klan.

President Johnson subsequently convened a joint session of Congress and urged passage of a bill extending federal protection to voting rights in every state. It was signed into law five months later, the crowning achievement of the southern civil rights era that has been called the Second Reconstruction.

Location: Pettis Bridge empties directly onto Broad St., U.S. 80, the main business thoroughfare of Selma. A good view of it can be obtained from a cobblestoned riverside plaza along Water St., 1 block east. Five blocks east is Martin Luther King St., and along its length are 3 churches associated with the civil rights struggle. Most prominent is the Brown AME Chapel, at 410 Martin Luther King. This was the starting point of the march to Montgomery and the site of many rallies in 1965.

Exhibits: A bust of Dr. King, situated in front of the church, is part of a memorial to the marchers. There is also an interior room containing memorabilia of that period.

Telephone: (205) 874-7897; call in advance for admission.

Other attractions: The church itself was founded in 1867, and was the first AME congregation in Alabama. Nearby is First Baptist Church, also the location of many rallies in 1965 and regarded as one of the most architecturally distinguished houses of worship in the state. The Martin Luther King, Jr., Street Church of God was build in 1900 as the second black Presbyterian church in Alabama.

Talladega

Talladega College

Two former slaves founded this black liberal arts school in 1867. One of them, William Savery, is remembered in the name of the library building. The frescoes inside, depicting the revolt of blacks aboard the slave ship *Amistad,* were painted by Georgia-born artist Hale Woodruff. (For further information on the *Amistad,* see the entry on First Church of Christ, Farmington, Connecticut.) One of the oldest buildings on the tree-shaded campus, along West Battle Street, is Swayne Hall, dating from the 1870s.

> **Location:** From I-20, west of Birmingham, exit at southbound Alabama 77 and follow signs when you reach Talladega.
> **Hours:** Library hours vary for viewing the Woodruff murals. It is best to call in advance.
> **Telephone:** (205) 362-0206.

Tuskegee

Tuskegee Institute National Historic Site

There is not another black educational facility in America with the legacy and lore of Tuskegee. Molded by the most remarkable educator of the time, ornamented by a brilliant scientist and scholar, Tuskegee is much more than a college campus. It is a symbol of aspiration and triumph, and the ideas born here still resonate through the black experience.

Booker T. Washington

Tuskegee is a living monument to two men: its first president, Booker T. Washington, and its most famous teacher, George Washington Carver. Both men were born into slavery and through their work at Tuskegee were numbered among the most admired Americans of their time.

Washington came here in 1881 to run the school, funded by a skimpy $2,000 grant from the Alabama legislature. He had been a teacher at Hampton Institute in Virginia (see the entry on Hampton Institute, Hampton, Virginia), and at the time of his arrival here he was twenty-six years old. He came to a place that had no faculty, no campus, no land. It didn't seem to matter to him. He had a vision of what black education should be in that time and place, and that was enough.

Holding classes that first year in a shanty and a church for an enrollment of thirty students, Washington began putting together his concept. His students would learn by doing, and when they understood they would go out and teach others. They would learn how to put up buildings and raise crops, to practice a trade that would enable them to live with dignity. He said that it was more important to earn a dollar in a factory than to spend a dollar in an opera house. The emphasis was always on the practical, on solving problems in the here and now. There were no buildings, so students built the campus themselves, brick by brick, as a class project. They ate food they raised in the adjacent fields. Then they went out and showed others how to do what they had done. All this was combined with moral instruction and the instilling of personal discipline.

For many in those first classes, these were the first ventilated buildings, the first balanced meals, they had ever known. Impoverished blacks across Alabama donated what they could give: eggs, livestock, a few coins. Eventually, people with names like Rockefeller and Carnegie would donate hundreds of thousands for new classroom facilities. But in the early years it was Washington's will and the scraps, painfully saved by blacks who believed, that kept Tuskegee alive.

By 1895, with the first Jim Crow laws being enacted by southern legislatures, Washington saw what was coming. In a speech which has come to be known as the Atlanta Compromise, delivered at the Cotton States Exposition, he outlined a place for blacks in this system. He would eschew demands for social equality but "interlace our industrial, commercial, civil, and religious life with yours in a way that shall make the interests of both races one. In all things that are purely social, we can be as separate as the fingers, yet one as the hand in all things essential to mutual progress."

This speech gave Washington a national reputation, but it meant different things to different audiences. To white southerners, it sounded like acceptance of the emerging system of segregation that was then replacing the shattered hopes of Reconstruction. To northern liberals, it sounded like a hopeful and reasonable response to an oppressive system, and Washington became the leading black spokesperson in America, invited to dine at the White House by

President Theodore Roosevelt and welcomed in the parlors of Fifth Avenue millionaires. But to many blacks, it sounded like surrender. Led by W. E. B. Du Bois, several leaders of the black community vowed to carry on the fight for social and political equality, and for scholastic as well as vocational education. Their opposition to the Atlanta Compromise led directly to the formation of what became the National Association for the Advancement of Colored People, the most powerful black organization of the twentieth century. After Washington's death in 1915, the Tuskegee curriculum was revised to encompass the pursuit of academic excellence. But it has never forsaken his original concept.

One year after delivering his Atlanta speech, Washington made his most significant appointment. He hired a young botanist from Iowa State College to head the new agricultural department. George W. Carver would stay on for forty-seven years until his death and become one of the most revered figures in American science. He had wanted to be an artist and he continued to paint for the rest of his life. But he shared Washington's practical turn of mind and shifted his attention instead to growing the things he depicted in his still-life canvases. Putting aside a promising career at an established school, Carver came to the makeshift laboratories and uncharted future of Tuskegee.

He emphasized "found" materials to his students, making things out of the stuff that was at hand. That's what led him to his famed research with the peanut. Driven by curiosity and an innovative mind, he tried devising the greatest number of possible uses for the most ordinary material in the southern fields. He made paint out of the red Alabama clay, paving blocks from cotton. He found 188 uses for the sweet potato. And from the humble peanut, he devised three hundred items of practical use—from milk to plastic. It was this work, this unlocking of fantastic secrets from even the most ordinary of products, that elevated Carver's reputation to an almost mystical level. Henry Ford was one of his most outspoken admirers, and donated funds to further his work.

Carver's achievements remain the focus of a visit to the Tuskegee campus. The Orientation Center of the National Historic Site is also a museum of his life and work. This is the best place to begin any tour of the campus. The center will impart a good historical perspective of Tuskegee and the lives of its two most prominent figures. You can even pick up a headset and listen to an ancient recording of Washington reading part of his Atlanta Compromise address.

The main part of the campus is to your left as you leave the Orientation Center. Many landmarks are situated around a central oval, with the clock tower and pillared front of White Hall, built by student workmen in 1910, dominating the site. It faces Tomkins Hall, built that same year in the same manner. At the far end of the oval is the oldest building on this part of the campus, Huntington Hall, built in 1900. At the near end are Carnegie Library and the Administration Building, constructed in the following two years. Between the last two structures and across Old Montgomery Road is The Oaks, Washington's stately home, which also was built by students, in 1899.

On the opposite side of the Orientation Center, near the traffic circle at the automobile entrance to the campus, is the famed sculpture of Washington "lifting the veil of ignorance from his fellow men." It was erected in 1922. A few steps north of that is the imposing campus chapel, a modern structure built to replace the original, which burned down in 1957. Behind the chapel on a hillside are the graves of several of Tuskegee's founders.

Continuing west along the main campus drive, you'll come to the Daniel "Chappie" James Aerospace Center. A Tuskegee graduate and the first black four-star general in the U.S. army, James was a fighter pilot, a war hero, and also an early civil rights activist. He liked to say in his later years that he participated in the first "sit-in" ever, as a member of the Tuskegee Airmen.

This group of black pilots was trained at nearby Moton Field, under the auspices of C. Alfred Anderson, who founded the school of aviation at Tuskegee. In the early days of World War II, black pilots, barred from combat training by the segregated U.S. Army Air Force, were sent here for instruction. Afterwards, they had to fight both for the chance to get into combat and for equal treatment on bases throughout the South. Officer's club sit-ins, led by James and many other Tuskegee Airmen, succeeded in breaking down segregated facilities at several installations. When given the chance to fight, their combat record was exceptional. Among the Tuskegee Airmen were Percy Sutton, who would become Manhattan borough president, and Coleman A. Young, future mayor of Detroit. A plaque honoring the Airmen is in the plaza of the Aerospace Center. Nearby is a jet like the one James flew in combat in Vietnam. The center was designed by another Tuskegee graduate, Tarlee W. Brown.

> **Location:** From I-85, east of Montgomery, take south-bound Alabama 81. The road will take you through the center of Tuskegee, then loop back to the campus on Old Montgomery Rd.
> **Hours:** The Orientation Center and Carver Museum are open daily, 9-5. The Oaks offers tours on the hour Monday to Friday, 9-11 and 2-4.
> **Admission charge:** None.
> **Telephone:** (205) 727-8011.

A R K A N S A S

Camden, New Edinburgh, Sheridan

Red River Campaign

In April of 1864, the Union Army occupying Little Rock began moving south, hoping to link up at the Red River with federal troops coming north from Louisiana and destroy the Confederate forces between them in a pincer. General Frederick Steele quickly seized Camden, but was harassed by Confederate raiders who cut off his supplies. One large wagon train was attacked on April 18, northwest of the city at Poison Spring. The First Kansas Colored Regiment, guarding the supply train, was in the thick of the battle and suffered its heaviest casualties of the war, with 117 dead and sixty-five wounded. Moreover, there were reports that captured black soldiers had been shot.

The battle at Poison Spring was fought five days after the fall of Fort Pillow in Tennessee, another engagement in which black soldiers were executed by the Confederates (see entry on Fort Pillow State Park, Henning, Tennessee). On April 25, racial retaliation took place again, when another supply train was attacked at Mark's Mill, near the village of New Edinburgh, northeast of Camden. "This battlefield was sickening to behold," reported one Confederate commander. "No orders, threats, or commands could restrain the men from vengeance on the Negroes and they were piled in great heaps about the wagons, in the tangled brushwood, and upon the muddy and trampled road."

The black soldiers from Kansas were enraged as reports of this slaughter came in. They vowed to take no southern prisoners in future battles.

With his supplies captured, Steele's position in Camden became untenable and he began retreating to Little Rock. The Confederates caught him at the Saline River on April 30 and moved in to pin down his forces before he could cross. But the Kansas troopers, in an act of desperate heroism mixed with revenge, charged the Confederate guns shelling the Federals at the river. The Kansans, shouting "Remember Poison Spring," suffered fifteen fatalities in the melee, compared to 150 Confederate dead. The action enabled Steele to withdraw safely and retreat unpursued to Little Rock.

Location: Three state parks commemorating the Red River campaign are within a few miles of each other in southern Alabama. Poison Spring is located 12 miles northwest of Camden by way of Arkansas 4, 24, and 76. **Facilities:** A picnic area, battle diorama, and foot trails are at the site.

Return to Camden and head north on U.S. 79 to Fordyce, then east on Arkansas 8. Mark's Mill is at the junction with Arkansas 97.

Facilities: There is also a picnic area here.

Return to Fordyce and head north on U.S. 167 to Farindale, then west on Arkansas 48, north on Arkansas 229, and east on Arkansas 46 to Jenkins Ferry.

Facilities: This is the best developed of the three parks, with swimming and fishing on the Saline River and an interpretive center about the battle. **Hours:** The 3 parks are open all year, but some facilities are available only during the summer season.

Carthage

Hampton Springs Cemetery

The entirely black community of Carthage, in central Arkansas, is the focus of a puzzle involving the studies of archeology and anthropology. A dig in the nineteenth-century graveyard uncovered burial sites in which shards of pottery were placed in a deliberate pattern. Such burial practices have been traced back to tribes of West Africa, but rarely occur in the United States. Even more unusual was their appearance in a comparatively remote frontier community, far from coastal cities in which former tribal groupings could be expected to remain more cohesive. The find is still being analyzed by historians.

Location: Carthage is about 60 miles southwest of Little Rock, by way of U.S. 167 and westbound Arkansas 48. It is also 10 miles south of the Jenkins Ferry battlefield (see entry above), by way of westbound Arkansas 46 and southbound Arkansas 229. There are signs to the cemetery from the city hall in the center of town. **Exhibits:** Several of the old gravestones and shards can be seen on the grounds. **Hours:** Dawn to dusk, all year.

Elaine

Riots of 1919

In the months following the armistice that ended World War I, the United States was gripped by what came to be known as "The Great Red Scare." Alarmed by developments in Russia and Germany, members of President Woodrow Wilson's administration were convinced that this country was also threatened by communist revolutionaries. In many parts of the country, blacks identified with radical political causes became targets.

In the Arkansas Delta, grievances over the sharecropper system and its pervasive poverty created widespread sympathy for an organization called the Progressive Farmers and Household Union of America. They were watched suspiciously by Phillips County authorities, and on the night of September 30, 1919, the situation blew up.

Two deputies approached a schoolhouse near the town of Elaine at which a union meeting was being held. One of them was shot and killed. The survivor claimed that they had been fired on without provocation, while blacks inside the schoolhouse insisted that they were returning gunfire. Within days, a full-scale war erupted around Elaine. Armed posses converged on the town and, by the count of one newspaper, killed fifteen blacks. Running battles through the back country lasted another week before five hundred regular army troops were sent in to end the unrest.

In the aftermath, ninety-nine blacks were arrested and sentenced to death. Those verdicts were reversed by the U.S. Supreme Court and all of the defendants eventually were freed. The incident today is virtually forgotten.

> **Location:** Elaine is now a sleepy Delta town, 25 miles south of Helena, by way of Arkansas 20. No memorial to the events of 1919 exists.

Little Rock

Central High School

"For us, the bottom line was every single morning of our lives, for nine months, we got up, we polished our saddle shoes, and we went to war."

The speaker was Melba Pattillo Beals, at her return to Central High School in 1987 for the thirtieth anniversary of the most celebrated case of school integration in American history. Along with eight other black teenagers selected for academic ability, she walked into the firestorm that pitted a governor against a president and gave the nation its first inkling of how bitter the fight to desegregate southern schools would be.

Central High School in 1957

Brown v. Topeka Board of Education established the legal principle that ended school segregation in 1954. The decision instructed the nation's public schools to open their facilities on a nonracial basis "with all deliberate speed." For three years, the schools complied and 712 districts, mostly in the mid-South, were desegregated with minimal protest.

Then came Little Rock's turn, and it soon became clear that while a U.S. Supreme Court ruling was one thing, putting it into effect was another.

Governor Orville Faubus was elected as a moderate on racial issues and Little Rock was regarded as less a potential trouble spot than cities further south. But in the first week of September, 1957, Faubus called out the National Guard to encircle Central High and turn away black students. A federal court order directed him to remove the troops, but when the students arrived for classes on September 23, they were met by a cursing, spitting mob and were forced to leave.

The mayor of Little Rock and the head of the city's board of education were outraged. They had carefully prepared for integration and were convinced their plan would have worked. The mayor even asked for a legal opinion about using city police to escort the black children. Events supplied an answer the following day. President Dwight D. Eisenhower, who had stated a week before that he could not conceive of a situation in which federal troops would be sent to Little Rock, did exactly that, calling up the 101st Airborne Division to fly into Arkansas's capital and occupy the school area. While regular army soldiers held back the jeering throng with fixed bayonets, the nine black children walked silently into the high school.

Eight of them made it through the year, with Ernest Green graduating in June. But Minnijean Brown was expelled when she responded to repeated taunts by calling her tormentors "white trash." The others did not enjoy an uninterrupted education after the initial victory. Faubus closed all the city's public schools before classes began in 1958 and his segregationist allies set up a system of private, all-white academies. Most people of Little Rock did not support this action and when the superintendent and forty-four white teachers were fired for supporting insurrection, the city struck back. In a recall election, three segregationist school board members were recalled from office and the schools reopened for keeps in the fall of 1959.

The sight of federal troops occupying a southern city for the first time since Reconstruction struck a nerve. As one commentator put it, "The lights of reason began going out all over the South" after Little Rock. Massive resistance to school integration began and the "deliberate speed" ordered by the Supreme Court slowed to a crawl for the next three years. Poignant scenes of tiny children in elementary school walking past cursing mobs became familiar. Even Norman Rockwell, who normally depicted only the sunny side of American life in his magazine covers, was moved to draw a little black girl, in shiny patent shoes and starched white dress, escorted by a huge federal marshal past a mob. It became one of the most-requested covers he ever did.

> **Location:** From downtown, take Broadway south to 14th St. and head west. The school is at the corner of Park Ave. and 14th St.
>
> **Exhibits:** A stately, well-landscaped facility built in 1927, the school is built around a five-story central tower. It now has about a 60 percent black enrollment.

K E N T U C K Y

Berea

Berea College

This little school in the Cumberland mountains became well known for its innovative tuition plan: students, most of them drawn from poor mountain families, work for the college in return for an education. But Berea was touched with innovation from its very beginning in 1855. Its founders were Cassius M. Clay and John G. Fee, two ardent Kentucky abolitionists who were convinced that racial equality had to begin with educational equality. Berea was the first college formed for the purpose of admitting both black and white students, a wildly controversial idea for any part of the country, let alone a southern border state.

It worked for almost fifty years. But in 1904, Jim Crow accomplished what even the slavery era could not, and Kentucky passed a law barring blacks from Berea. The endowment for black students was used to found a separate black facility near Louisville, and for the next fifty years Berea was a whites-only school.

Lincoln Hall, dating from 1887, is the oldest building on the Berea campus, a national historic site and the last surviving structure from the old college.

> **Location:** Berea is located just west of I-75, about 35 miles south of Lexington.
> **Hours:** Tours of the college and its crafts shops begin at the Boone Tavern, on campus, and are conducted Monday to Friday at 9 and 2, September to May; morning tours only on Saturday.
> **Admission charge:** None.
> **Telephone:** (606) 986-9341.

Frankfort

Kentucky Military History Museum

Kentucky was a border state during the Civil War, permitting slavery, but not seceding from the Union. The long Ohio River

149

border with the northern states of Ohio, Indiana, and Illinois had substantially weakened slavery in Kentucky long before the war began, and the physical brutality of slavery may not have been as harsh here as in states further south. Knowing that freedom lay on the far side of the river, however, and that the Underground Railroad was in place to assist the flight north, the rate of escape from Kentucky ran far higher than in any other slaveholding state.

With a deep tradition of resistance, black Kentuckians were ready to fight when the chance came. As a result, it provided some of the richest recruiting in the country for the federal army. One historian estimates that former slaves enlisted at the rate of one hundred a day after 1863.

The Military History Museum in the state capital has a special section devoted to the black units recruited during the Civil War.

> **Location:** The museum is located on U.S. 60 at Capitol Ave., just north of the Kentucky River bridge.
> **Exhibits:** It contains displays on 250 years of the state's armed heritage, from the long rifles of Daniel Boone to the Vietnam War, as well as the black military history displays.
> **Hours:** Monday to Saturday, 9-4, and Sunday, 1-5.
> **Admission charge:** None.
> **Telephone:** (502) 564-3265.

Lexington

Fieldstone Fences

One of the most distinctive features of the Bluegrass landscape is its fences. The patterns they make over the rolling countryside give a sense of order and serenity to the lush Kentucky horse farms.

White plank fences are the visual signature of the Lexington area, but far older are the fieldstone fences along some of the back roads. Some of these fences date from the 1820s and were crafted by slave labor. The stones were cleared from the fields and the fence made without mortar, each rock supported by the sureness of its fit with the rocks around it.

Building them became a highly valued skill and for generations many black families continued to make their livings as fence masons. The Guy family in Woodford County carried on this tradition for six generations, and in the 1950s they were called upon to repair fences their own ancestors had made while slaves.

> **Location:** For a look at some of the old fieldstone fences, head west from Lexington along the Old Frankfort Pike, Kentucky Hwy. 1681. Many fences in this area were built and then restored by the Guys.

Kentucky Horse Park

Isaac Murphy Memorial, Kentucky Horse Park

There are two memorial graves outside the front gate of this shrine to the Kentucky thoroughbred. One is to the greatest horse the state ever produced, Man O'War. The other is to its greatest jockey, Isaac Burns Murphy.

In his twenty-year career, Murphy mounted up more than fourteen hundred times and won an incredible forty-four percent of his rides. He was the first rider to win the Kentucky Derby three times, a record that stood for fifty-seven years until broken by Eddie Arcaro in 1948.

He was born outside Lexington in 1861 and started riding professionally at the age of fourteen. He learned his trade galloping horses for some of the stables in this heart of Bluegrass Country and came under the wing of "Uncle" Eli Jordan, a black trainer who took a liking to him. By 1877, he was riding in big stakes races at Louisville's Churchill Downs.

In a time when any sort of honesty in professional sports was regarded as remarkable, Murphy won a reputation for his unshakable rectitude. Jockeys routinely sold out, getting rich by taking bribes from heavy bettors. But in Murphy's obituary in the *Thoroughbred*

Record, he is quoted as giving this advice to a young jockey: "You just ride to win. They get you to pull a horse in a selling race, but when it comes to a stake race they get Isaac to ride. A jockey that'll sell out to one man will sell out to another. Just be honest. You may only become rich in reputation but they will record you as a success."

Murphy won his first Derby in 1884 aboard Buchanan, repeating in 1890 on Riley and the following year on Kingman. His last win was famed for being the slowest Derby ever run. The winner's time was two minutes, fifty-two and one-quarter seconds over a mile and a half (the race was shortened to a mile and a quarter in 1896). Murphy explained later that he had been instructed to pace himself with the favorite, Balsowan, "and if he walked, then I was to walk." This Derby came to be known as the "walking Derby."

Murphy was better known to his contemporaries for winning four of the first five American Derbies ever run and five Latonia Derbies. In those days, these races were regarded as more prestigious than the Kentucky Derby. It was only after his death that the race in Louisville assumed such a central place in thoroughbred lore, magnifying his achievements posthumously.

Constantly fighting a battle with weight, he tried to keep himself at one hundred pounds during the season, as much as forty pounds less than his off-season weight. He was charged with riding drunk in 1890, although he protested that he was simply weak from losing weight. His career started going downhill and he retired after the 1895 season, when he won only twice in twenty rides. He died the following year and was given an elaborate burial in Lexington.

Over the years, however, his grave was neglected, its very location being lost for a time, and the cemetery was abandoned. Finally, in 1967, his remains were moved to their present location.

Location: The Kentucky Horse Park is located just north of Lexington at the Ironworks Pike exit of I-75.
Exhibits: It is a sprawling state park, featuring horse-drawn rides, a museum of the horse, twice-daily shows of various breeds, pony rides, and a celebration of the area's equine tradition. Murphy's grave is a short walk to the left, just before you reach the main gate of the park from the parking lot. It is not necessary to buy a ticket to the park to view it, although a $1 parking fee is collected.
Hours: Daily, 9-5, mid-March to October; Wednesday to Sunday, 9-5, the rest of the year.
Admission charge: Adults, $5.95; children under 12, $2.50.
Telephone: (606) 233-4303.

Louisville

The Kentucky Derby Museum

The first Kentucky Derby was run in 1875 and a black jockey was aboard the winning horse. Any other result would have been difficult to obtain: of the fourteen horses entered in that first race, thirteen were ridden by black men. Blacks frequently worked as trainers and riders in Kentucky before the Civil War, and the knowledge they acquired in this field enabled them to dominate horse racing the late nineteenth century.

The museum documents the accomplishments of these men, many of them record-setters, but regarded with slightly less concern than the thoroughbreds they rode. While the lineage of the horses was painstakingly documented, the first names of several Derby-winning jockeys were never registered and are unknown. The museum, however, does present a fair account of their achievements in this most celebrated of American races.

> **Location:** The museum is part of Churchill Downs, the track at which the Derby is run, at 700 Central Ave. From downtown Louisville, head south on 3d St. and then right on Central, or take southbound I-65 to westbound Eastern Pkwy., and then south on 3d to Central.
> **Exhibits:** The history of the Derby is presented with displays about the famous horses who ran here, and the people who owned, trained, and rode them. There is also a multi-media show.
> **Hours:** Daily, 9-5.
> **Telephone:** (502) 637-1111.
> **Admission charge:** Adults, $3.50; seniors, $2.50; children 5-12, $1.50; children under 5, free.

Mammoth Cave

Mammoth Cave National Park

It is probably the best known hole in the ground in America. The cave has the longest trail network of any cavern system in the world, with more than three hundred miles of subterranean passages. But for forty years after its discovery, only a small portion of it was known. Not until Stephen Bishop, a black slave, dared to explore its hidden recesses and unknown corners did the extent of Mammoth Cave become known. For many years, he was almost as famed an attraction as the big cave itself for the tourists who made the trip here.

Credit for Mammoth Cave's discovery is traditionally given to a man named Houchins, who stumbled upon it in pursuit of a wounded bear in 1798 at what is now known as the Historic Entrance. Its first owners concluded that its greatest value was in the rich deposits of saltpeter, a source of gunpowder. The vats in which the mineral was worked are still on display. But when the War of 1812 ended, so did the demand for saltpeter.

Its second owner, Frank Gorin, hit upon the idea of developing the cave as a tourist attraction. This was complicated somewhat by the fact that there were no roads to the place. But Gorin was a man who thought big, and he built his own. He also encouraged Bishop to familiarize himself with the cave and become a guide. In those days, the cave was thought to end at the Bottomless Pit, a gap two hundred-feet deep. Bishop wasn't convinced. He managed to get a ladder down into the cave and used it to cross the pit, finding a new, completely unexpected world to explore on the far side.

From that time on, Bishop became Mammoth Cave's Columbus. Even today, guides say they come upon Bishop's name smoked into the walls in the deepest portions of the cavern system. By the late 1830s, the cave had become an international attraction and Bishop's tours a staple of American travel. It is said he learned to write by watching tourists smoke their names on the walls with their lanterns. It was also here, under the soil of Kentucky, that white tourists invited a black man to sit down with them at a picnic lunch, an act that would have been inconceivable on the surface.

Bishop died in 1859 and his protégé, Matt Bransford, took over as chief guide. Guides say that most of what is known about the cave today still dates back to Bishop's explorations and the map he drew of the caverns in 1842.

> **Location:** Mammoth Cave National Park is reached from I-65, about 85 miles south of Louisville, by taking Kentucky 90 west to the park road. There are a variety of tours available, ranging in length from 75 minutes to 6 hours. Some of the longer tours are fairly strenuous.
> **Hours:** Open daily 8-6:30 during the summer months; 8-5:30 the rest of the year. In summer, tickets for specific tours may be purchased in advance at Ticketron outlets.
> **Admission charge:** Prices vary widely depending on the length of the tour.
> **Telephone:** (502) 758-2328.

Owensboro

Josiah Henson Trail

Isaac Riley was a Maryland landowner who came upon hard times and wasn't able to maintain the eighteen slaves he owned. In 1825 he shipped them all to his brother Amos in Kentucky, including Josiah Henson, his wife, and their two children. After three years, he instructed his brother to sell them, except for Henson, whom he wanted sent back to Maryland. Henson, who was about thirty-six years old when he arrived in Kentucky, had been given access to education and had been ordained as a minister in the Methodist Episcopal Church. On the trip back to Maryland, he raised money by his preaching and upon his return gave Isaac Riley a $275 payment toward his freedom. But after a few months, Riley sent him back to Kentucky and told him the price had been upped to $1,000.

Henson decided his only alternative was escape. He located his wife and children and together, late in the summer of 1830, they made a run for freedom. They managed to get a rowboat and crossed the Ohio River at Rockport, Indiana. From there, the Underground Railroad spirited them off to Canada. Henson's autobiography and interviews with Harriet Beecher Stowe many years later supplied much of the material for her influential novel *Uncle Tom's Cabin*. (For more on Henson's life, see the entry on *Uncle Tom's Cabin*, Dresden, Ontario.)

> **Location:** The site of the Riley plantation is designated by a historical marker on U.S. 60, near the village of Maceo, just west of the Daviess county line. No other evidence of the place remains.
>
> **Exhibits:** Local historical enthusiasts have collected many artifacts relating to *Uncle Tom's Cabin* and slavery in the area, and are trying to raise funds to build a museum and park in the vicinity of the Riley plantation. Their efforts also led to the renaming of U.S. 60 to the Josiah Henson Trail between Owensboro and the county line.

Washington

Old Slave Market

Washington was the second-largest town in Kentucky in the days after the Revolutionary War. It grew because the hill leading up from the Ohio River landing at Maysville was such an arduous climb that it took an entire day, and travelers needed a place to stay before proceeding. Pioneer Simon Kenton owned land here and organized the community. Among those who moved to Washington was the Marshall Key family. When their daughter was sent to school in Cincinnati, she became a friend of Harriet Beecher, daughter of the minister Lyman Beecher, who headed Lane Seminary. Miss Beecher paid her friend in Kentucky a visit in 1835, her first.

A few doors down from the Key home, which still stands on the main street, was the courthouse. On the broad lawn in front of the building, slaves were sold for transport to states further south. Miss Beecher was horrified by what she saw at one of these auctions, and the images stayed with her for the rest of her life. She married Calvin

Ellis Stowe and later moved to New England, but she could never entirely erase the memory of families being split up and sold. Seventeen years later, after passage of the Fugitive Slave Act, she was moved to start her famed book, *Uncle Tom's Cabin.* The abhorrence of slavery which animated the novel, she later wrote, had its beginning in her visit to the slave market in Washington.

> **Location:** Washington is just off U.S. 68, about 5 miles south of Maysville. Watch for the turnoff to the east.
> **Exhibits:** There are several historic buildings in the village and many of them can be visited during a short walk along the single business street. The Key House is private. A historic marker indicates the site of the old courthouse and slave market in the center of town.
> **Hours:** The Washington visitor center is open daily, 11-5, April to December.
> **Telephone:** (606) 759-7411.

L O U I S I A N A

Baton Rouge

Southern University

With a campus high atop a bluff overlooking the Mississippi River, just north of Louisiana's capital, this is among the loveliest collegiate settings in the country. Southern moved to the Scott's Bluff plantation in the Scotlandville area of Baton Rouge in 1914. That was thirty-four years after it opened its doors as a technical high school for blacks in New Orleans.

The loop drive around campus leads to a parking overlook on the bluff, a fine spot for viewing the river and its waterborne activity as well as the rail and highway traffic on the bridges to the south. A few hundred yards further east is the center of the campus, with classroom buildings grouped around a large pond and shaded by

The campus of Southern University

157

huge, moss-draped trees. If someone asked you to picture the ideal southern campus in your mind, it probably would look a lot like Southern's.

> **Location:** From central Baton Rouge, take I-110 north to the westbound Harding Blvd. exit (Louisiana 408). The road runs right into the campus and becomes the loop drive.
> **Hours:** The drive is open to visitors during daylight hours.

Melrose

Melrose Plantation

If they tried to put the story of this plantation into a novel, it would sound too romantic to be true. While some of its strands are wrapped in legend going back more than two hundred years, the main elements are a matter of verifiable historical fact, and a tribute to two remarkable black women born two centuries apart.

The first was Marie Therese Coincoin, who built Melrose. The second was Clementine Hunter, who celebrated its life on canvas. Melrose is not one of Louisiana's better-known plantations. It is a bit out of the way, situated on a back road along the Cain River near the town of Natchitoches in the northwest part of the state. The town became celebrated in 1989 as the locale of the hit movie *Steel Magnolias,* an accolade to the indomitable spirit of southern women.

Melrose Plantation

The same spirit might be attributed to the founder of the Metoyer family dynasty here.

Marie Therese Coincoin was born in Natchitoches around 1742, a household slave in the family of the town's leading citizen, Louis Juchereau St. Denis. He had been sent out from New Orleans twenty-eight years before to establish a post there and open trade with Spanish settlements in what is now Texas. A resourceful adventurer, St. Denis tried to solidify relations by marrying the daughter of the Spanish commandant, but later had to fight off repeated attacks by both Spanish and Natchez Indian parties. By the time of Marie Therese's birth he was an honored elder statesman, sixty-six years of age. He lived only two years more and she grew up working in the home of his widow.

When Madame St. Denis died, Marie Therese was a woman of thirty-four, the mother of four children. With the estate dissolved, the entire family was sold to Thomas Pierre Metoyer, a French planter on the Cain River. Within four years, she had been granted her freedom and had borne Metoyer the first of ten children she would have by him. Eventually, he freed all their children and gave her several grants of land along the river. Never forgetting her four other children, however, Marie Therese used the proceeds from her land to buy their freedom and establish them on land of their own.

By 1796, the family was well established on several tracts along the river. The largest of them became Melrose, run by Marie Therese's oldest son by Metoyer, Louis. He built Yucca House that year, the oldest structure on the property and the original main house of the plantation. The beams were cypress, the walls of mud from the river bottom mixed with Spanish moss and deer hair. From here, the Metoyers cleared the land and started cultivation of tobacco, indigo, and cattle, with slaves of their own. African House was put up in 1800, and is regarded as the most architecturally distinctive building at Melrose. It was intended as a storehouse and jail, and got its name from the outwardly extending second story, which resembles huts found in the Congo region of Africa.

Marie Therese died in 1817, but lived to see her descendants prosper. Melrose plantation house was built by Louis sixteen years later in the stately style of southern planters, with an imposing pillared front and brick lower floor. Within ten years, however, the Metoyers lost the land in the aftermath of a national depression.

For the next forty years, Melrose passed through the hands of several owners, finally being purchased by the Henry family in 1884. By the turn of the century, it was in severe disrepair, with several buildings in a dilapidated state and the fields overgrown. But Cammie Garrett Henry was a woman fascinated by the region and its lore, and she dedicated herself to restoring Melrose and turning it into an artistic center. Over the years, many prominent writers were her guests, put up at Yucca House for as long as they cared to stay. Some of them celebrated the Cane River in their works.

The cook at many of the gatherings here was a black woman who had grown up working at Melrose, Clementine Hunter. When the

Henrys found that she had a talent for painting, they encouraged her to leave the kitchen and spend her time at the easel. The results gave Melrose its second element of importance. Many of her works are displayed throughout the buildings, especially in African House, and have made Melrose a significant art center. She depicted scenes of the black plantation life of her childhood, a way of life that was quickly disappearing even while she worked in the 1940s and 1950s. Acclaimed as Louisiana's most outstanding primitive artist, her works are a historic treasure, a touching and priceless visual record of everyday rural black life of a century ago.

Location: Melrose is located on Louisiana 119, a meandering back road that follows the course of the Cane River, about 15 miles southeast of Natchitoches. From Natchitoches follow Louisiana 1 to Natchez and turn left on Hwy. 119. From the east, take I-49 to the northbound Hwy. 119 exit, at Derry.

Exhibits: An excellent tour of all the buildings on the property, starting with an audiovisual presentation that sets the historic perspective, is given by guides who live on the site. Allow at least 90 minutes.

Hours: Daily, 12-4.

Admission charge: Adults, $4; children 13-18, $2; children 6-12, $1; children under 6, free.

Telephone: (318) 379-0171.

Other attractions: Directly across the Cane River, by way of Louisiana 493, is the church still attended by members of the Metoyer family living in the area. The graveyard in back, with the tombs aboveground in the Louisiana manner, contains the remains of several generations of this remarkable family. It is open during daylight hours.

New Orleans

Amistad Research Center

The largest collection of material on African-American culture and race relations in the United States, this facility is part of Tulane University. There are over eight million pieces of material in its library, and its primary source documents are regarded as unmatched in the field.

Location: 6823 St. Charles Ave., in the eastern end of the city.

Hours: Daily, 8:30-5.

Admission charge: None.

Telephone: (504) 865-5535.

Amistad Research Center

Chalmette Battlefield

The final battle of the War of 1812 can't really be called a turning point in history. It was fought two weeks after the treaty that ended the war had been signed in Europe. But the Battle of New Orleans has become a legendary fight in American history. The image of a motley bunch of frontiersmen, Cajuns from the Louisiana swamps, pirates from Jean Lafitte's band of brigands, and regulars under the command of Gen. Andrew Jackson, mowing down the finest troops in the British army, touched a proud chord in the young country.

The battle propelled Jackson into the White House, and almost a century and a half later it was still powerful enough in the American imagination to furnish the material for a hit song by Johnny Horton. What is far less widely known is the role black soldiers played in the battle and Jackson's own statement that one of them fired the critical shot of the engagement.

New Orleans was the prize towards which Britain's grand strategy was directed. Its capture would have secured a foothold on the Mississippi River and possibly detached the rest of the United States from its new possessions in the West. The British force had gathered in the West Indies and moved to take the city by stealth, sailing in from the Gulf of Mexico through the back bayous before the Americans suspected the threat. But the civil authorities were alerted by Lafitte, who had been approached by British agents seeking his aid. Desperately gathering whatever troops he could muster, Jackson enlisted two black battalions, the largest force of black men ever assembled to fight for America up to that time.

Blacks participating in the Battle of New Orleans

The idea had originated with Louisiana Gov. William C. C. Claiborne, and Jackson accepted it enthusiastically. "Our country has been invaded and threatened with destruction," he responded. "She wants soldiers to fight her battles. The free men of colour in your city are inured to the southern climate and would make excellent soldiers. They will not remain quiet spectators of the interesting contest. . . . Distrust them, and you make them your enemies. Place confidence in them and you engage them by every dear and honorable tie to the interest of the country who extends to them the equal rights and privileges with white men."

Jackson personally reviewed these battalions, and when questioned about their use by the assistant district paymaster, he angrily responded: "Be pleased to keep to yourself your opinions upon the role of policy of making payments of the troops with the necessary muster rolls without inquiring whether the troops are white, black, or tea."

On the morning of January 8, 1815, these battalions occupied the center of the American line facing British commander Sir Edward Pakenham. Two earlier attempts at breaching this line had failed, but Pakenham decided his only recourse was a full frontal assault. Despite the battle-tested discipline of the British troops, many of them veterans of the Duke of Wellington's campaigns, their line disintegrated under the withering fire from the Americans. Pakenham desperately tried to rally his forces, although one horse was shot out from under him and his arm shattered by a musket ball. As he called on his Highlanders to advance, a torrent of fire ripped into the position, striking him in the thigh and the groin. He died moments later, effectively ending any British resistance. The battle became a massacre, and before it ended, the British had lost seven hundred men, compared to thirteen for the Americans.

In his final report to President James Monroe, Jackson wrote: "I heard a single rifle shot from a group of country carts we had been using, and a moment thereafter I saw Pakenham reel and pitch out of his saddle. I have always believed he fell from the bullet of a free man of color, who was a famous rifle shot and came from the Attakapas region of Louisiana."

> **Location:** Chalmette Battlefield is now part of the Jean Lafitte National Historical Park. It is 6 miles east of central New Orleans by way of St. Claude Ave. and St. Bernard Hwy., Louisiana 46.
>
> **Exhibits:** Self-guided auto tours take you to the major points of interest on the battlefield. There is an audiovisual presentation in the visitor center, which is in the Beauregard House, a country residence built about 18 years after the battle. The Chalmette Battle Monument is situated close to the position of the American lines occupied by the black battalions. Its cornerstone was laid on the 25th anniversary of the battle, but it wasn't completed until 68 years later, in 1908.
>
> **Hours:** Daily, 8-5.
>
> **Admission charge:** None.
>
> **Telephone:** (504) 589-4428.
>
> **Handicapped access:** Yes.
>
> **Other attractions:** The adjacent National Cemetery contains graves of Union soldiers who died in Louisiana in the Civil War and veterans of all subsequent wars.

Louis Armstrong Park, Preservation Hall, Old Mint Museum

Possibly the best-known nondefinition in American musical lore is the one that Louis Armstrong gave in response to an inquiry about the meaning of jazz: "If you have to ask, you'll never know."

There are about as many theories about the creation of jazz as there are keys on a piano. Some say it evolved in Congo Square, the one place in New Orleans where black slaves were allowed to gather on Sunday afternoons. The rhythmic chants and dances performed there, with origins deep in Africa, were a tourist attraction long before the Civil War. Others insist the music developed in Storyville, the city's legalized red light district, where black musicians were esteemed as entertainers by the white clientele of the bawdy houses. There is even one theory that the imposition of segregation in New Orleans in the 1890s was responsible for jazz, in that formally trained Creole musicians gave structure to the music of poorer blacks with whom they previously would not have been associated.

Musicians outside Preservation Hall in the French Quarter

By the start of the twentieth century, this music was emerging throughout New Orleans, in brass bands and street "spasm" bands, on the riverboats, and in the back streets of the black neighborhoods. Musicians whose names have been forgotten were creating something new, borrowing a bit from the blues, a bit from the church, and rhythmic snatches that may have originated in Louisiana's old French or Spanish dances. This was the city in which Armstrong was born and these were the sounds he heard. In time, the name of the city, the music, and the man would become so intertwined that it would be almost impossible to hear one without thinking of the others.

When Armstrong was born on July 4, 1900, the music was known as "jass," which was then a slang word for the sex act. Congo Square was only a memory, but Storyville was thriving, and as a child Armstrong wandered its streets. The district was created in 1897 at the behest of a city alderman who felt it would allow better control of prostitution. To his embarrassment, it was soon named for him and for the next twenty years, until it was shut down by the U.S. Navy, it was a leading attraction of New Orleans. An official guide, the *Blue Book*, was published annually, listing the delights of each house in the district. This is where men who became giants of early jazz—Jelly Roll Morton, Bunk Johnson, King Oliver—developed their styles, and it is easy to discern how the name for their music evolved from "jass."

"We kids, even in our teens, we would hang around the honky tonks all night, afraid we would miss something," said Armstrong in a seventieth-birthday interview with the *New York Times*. "We used to go around and pass the hat, because I had to pay my mother's rent. Things were awfully rough. I played at as many funerals as I could get and cats died like flies so I got a lot of nice little gigs out of that."

When he was thirteen Armstrong got into trouble for shooting off a pistol during a New Year's Eve celebration and wound up in the Colored Waif's Home. Someone in that institution recognized his musical talent and handed him a cornet. When he got out, he became a protégé of Oliver, regarded as the city's most talented trumpet player. Later, Oliver would summon his young friend to Chicago to play second cornet in his band, launching the career that eventually eclipsed his own.

Two groups from New Orleans, the Original Dixieland Jass Band and the New Orleans Rhythm Kings, signed recording contracts in 1917, and the regional music soon was being heard all over the country. But the New Orleans style started to be modified by musicians in Kansas City, Chicago, and New York. By the end of the 1920s, the music was starting to shade into swing. Armstrong changed with it and with his gravelly voice and "scat" singing—vocal phrases without words that duplicated the solo line of an instrument—he rose to a popularity that never wavered. Even when New Orleans jazz was regarded as hopelessly old hat, in the forties and fifties, Armstrong's style and bubbling personality made him a renowned figure worldwide, an ambassador of American music. Even though his hometown remained a tightly segregated city, he returned in 1949 to become the first black man ever to reign over Mardi Gras, an honor that moved him deeply. After his death in 1971, a park was named for him and a statue by black sculptor Elizabeth Catlett erected.

As Armstrong went on to global success, the music nearly died. By the late 1950s, there were no clubs in New Orleans playing the city's traditional jazz and the musicians who were trained in the style were dying off or working other jobs. Then a group of aficionados began holding small, pass-the-hat concerts in an old building in the French Quarter, which became known as Preservation Hall. Enthusiasm started to build and performers who hadn't played publicly in years emerged to join old colleagues. A touring band was formed and the vitality of the players and their music captured audiences around the country. Soon Preservation Hall had become a major tourist attraction, and as the older musicians passed away, younger people whom they had trained took their places to sustain the legacy.

At about the same time, a jazz museum was assembled in the Quarter. But the collection outgrew its quarters and in the 1970s it was decided to transfer the museum to the renovated U.S. Mint on Esplanade. This imposing, fortress-like structure with three-foot-thick walls was opened in 1838 and coins were made here until 1909. For a brief period during 1861 it was the Confederacy's mint. It occupies the site on which Gen. Andrew Jackson reviewed his troops, including two battalions of black soldiers, before the Battle of New Orleans (see the entry on Chalmette National Historical Park above.) After the government shut down the coinage operation, it became a Veterans' Bureau office and then a prison. Finally taken over by the Louisiana State Museum, it now houses the city's vast collection of material relating to jazz history and Mardi Gras.

> **Location:** Louis Armstrong Park is a redeveloped area of the city which has become a cultural center, located just across Rampart St. from the French Quarter. This is the perfect place for a park honoring Armstrong, because it is within steps of the traditional birthplaces of jazz, Congo Square and Storyville. The square was located in what is now the southwestern corner of the park, on N. Rampart St. between St. Peter St. and St. Ann St. Later, it was renamed Beauregard Square. The Municipal Auditorium, site of many Mardi Gras balls and cultural events throughout the year, is at the northern edge of the old square. Storyville was a few blocks to the west, in the area bounded by Basin, Robertson, St. Louis, and Iberville streets. The area is now public housing. Armstrong's statue, depicting him with trumpet in hand, is just to the east of the park's main entrance gate from Rampart St. Preservation Hall is located near the heart of the Quarter, at 726 St. Peter St.
> **Hours:** Performances are given nightly at Preservation Hall, with the doors opening at 8 P.M. and the closing hour

usually at 12:30 A.M. Seating capacity is very limited and you should expect to stand.
Admission charge: $2.50.
Telephone: (504) 522-2841.

The U.S. Mint Museum is in the southeastern corner of the Quarter, at Esplanade at Decatur St.

Hours: Wednesday to Sunday, 10-5.
Admission charge: $3.50, with a combination ticket available to both the jazz and Mardi Gras collections. Tickets are also sold individually, and there is a reduced rate for senior citizens. Children under 12 are admitted free.
Exhibits: Jazz exhibits occupy about a dozen galleries on the second floor, with many audio displays. Plan to spend at least 90 minutes.
Telephone: (504) 568-6968.

St. Louis Cemetery Number One

This is one place in which the dead continue to serve their hometown as a tourist attraction. New Orleans's cemeteries are the most unusual in the country, looking more like miniature marble cities. Because the water table is so high, all burials are above ground in ornate tombs. St. Louis Number One is the city's oldest cemetery, dating back to 1789. Its below-ground predecessor had to be abandoned when water broke through the levee system and coffins started floating away.

New Orleans was almost entirely a Catholic city then, and Protestants and blacks were buried in the swampy back end of the cemetery. One of the most frequently visited tombs in this section belongs to Marie Laveau, a legendary figure from the city's past. Known as the Voodoo Queen, she occupied an unchallenged position in the black community in the years immediately following Emancipation. Playing upon supernatural dread, she wove together strands of old forbidden tribal religions that had flourished underground among slaves who were nominally Christians and used them to exert control. Music historians say that rhythms which eventually became identified as jazz grew out of the secret rites over which she presided. Believers still visit her grave on June 23, St. John's Eve, and take away bits of dirt as a token of her power.

Location: The cemetery is entered from Basin St. between St. Louis St. and Conti St., just north of the French Quarter.
Hours: Daily, 8-4.
Admission charge : None.
Telephone: (504) 482-5065.

M I S S I S S I P P I

Alcorn

Alcorn State University

In the summer of 1862, as Union and Confederate forces battled in a bloody stalemate across the American map, the U.S. Congress passed a piece of legislation that would shape the country that emerged from the Civil War. The Morrill Land Grant Act provided for the sale of public lands to fund agricultural colleges in every state, extending opportunities for higher education to those who never thought of attending college before.

The first black school chartered under this system was Mississippi's Alcorn A&M (now Alcorn State). In 1871, with most white southerners barred from holding state office by a constitution imposed by the occupying Union Army, black legislators and their allies held the balance of power in Mississippi. They took the opportunity to allocate $50,000 for a black land grant school, a far greater sum than such schools could have expected to see in that era. Ironically, it was named for the governor, James I. Alcorn, who had been elected by the white branch of the Republican party. An antagonist of black legislators throughout his term, Alcorn was voted out of office in 1873 as blacks united behind his opponent. But in 1875, in an election that virtually ended Reconstruction in Mississippi, Alcorn's organization swept the state and forced the resignation of all black officeholders. Nonetheless, the university still carries his name.

Alcorn State started up on grounds occupied by Oakland College, which had been established in 1830 by the Presbyterian Mission Board of Philadelphia. Its president, Rev. Jeremiah Chamberlain, was an outspoken Unionist, and in 1851 he was stabbed to death by a secessionist in front of his home on the college grounds. The school declined afterwards and suspended operations during the war.

Oakland Memorial Chapel, designated as a National Historic Site, was one of the original structures of the earlier school and is regarded as an outstanding example of southern Greek Revival architecture. Its plain brick facade and six white columns make an imposing sight and its interior walnut pews are original. The front steps of the building were taken from Windsor, a nearby antebellum mansion which burned down in 1890—whose bare, ruined Corinthian columns are

168

one of the state's most haunting sights. The President's Mansion at Alcorn was built in the same style.

> **Location:** From U.S. 61 and the Natchez Trace Pkwy., take westbound Mississippi 552 to Alcorn.
> **Hours:** Oakland Chapel is open Monday to Friday, 8-4, or by appointment.
> **Telephone:** (601) 877-6100.

Bay St. Louis

St. Augustine Seminary

Mississippi is an overwhelmingly Protestant state. Along the Gulf Coast, though, ties to its French and Spanish origins remain strong and the population is predominantly Roman Catholic. This resort town and its bay were named for the sainted French king by the Sieur de Rienville, who explored the area in 1699.

It was here that the Society for the Divine Word opened the country's first facility for training black seminarians, St. Augustine, in 1926. It was endowed by Sister Catherine Drexel, a member of a wealthy Philadelphia family who used part of her own inheritance to further the work of training black men for the priesthood. Its library, concentrating on works dealing with the black Catholic experience in America, is open to researchers by application.

> **Location:** The seminary is located off U.S. 90, just west of the St. Louis Bay Bridge. Call in advance for information on visits.
> **Telephone:** (601) 467-6414.

Canton

Black Confederate Memorial

Of all the Civil War memorials and monuments dotting the South, the most unusual may be in this town, north of Jackson. It is a tribute to the black slaves who went into battle with Confederate forces.

The South was never able to bring itself to use blacks as soldiers. That would have been an absurdity, calling on slaves to fight for the very system that enslaved them. On a more subtle level, the practice would have destroyed the philosophical foundation of that peculiar institution. If black men were capable of fighting in the lines with white soldiers, on what basis could they be deemed inferior human beings, fit only for slavery? Throughout the war, both slaves and freedmen were impressed into service behind the lines, to build fortifications and the like, especially in the Richmond campaigns. But a suggestion to arm blacks as soldiers was rejected out of hand when proposed by an increasingly desperate Confederacy in late 1864.

At last, three weeks before the war ended, Jefferson Davis was authorized to raise 300,000 black troops, with the implication that they would be given their freedom afterwards. But the order was never put into effect.

The monument in Canton was erected in 1894 by William H. Howcott to honor the memory of his personal servant, Hollis. Howcott was a member of Harvey's Scouts, a locally recruited unit of raiders who operated behind Union lines to harass supply shipments. Hollis was killed in one of these engagements, and Howcott never forgot his loyalty. The twenty-foot-high obelisk honors, in particular, his "rare loyalty and faithfulness whose memory I cherish with deep gratitude." An adjacent inscription honors all blacks who accompanied the Scouts.

The monument was virtually forgotten until a journalist from Jackson chanced upon it in 1984. One of Howcott's descendants saw the resulting article and funded its restoration. At rededication ceremonies in 1985, a local choir sang "Go Down, Moses," while three ministers, two black and one white, called it a symbol of "a second age" of racial unity and an end to intolerance.

> **Location:** Canton is 25 miles north of Jackson along I-55. Take the eastbound Mississippi 16 exit. The monument is located on E. Academy St., adjacent to Canton Cemetery, in Howcott Memorial Park.
> **Hours:** Always open.

Clarksdale

Delta Blues Museum

Where U.S. 61 crosses U.S. 49 is ground zero for the blues. The semi-mystical reverence in which musicians hold this corner of the Mississippi Delta was celebrated in the film *Crossroads,* made in the late 1980s. The crossroads of the title is outside of Clarksdale, the first big town south of Memphis in the Delta.

It was near here, on the Stovall plantation, that legendary blues musician Muddy Waters grew up. And it was in Clarksdale, in 1941, that Library of Congress musicologist Alan Lomax first recorded Waters and his distinctive guitar style.

Waters subsequently moved to Chicago, added electrical amplification, and is credited with inventing the urban blues. This, in turn, inspired a younger generation of musicians who transformed it into rock and roll.

The Delta Blues Museum in Clarksdale's Carnegie Library is meant to preserve and present the music of many of the area's blues musicians. But it is primarily dedicated to Waters, who died in 1983. It undertook a multimillion dollar expansion in the early nineties,

Muddy Waters

funded partially by many rock musicians who were influenced by Waters.

Waters was born McKinley Morganfield in 1915, and as a child was sent to Stovall to be raised by his grandmother. She gave him the nickname Muddy because he liked playing in the mud. By the time he reached his teens, he was performing at weekend social events in the area and had added the second name as a slang joke. He learned the blues from dozens of older men whose musical roots reached back to the cotton fields and the levees, where the music had evolved from work songs.

"Blacks don't always accept this music because they thought it was disgraceful," he said in a 1977 interview. "That's bad because they should stay with it. It's our music. But it reminds them of something old—slavery time."

Moving to Chicago in 1943, Waters developed his distinctive style, a deceptively simple expansion of traditional Delta blues guitar. For years, his records sold exclusively on the "race" market to a black audience, but in the 1950s his work came to the attention of a wider market. His song "Rollin' Stone" inspired a Bob Dylan composition, the title of a new magazine created to cover rock music, and, when he sang it on a trip to England, the name of a new rock group being formed by a young fan named Mick Jagger.

Waters was admired not only for his skill with the guitar—the uncanny ability to coax a mournful, achingly intense sound from it—but his vocal stylings, which sounded almost like improvised conversation rather than song. His music kept an entire generation of southern blacks who had moved to northern cities in touch with the musical heritage of their birthplaces.

> **Location:** Signs from the crossroads of U.S. 61 and U.S. 49 on the outskirts of Clarksdale direct you west to the museum, at 114 Delta Ave., downtown.
> **Hours:** Monday to Friday, 9-5.
> **Admission charge:** None.
> **Telephone:** (601) 624-4461.

Holly Springs

Rust College, Leontyne Price Library

Rust College was the first institution of higher education for blacks in Mississippi, its roots going back to 1868. Its early curriculum stressed science and mechanics, but its present campus was created by song, part of the debt a great artist owed her mother.

Leontyne Price appeared here in 1964 in a concert to raise funds for campus facilities, including a new library. Three years before, the Mississippi-born soprano had been the first black singer to perform the lead role of the New York Metropolitan Opera Company on opening night.

Throughout her illustrious career, she said that the greatest influence on her life had been her mother. Kate Price was an iron-willed woman who became a midwife to enhance her family income and finance some of her daughter's early vocal training. "She was an incredible woman," Price said in a 1973 interview. "I always say it's Mama who gets me on the stage. She has fire to burn. She has always been my strongest source of inspiration. I'm not even ashamed to admit that I was immature enough to call her before I left home for a performance. She always said: 'If you can't be first, get out of the ballgame'."

After her triumphant Met debut in Puccini's *Girl of the Golden West,* Rust College invited Price and her family to Holly Springs. She had given several concerts in her native state. In many cities, her concerts were the first integrated performances within memory. But this one was special. Rust was Kate Price's alma mater, and the concert her daughter gave there raised $50,000, an incredible sum for a concert performance in 1964.

Kate Price died eight years later. Her daughter had returned to Rust frequently, and her portrait now hangs over the main desk of

Leontyne Price

the library named in her honor. The college hopes eventually to assemble a collection of memorabilia from her long career.

Location: Holly Springs is located southeast of Memphis, and the college is off U.S. 79 business.
Hours: Hours vary, so it is best to call in advance.
Telephone: (601) 252-4661.
Handicapped access: Yes.

Jackson

Jackson State University

On May 14, 1970, headlines around the country reported the latest development in the investigation into the shooting deaths of four college students by Ohio National Guardsmen ten days before at Kent State University. Scant attention was paid to the ongoing demonstrations at Mississippi's Jackson State University, protests relating to the recent incursion of U.S. forces into Cambodia and the drafting of young black men to fight the Vietnam War. Police had been called out a few nights before, but by this Thursday it seemed that calm was returning to the campus area in the heart of the capital city.

No one knew it at the time, but the era of campus protest in America was drawing to a close. Civil rights demonstrations had shaded into antiwar demonstrations as the sixties progressed. But a sense of exhaustion, coupled with a dangerous escalation in violence, was turning over this page of campus history. Ironically, it was Tougaloo College, a few miles away in the northern part of Jackson, that had been Mississippi's center of campus activism throughout the civil rights struggle. Tougaloo was headquarters for the major voter registration drives and supplied a steady stream of student volunteers to the civil rights movement. If a major protest was to erupt anywhere, it was likely to be there. Instead, it happened across town at Jackson State.

Shortly after 11 P.M., Jackson police received a call that a city fire truck had drawn sniper fire as it attempted to put out a blaze at the edge of campus. Within minutes, about seventy city police and state troopers had swarmed into the area and surrounded Alexander Hall, a women's dormitory. A large body of angry students confronted them. Later reports indicated that taunts and obscenities were exchanged for several minutes.

Then without warning the police opened fire. The fusillade lasted thirty seconds, during which time 150 rounds of shotgun, rifle, and submachine gun fire were pumped into the building as students scattered. When the deadly hail ended, twelve students had fallen wounded. Two more were dead: Phillip I. Gibbs, a Jackson State senior, and James F. Green, a high school student who happened to be crossing the campus and was caught up in the demonstration.

The view from a bullet-riddled window at Alexander Hall photographed shortly after
the building was fired upon by Jackson police

The rest of the school term was cancelled and a grand jury convened to investigate the attack. Its report, issued two months later, exonerated law enforcement officers, declaring that they used only "necessary force" and were justified in discharging their firearms. But a federal report on campus unrest that appeared in October excoriated the police, calling their behavior, "unreasonable, unjustifiable overreaction," and charging that the weapons were fired indiscriminately.

Nonetheless, a suit seeking damages, brought by the victims of the shooting and their relatives, was dismissed in a ruling upheld by the U.S. Supreme Court in 1975 on the grounds of sovereign immunity.

> **Location:** The university is west of downtown Jackson, along Lynch St. From I-20, take the northbound Ellis Ave. exit to Lynch, then turn right. At the corner of Lynch and Prentiss, near Alexander Hall, there is a memorial marker to the two men killed on the campus.

Smith Robertson Museum

Until 1894, the few black children in Jackson who received any formal education had to rely on church schools or informal family arrangements. But Smith Robertson, a prominent businessman and the first black alderman in the city's history, made the founding of a public school for blacks a matter of urgent priority. This was also the period in which the doctrine of "separate but equal" was being shaped across the South as a legal justification for segregation. With that in mind, this school near the main thoroughfare of the city's black community, Fair Street, was established.

The school, eventually named for Robertson, stayed open for seventy-six years, until court orders desegregating Mississippi schools resulted in its closing in 1970. Fourteen years later it opened its doors again with a new educational mission. It is now a museum of the black experience in Mississippi.

The exhibits, some of them assembled and organized by members of the community, explore the Fair Street Historic District and the history of the school. Other rooms concentrate on family life and those who chose to stay on in the state despite its long history of oppression of blacks. Memorabilia of the civil rights struggle and African-American contributions to Mississippi are also displayed.

> **Location:** The museum is located just north of downtown Jackson at 528 Bloom St.
> **Hours:** Monday to Friday, 9-5, and by appointment on weekends.
> **Admission charge:** Adults, $1; children, $.50.
> **Telephone:** (601) 969-9638.

Lexington

Booker-Thomas Museum

Fannye Booker saw the Mississippi countryside that she knew as a child vanishing before her eyes. The country store her family had run, the people who shopped there, the farms they worked—all were disappearing. So she decided to bring part of it back to life.

On Honeysuckle Hill, just west of Lexington, she started to assemble artifacts, bits and pieces of everyday life that you might have seen on sale at a country store fifty years ago. Much of it came from her own family's possessions, and from residents of the country's retirement homes who wanted to bequeath some part of their own lives to posterity.

Mrs. Booker built a museum in 1980 to house her growing collection. Set up like an old-fashioned store, it is really an exhibit of life in black, rural Mississippi as it was earlier in this century. A lake, picnic area, and hiking trails are on the site, as well as two log cabins which she moved here from nearby farms and plans to renovate.

> **Location:** From I-55, take westbound Mississippi 12 through Lexington. It is just west of town, on the road to Tchula.
> **Hours:** The museum is open all year, by appointment.
> **Admission charge:** None.
> **Telephone:** (601) 834-2672.

Mound Bayou

Largest Black Municipality in America

If Isaiah T. Montgomery had been a slave on any other plantation in Mississippi, the history of this part of the Delta would have been much different. But Montgomery, the founder and first mayor of Mound Bayou, had labored on the holdings of Joseph F. Davis, the brother of the Confederacy's president, Jefferson Davis.

A few years after the war, Montgomery purchased the plantation on which he had been a slave, Davis Bend, south of Vicksburg. Although the transaction was legal, the state courts ruled subsequently that the Davis family, who were revered in Mississippi, retained title to the property. Montgomery's family was forced to move.

Montgomery came to the conclusion that the only way black people could survive in the increasingly hostile environment of post-Reconstruction Mississippi was to form their own municipalities completely separate from whites. At this time, the Yazoo and Mississippi Valley Railroad was laying track through Bolivar Country and recruiting settlers for new towns it wanted to form along the right-of-way. Montgomery and the railroad found a common interest.

With his cousin, Benjamin T. Green, and twelve other families, the former slave established the community of Mound Bayou in 1887.

With a population of just under three thousand, it is the largest all-black community in the country. It has been self-governing since 1898. Montgomery's handsome three-story house near the tracks remains the most prominent building in town. A modern red-brick city hall a few blocks away is the focus of the community and carries a massive wood sculpture at its entrance, depicting famous black Americans and their achievements.

> **Location:** Mound Bayou is located on U.S. 61, about 25 miles south of Clarksdale. The business district is west of the highway, across the railroad tracks.
> **Hours:** Check with City Hall in advance for information about visiting hours to the Montgomery house.
> **Telephone:** (601) 741-2193.

Philadelphia

Mount Zion United Methodist Church, Neshoba County Courthouse

The film *Mississippi Burning* made few friends among black moviegoers when it was released in 1988. They complained that it built up the role of the FBI in the dramatization and made it seem as if blacks were simply victims and passive spectators of their own struggle for justice.

Nevertheless, the movie focused attention once more on this little eastern Mississippi town and the events of the Freedom Summer of 1964, when three civil rights workers were murdered, with police complicity, by the Ku Klux Klan near Philadelphia. The killings and their aftermath drove home the realization to the country that Mississippi was dangerously close to being a police state, a closed society in which equal justice under the law was a fiction.

State civil rights leaders, assisted by volunteers from around the country, had begun a campaign to register black voters. Michael Schwerner of New York, an organizer for the Congress of Racial Equality, recruited James Earl Chaney of nearby Meridian to help out in Neshoba County. Joining them on June 21, his first day on the job, was Andrew Goodman, a college student from New York. Chaney was black, Schwerner and Goodman were Jewish.

This rural area has one of the lowest concentrations of black residents in the state. But the Klan reacted with special fury to the registration drive. The three men were detained on a speeding charge for six hours that afternoon by a sheriff's deputy, who alerted the Klan when he released them after dark. Their car was intercepted, the three men brutally beaten and shot, and their bodies buried in a nearby pond dam.

Downtown Philadelphia, Miss., in 1964. The Neshoba County Courthouse is at the far left.

Six weeks later, after President Lyndon B. Johnson ordered hundreds of FBI agents into the state, the bodies were unearthed. At a joint funeral in New York, as the mothers of the three men linked arms, Dr. Algernon D. Black closed the service by saying "Wherever Negro and white stand up together, there will be the spirit of these three young men. And it's got to happen to every one of us personally."

In December the FBI arrested twenty-one men in Philadelphia, including the sheriff, his top deputy, Cecil Price, and Klan Imperial Wizard Sam Bowers. But the grand jury refused to return a murder indictment. The photographs of the accused men, sitting cockily in the federal courtroom, tobacco plugs in their mouths, secure in the knowledge that they would not be touched by the law, underlined the nature of justice in Mississippi.

Three years later, in October 1967, Price, Bowers, and five other men were convicted by an all-white federal jury in Meridian of conspiracy to deprive the three slain men of their civil rights. No one was ever convicted of murder in the case.

At the twenty-fifth-anniversary commemoration of the deaths in 1989, Mississippi's secretary of state, Dick Molpus, who grew up in Philadelphia, spoke to the families of the three slain men. "We deeply regret what happened here twenty-five years ago," he said. "We wish we could undo it. We are profoundly sorry that they are gone. We wish we could bring them back. Every decent person in Philadelphia and Neshoba County and Mississippi feels that way."

Location: Philadelphia is located about 40 miles northwest of Meridian, by way of Mississippi 19. The Neshoba County Courthouse, in which many of the events of the tragedy were played out, including the jailing of the 3 civil rights workers and the later arrest of local lawmen by federal marshals, is in the center of town. There is a memorial marker to Chaney, Schwerner, and Goodman at Mount Zion United Methodist Church, east of town. The church was one of the bases for voter registration in Neshoba County and the former edifice was blown up in 1964. Leave Philadelphia on eastbound Mississippi 16, then turn north at Mississippi 482. Watch for the sign pointing to Mount Zion at the crossroad in front of the Sandtown Methodist Church, then take that road for 9 miles. There is no phone at the church.

Vaughan

Casey Jones Museum

On April 30, 1900, the six-coach Cannonball Express of the Illinois Central Line rounded a curve near this town and plowed into the rear of a parked freight train. The collision killed the Cannonball's engineer, Casey Jones.

Ordinarily, the incident would have been quickly forgotten. Rail disasters were a fairly common occurrence in that era of casual safety. During the year 1900 more than fifty-eight thousand people were either killed or injured in railroad accidents in the United States.

But Wallace Saunders, a black engine wiper from the nearby town of Canton, was an admirer of Jones, and when he heard of his death, he made up a song about it. It turned the tale of a routine crash into a historic epic and immortalized Casey Jones. When the song, whose refrain seemed to echo the mournful call of a locomotive whistle, was transcribed and published, it swept the country. It almost has the feel of folk music today, and most people are surprised to learn that it carries a composer's credit.

Saunders embellished a tiny bit, and in the most popular version of the song Casey is made out to be something of a womanizer. His wife detested the song and refused to hear it played. Saunders didn't make out much better from his composition. He sold all rights to it for a bottle of gin.

Location: Vaughan is located just off I-55, north of Jackson about 35 miles. The museum, housed in a restored railroad station, contains items relating to the crash, including some of Saunders's original sheet music.
Hours: Tuesday to Saturday, 9-5.

Admission charge: Adults, $1; children 3-11, $.50.
Telephone: (601) 673-9864.

M I S S O U R I

Diamond

George Washington Carver National Monument

As a great scientist, George Washington Carver found worldwide fame on the faculty of Tuskegee University in Alabama (see the entry on Tuskegee Institute National Historic Site in Tuskegee, Alabama). But the early years of his life were spent in the Midwest, and his experiences in these farms and fields were the shaping influences of his work.

He was born a slave on the farm of Moses Carver, outside this little town southeast of Joplin, in 1864. These were chaotic times in this section of Missouri. Confederate raiders from Arkansas and Kansas battled with federal forces for control of the area. On one of these incursions, the infant Carver and his mother were carried off to Arkansas. Nothing was ever heard of his mother again, but Carver was returned to his birthplace in exchange for a $300 racehorse. He was raised by his former owners as one of their own children, until he left to seek a high school education at the only nearby school that would accept him, in Kansas.

The Carver farm, watered by the springs that abound in this area, was where the future scientist first indulged his curiosity for his natural surroundings. He collected rocks and plants, and kept them in his room, marveling at the wonders within the most common everyday objects. A statue of him on the site depicts a moment of childhood reflection as he ponders the secrets of the world around him.

> **Location:** The national monument is located 3 miles southwest of Diamond. From the Joplin area, head east on I-44, take the southbound U.S. 71 exit to Diamond, then west on County Road "V". A park road leads south to the birthplace site.
>
> **Exhibits:** A visitors' center contains exhibits on Carver's life and works. From that point, a short walking trip leads to the birthplace, Carver statue, and many of the farm's natural features. The farmhouse on the site was built in 1881, and while Carver never lived there, he was a visitor on several occasions. Moses Carver and his wife, Susan, are

The statue of young George Washington Carver that stands at his birthplace

buried in a family cemetery on the southern edge of the property.

Hours: The George Washington Carver birthplace is open daily, 8:30-5.

Admission charge: None.

Telephone: (417) 325-4151.

Handicapped access: Yes.

Jefferson City

Lincoln University

It began as an idea among black troops as they talked around their campfires in the last days of the Civil War. It became a milestone on the road to equal education. It then found itself transformed from a small, all-black institution into a school four times its former size, with a white student majority.

From its hilltop location in the capitol city, Lincoln University has witnessed a lot of Missouri history. One of the state's best-known citizens, Jesse James, is even said to have contributed $15 to the school in its early years.

Lincoln opened in 1866, funded by soldiers of the Sixty-second and Sixty-fifth U.S. Colored Infantry. Most of the men in these units were Missourians, and as the war wound down they wondered about the kind of place to which they would be returning. The Sixty-second raised $5,000 to start a college that would train teachers. A state law of 1847 had made it a criminal offence to educate blacks and the troopers knew they had a lot of ground to make up. The Sixty-fifth heard of the idea and chipped in another $1,324, which enabled the men to buy a building in Jefferson City and install their former commander, Lieutenant Richard B. Foster, as president. The amounts seem small, but when you consider that these soldiers were paid about $13 a month, you can understand the degree of financial sacrifice involved.

The property was deeded to the state in 1879, leading to increased financial benefits and, eventually, to an important civil rights decision. When Lincoln graduate Lloyd L. Gaines was turned down at the University of Missouri Law School because of his race, he appealed his case to the U.S. Supreme Court. The high court, in 1938, ordered Missouri to establish a law school at Lincoln and provide equal educational opportunities to black students.

The law school remained open only seventeen years. It closed with the advent of school integration. But those doors swung in both directions, and Lincoln, with its central location in a heavily populated area, suddenly found itself an attractive educational choice for white students. By the 1960s, black students had become a minority at the school and the enrollment ratio has remained about the same since. Most white students are commuters, returning home at night and on weekends, while the vast majority of blacks are residential students and far more active in campus activities.

> **Location:** The school is located in the eastern part of Jefferson City. From the state capitol area, follow Capitol Ave. east to Chestnut St. and turn right. The campus in on the far side of U.S. 50. Tours of the campus are available. **Telephone:** (314) 681-5000.

Kansas City

The Black Archives of MidAmerica

This museum and library, located in the first black fire hall in Kansas City, focuses on black history in the states of Missouri, Kansas, Nebraska, and Iowa. It features displays on the Buffalo Soldiers, the black Ninth and Tenth Cavalry units organized in nearby Kansas, and the formidable Kansas City style of jazz, which produced many of the founders of early swing and seminal figures in the development of bop.

Count Basie

Location: The archives are at 2033 Vine St., just a few blocks south of the heart of downtown.
Hours: Monday to Friday, 9-4:30.
Admission charge: None.
Telephone: (816) 483-1300.

Mutual Musicians Association

This was one of the great jazz centers of the country in the 1920s and 1930s, and a wealth of talented musicians based themselves here. They developed a distinct sound during the swing era which became known as the Kansas City Style. It consisted of solo improvisations backed by riffs in the brass section. The Count Basie Band, which was organized here, became its best-known exponent.

Many of Basie's top soloists, including Lester Young and Herschel Evans, came from Kansas City. Both men are credited by jazz historians with leading the way, in their phrasing and ideas, to the postwar school of cool jazz. Another Kansas City–born sax man, Charlie "Bird" Parker, became the symbol of that style. Most of these men visited this building, which was the headquarters for the black musicians' union. It is now a private club, but tours of the facility, and exhibits relating to this era, can be arranged by phoning in advance.

Location: The building is just south of the city's central business district, at Highland St. near 18th St.
Exhibits: Mostly photographs of the performers who were associated with this building, which is itself a National Historic Landmark and dates from 1904.
Hours: Monday to Friday, 11-6.
Admission charge: Donation requested.
Telephone: (816) 421-9297.

St. Louis

The Old Courthouse and Dred Scott Case

From all accounts, he was frail and in late middle age, no longer capable of hard physical labor, but used as a sort of odd job man. But when the U.S. Supreme Court decreed that as a slave he had no legal rights as a citizen, the name of Dred Scott became a towering milepost on the road to civil war.

The lawsuit filed in his behalf was actually a test case. He had passed into the ownership of a dedicated abolitionist, who wanted a definitive ruling on the rights of a slave in free territory. This was becoming a vital issue, as the country debated whether slavery could be carried into the new territories in the West. Both slaveholders and antislavery settlers were pouring into Kansas, and it seemed only a

The Old Courthouse in St. Louis

matter of time before some explosion would occur there. Abolitionists hoped that a clear legal ruling would help their cause.

Scott was born in Virginia in the last years of the eighteenth century and was brought to Missouri in 1827. A few years later, he was sold to Dr. John Emerson, an Army doctor who was soon transferred to Fort Snelling, located in what would become Minnesota (see the entry on Fort Snelling State Historical Park, Minneapolis-St. Paul, Minnesota). This was part of the old Northwest Territory, an area in which slavery had been expressly forbidden by the Northwest Ordinance of 1787.

Scott lived there for five years before returning to Missouri, and when Emerson died, Scott's title passed to his widow. Mrs. Emerson was decidedly against slavery, and attorneys devised the plan of having Scott sue her in 1847 for assault, battery, and false imprisonment on the basis that his residence on free soil had ended her legal rights to him as a slave.

The suit was heard at the courthouse in St. Louis, a proud Greek Revival structure which had been completed only two years before, in the heart of the city. Its dome was a forerunner of a style in public architecture that would soon sweep the country, although skeptical local officials had to be convinced by a thirteen-thousand-pound scale model that it could actually be supported. This dome is two years older than that of the U.S. Capitol.

In three separate trials held over the next five years, the first two in this building, Scott's case was denied, then upheld on appeals, and finally reversed by Missouri's supreme court. With the situation in Kansas worsening, the trials drew national attention, and the case became a leading cause among abolitionists. They appealed to the federal courts in 1854 and lost. Finally, the case went to the U.S. Supreme Court.

This was one of the most anxiously awaited legal decisions in American history. Civil War historian Bruce Catton implies that newly elected president James Buchanan skirted the edge of propriety in encouraging the court, which contained a southern majority, to uphold the ruling and take the political pressure off of him. It did, in a seven-to-two vote, which contained nine separate opinions. But it was the opinion of Chief Justice Roger B. Taney that astonished the country. Taney ruled that Congress had no power to prohibit slavery in the new territories, and so Scott's argument was void and the Missouri Compromise illegal. Moreover, Taney wrote that Scott, born a slave, could never become a U.S. citizen, and that the framers of the Constitution regarded blacks as "being of an inferior order. . . with no rights which the white man was bound to respect."

Historians stress that Taney was expressing his understanding of the framers' intent, and not his personal convictions. Nonetheless, his words infuriated the abolitionists, leading many of them to conclude that violence was the only avenue open to gaining freedom for slaves. Scott himself was freed immediately after the decision was handed down in March, 1857. He died the next year of tuberculosis, and Mrs. Emerson paid his funeral expenses.

> **Location:** The Old Courthouse is a landmark of downtown St. Louis, part of the Jefferson National Expansion Memorial and administered by the U.S. National Park Service. It is located a few steps west of the soaring Memorial Arch, at North Forth St. and Market St.
>
> **Exhibits:** The courtroom in which the Dred Scott trials were held no longer exists, although others from the same era have been restored and displays relating to the case are on exhibit. The building is a museum of St. Louis history and the westward expansion. Rangers give guided tours.
>
> **Hours:** Daily, 8-4:30.
>
> **Admission charge:** None.
>
> **Telephone:** (314) 425-4465.

Scott Joplin House

When Scott Joplin came to live in St. Louis, it was a city bursting with energy. The biggest city in what was then regarded as the West was about to host a World's Fair. The rich and famous were flocking there, and in 1900 there were few more famous composers than Joplin.

He had come out of the west Missouri town of Sedalia (see the entry on the Scott Joplin Ragtime Festival and Sedalia Ragtime Archives in Sedalia, Missouri), the master of a new kind of music. They called it ragtime, and its rhythm seemed to measure the pace of a confident and growing America. It had its roots in the beat of African-

American music, and when it appeared in many parts of the nation, it was the topic of alarmed editorials and sermons. It was regarded as dangerous by moralizers, who were shocked by its irresistible invitation to dance, just as their counterparts in a previous generation were shocked by the waltz, and their successors would be by the two-step and the twist.

Joplin, born in Texarkana, first came to St. Louis as a teenager in 1885, when this music was developing in the city's black community. Eventually, he moved to Sedalia and studied advanced harmony and music theory at George Smith College. He made his living by playing piano at the Maple Leaf Club, and in 1897 he published a new rag that paid tribute to his place of employment in the title.

In the days before phonographs and radio, it took many years for a new song to make its way around the country in the form of sheet music. But the "Maple Leaf Rag" was a sensation. Within six months it had sold an unprecedented seventy-five thousand copies and the country embarked on a ragtime binge that would last for twenty years. Joplin, having obtained a degree of financial security, returned to St. Louis with his bride and bought a house at what is now 2658 Delmar Boulevard. He lived there for three years, writing many of his most enduring songs (including "The Cascades," a salute to the 1904 World's Fair), before moving into a larger house, which has since been demolished.

But while his fame grew, so did his frustration. Joplin was a serious composer, and with the rags he also wrote an opera, *Treemonisha.* No publisher would touch it. The idea of a black folk opera was regarded as preposterous. He published it at his own expense, and became obsessed with the idea of having it staged. In futile pursuit of this goal, he moved to New York and died there in 1919, his pockets empty and his career shattered, a prematurely old man.

Musical styles changed, and Joplin was forgotten by all except a few aficionados of ragtime. Then, in the early 1970s, a Boston music professor, Gunther Schuller, discovered a copy of some original Joplin arrangements. Ragtime had been sentimentalized and corrupted over the decades, and most musicians had no idea what it sounded like when the form was new. Schuller was astonished at what he found and at the extent of Joplin's genius. He managed to get backing for a recording of several Joplin rags and it became a top-selling record.

At about that time the producers of a new film, *The Sting,* were looking for a musical style that would reflect the period in which the film was set, the early 1920s. They heard Schuller's record and decided on ragtime. Suddenly, seventy-six years after he first delighted the American public, Joplin was a hit again. The film's theme, "The Entertainer," which he had written in the house on Delmar Boulevard, made an unlikely ascent up the charts and became the first ragtime composition to break into the Top Forty.

What Joplin would have relished even more, the Atlanta Symphony Orchestra, in conjunction with Atlanta and Morehouse universities, put on the premier performance of *Treemonisha* to a packed house in 1972. The work has since been performed frequently. Two years later, a New York researcher located Joplin's unmarked grave in Brooklyn's St. Michael's Cemetery, and the American Society of Composers, Authors, and Publishers erected a permanent marker on the site.

> **Location:** The Scott Joplin House was acquired by the state of Missouri in 1983, and a restoration program began. The intent is to reflect the period in which Joplin lived. Completion of the work has been repeatedly delayed. Delmar Blvd. runs west from downtown St. Louis, and the best way to reach the house is simply to follow the road out.
> **Hours:** Vary. Call in advance.
> **Telephone:** (314) 533-1003.

Shelley House

St. Louis was always a place with a distinct southern outlook. As the great wave of black migration reached the city in the early years of this century, St. Louis chose to deal with it discreetly through restrictive covenants. These were agreements limiting the sale of certain residential properties to whites, and were in common use in many parts of the country. In St. Louis, the practice was especially widespread, expanding to include entire city blocks and streets. Newly arriving blacks were shunted into an area known as the Ville, while surrounding streets were kept entirely white.

Blockwide covenants were declared unconstitutional in 1917, but remained enforceable on individual homes until 1948. The Shelley family's attempt to buy a restricted house on an all-white street led to a lawsuit that reached the U.S. Supreme Court. While not outlawing covenants, the court ruled that governments could not enforce them. The decision left them in a sort of legal limbo and was an initial step in breaking down residential segregation.

> **Location:** The 2-story brick Shelley House stands at 4600 Labadie Ave. From downtown, take westbound I-70 to the Kings Hwy. exit and head south. Labadie is a few blocks past Natural Bridge Road. The house is private, but a historic marker may be seen in front.

Vaughn Cultural Center

Funded by a grant from Mrs. Ermalene Vaughn, widow of a prominent physician, the center was established by the Urban League of Metropolitan St. Louis in 1977. It sponsors an ongoing series of historical and cultural exhibits relating to the black community, and has developed into a first-rate resource on the development of the city's African-American population.

> **Location:** The Vaughn Cultural Center moved to its expanded new home at 527 N. Grand in the city's restored theater district in 1989. It is located next to the restored Fox Theater. The area is just west of the central business district, north of Market St.
> **Hours:** Vary.
> **Telephone:** (314) 535-9227.

Sedalia

Scott Joplin Ragtime Festival, Sedalia Ragtime Archives

This bustling city of twenty-three thousand doesn't bear much resemblance to the rough-and-ready railroad town of the 1890s in which Scott Joplin mastered the ragtime piano. In those days, dozens of saloons catered to workers from the sprawling rail shops which were Sedalia's main employers, and musicians learned their craft in a tough setting. The site of the Maple Leaf Club, which Joplin immortalized in his best-known composition, is marked at the corner of Lamine Street and Main Street.

The Sedalia Ragtime Archives are housed in the State Fair Community College library. Students of music can examine rare and original pieces of sheet music, piano rolls, and taped conversations with some of the giants of the form, such as Eubie Blake.

Sedalia also puts on an all-out salute to Joplin and his music during the Scott Joplin Ragtime Festival, held annually in the first week of June.

> **Location:** Sedalia is located on U.S. 50, almost halfway between Jefferson City and Kansas City. From I-70, take the southbound U.S. 65 exit and proceed for 18 miles. State Fair Community College is located on Clarendon Rd.
> **Hours:** The Archives are open Monday to Friday, 9-5.
> **Telephone:** (816) 826-7100. For specific dates of the Ragtime Festival, call the Chamber of Commerce at (816) 826-2222.

T E N N E S S E E

Chattanooga

Afro-American Museum

Bessie Smith was just a teenaged girl when she was asked to perform for the famed singer Ma Rainey on one of the latter's trips through Chattanooga. When Rainey heard Smith's voice she immediately signed her up for her touring show and in the years ahead became her mentor. The Smith exhibits are the high point of this museum, which deals primarily with local African Americans.

By 1923, when she first stepped into a recording studio, Smith was already a top attraction on the black entertainment circuit. There had been nothing like her emotional, earthy delivery of the blues ever put on record before. Her first hit, "Down Hearted Blues," became one the biggest records in the history of the industry to that time, selling almost exclusively to a black audience. Its success convinced Columbia Records that there was a market for this sort of music, and made Smith one of the top black entertainers in the country. According to many of those who witnessed her live performances, the surviving records do not begin to capture the raw force of her singing. A large woman with a commanding presence, Smith was nervous in front of a microphone and, at times, tentative. But she held nothing back on the stage, and her shows sold out in the expanding black theaters of northern cities and the old tent show circuit in the South.

But musical tastes changed during the Depression. With reality sad enough, audiences didn't want to listen to the blues. Smith's career went into a steep decline, and she lapsed into heavy drinking. A final recording session was set up for her in New York in 1933, and it was here that she made the record that would become identified with the theme of her life, "Nobody Knows You When You're Down and Out." Four years later she was killed in an auto accident in Mississippi. The story persisted for many years that she died after being turned away from an all-white hospital. According to local records, however, she was immediately taken to a black facility, but was so seriously injured that nothing could be done.

Location: The museum is at 730 Martin Luther King, Jr., Blvd., which runs west, across I-124, from downtown, as a continuation of 9th St.

192

Bessie Smith

Exhibits: Smith's piano and many personal mementos are on display, along with photographs and artifacts relating to other notable Chattanooga African Americans.
Hours: Monday to Friday, 9-5.
Admission charge: None.
Telephone: (615) 267-1076.

Gallatin

Fairvue Plantation

The largest slave-trading operation in the old South was based here, on a two-thousand-acre plantation run by Isaac Franklin. He built Fairvue in 1832 when he was already a millionaire from the slave trade. Besides his holdings here, he owned thousands of acres in Texas and Louisiana to which most of the slaves were shipped. There were sixteen brick slave houses on the property. The mansion itself was regarded as one of the finest in the state, with a Georgian facade and wings built in the Spanish-influenced Louisiana style. The

Alex Haley House

plantation has been subdivided to less than one-third of its peak size, and the home is in private hands.

Location: Fairvue is about 3 miles west of Gallatin on U.S. 31 East. The site is a National Historic Landmark. The house is closed to the public.

Henning

Alex Haley House

In the middle of January, 1977, a show unlike anything presented before on network television captured the attention of America. For six straight nights, an estimated 130 million people watched a dramatized version of the black experience during the years of slavery. The miniseries was based on Alex Haley's book *Roots*, which had topped the *New York Times* best-seller list for twenty-two weeks the previous year. A genealogical detective story, as well as a work of history, the book and the television series seemed to tap something deep in the country's psyche. In an era noted for its sense of rootlessness, a single black man's attempt to learn where he came from elicited a response that transcended racial lines, and incidentally, gave millions of white viewers their first exposure to black history. *Roots* became a cultural phenomenon and made Haley one of the country's best-known writers.

He had spent twenty years of his life at sea, as a cook in the U.S. Coast Guard who enjoyed writing in his spare time. When Haley left the service in 1959, he turned to free-lancing, then landed a full-time job with *Playboy* magazine. One interview he worked on in the early sixties was with Malcolm X, and Haley developed a strong relationship with the revolutionary leader. He interviewed him over the course of a year, taking notes only in his memory, he said later, because "the sight of a tape recorder caused Malcolm to self-edit." The book that resulted from these sessions, *The Autobiography of Malcolm X,* was a stirring work that appeared in 1965, one year after Malcolm's assassination. It became a work that profoundly influenced the political ideas of an entire generation of young blacks.

In a 1988 interview with the *Washington Post,* Haley described the post-publication depression that hit him after this book. "All of a sudden it's done and you don't know what to do with yourself," he said. In this state of mind, he was walking around Washington, D.C., and passed the National Archives. On a sudden impulse, he walked inside, and, remembering stories he had heard from his mother, asked to see the 1870 census records for Alamance County, North Carolina. There he found the name of his great-grandfather, and the discovery triggered a search for more information about his forebears, based on tales he had heard from his aunts during boyhood visits to them in Henning.

The search would lead him all over the country and to Africa, take more than ten years of his life, and result in the tracing of his ancestor, Kunte Kinte, to his arrival as a slave in Maryland two hundred years before. The success of the book changed Haley's life. He found himself the object of adulation by people who had lost all hope of ever knowing their own roots.

In 1979, he decided to buy the old homestead in Henning and turn it into a museum. The house was built in 1918 by his grandfather, Will Palmer, whose lumberyard was the first black-owned business in western Tennessee. During the 1920s, Haley would return to the house to spend his summers, sitting on the cool front porch to hear the old family stories that became the basis of *Roots.* This is the era recaptured by the museum, which opened in 1986 and quickly became one of the biggest tourist attractions in this part of the state.

Location: From Memphis, head north on U.S. 51 for about 45 miles to Tennessee 209, the Henning turnoff. Then follow signs to the house, west of Main St. on Haley Ave. at S. Church St. From I-40 take northbound Tennessee 19 at the Brownsville exit. Continue to westbound Tennessee 87, which leads into Henning.

Exhibits: Local guides, many of whom knew Haley as a child, take you through the house. Many of the furnishings were owned by the Palmer family, and other items are consistent with the period of the restoration, the small-town South of the 1920s. The guides enliven the tours

The massacre at Fort Pillow

with personal recollections of Henning's past and Haley's visits there.

Hours: Tuesday to Saturday, 10-5, and Sunday, 1-5.
Admission charge: Adults, $2.50; students, $1.
Telephone: (901) 738-2240.

Fort Pillow State Park

On the morning of April 13, 1864, the defenders of Fort Pillow on the Mississippi River awoke to find themselves surrounded. Confederate raiders of Gen. Nathan Bedford Forrest, returning south after an incursion behind Union lines into western Kentucky, had seized the high ground on the river bluffs and demanded immediate surrender.

The fort, which guarded the river approach to Memphis from the north, had been captured two years earlier after an assault by Union gunboats. It was defended by East Tennessee Unionists and about 250 black soldiers, troops particularly hated by Forrest's men for reasons of race and sectional loyalty.

With its position hopeless, the garrison surrendered after a brief, fierce battle. What happened next has been a matter of controversy ever since. According to survivors, Forrest's troops when berserk, slaughtering black troops, many of them wounded, who had laid down their weapons. Historian Bruce Catton described it as "a lynching bee." Forrest insisted that those killed had been shot during battle and disavowed any knowledge of a massacre. Previous Confederate orders, however, had warned that any black soldiers captured while fighting for the Union would be summarily executed.

When news of Fort Pillow reached Washington, the cabinet met to decide on a response and ordered Gen. William Sherman to investigate. The fact that no retaliation was ordered was given as proof by historians sympathetic to the South that the massacre was propaganda. But the cabinet did consider executing southern prisoners in retaliation. President Lincoln, however, spoke against the plan, on the grounds that "blood cannot restore blood and government should not act for revenge. If once begun, there was no telling where [retaliation] would end." Sherman was instructed to punish any of Forrest's troops involved in the incident, but there is no record of this being done.

Recent historical research, including several articles published in the periodical *Civil War History,* indicates that "several dozen" black soldiers along with the garrison commander were, in fact, executed. "Fort Pillow" became a rallying cry among black soldiers for the remainder of the war. Forrest went on to become one of the leading figures in the founding of the Ku Klux Klan.

> **Location:** Fort Pillow is located 17 miles west of Henning along Tennessee 87.
> **Exhibits and Facilities:** The ruins of the Civil War works are maintained, and there is an interpretive center adjacent to them. Recreation grounds lie along the river.
> **Hours:** The park is open daily, but the interpretive center's hours vary.
> **Admission charge:** None.
> **Telephone:** (901) 738-5581.

Knoxville

Beck Cultural Exchange Center

This facility, located in a handsome twelve-room mansion on the city's east side, was originally the home of James and Ethel Beck. James Beck was the first black clerk ever hired by the U.S. Postal Service and went on to make a fortune in real estate. At the death of the Becks, the house was willed to the city, along with a bequest to turn it into something worthwhile in their memory.

The Cultural Exchange Center was the result, a museum and research center dedicated to the history and achievements of black people in eastern Tennessee. This part of the state was strongly Unionist in sympathy, with a higher percentage of freedmen than any other section of the Deep South. President Lincoln pressured his generals consistently to move into the area early in the war to rescue the multitude of Union sympathizers here. The center has traced the black experience in Knoxville back to 1791, and contains works of art, books, photograph collections, and oral histories relation to it.

Location: The center is located at 1927 Dandridge Ave.
From downtown, head north (away from the Tennessee
River) to Summit Hill Dr., and bear right. This road turns
into Dandridge. From I-40, take the downtown cutoff and
exit at eastbound Summit Hill Dr.
Hours: Tuesday to Saturday, 10-6.
Admission charge: None.
Telephone: (615) 524-8461.

Memphis

Beale Street Historic District

"This old town's all right, but Beale Street's paved with gold." Of
all the thoroughfares that run through black communities in the
United States, none is more celebrated in song and story than Beale
Street. Running only about one mile from its start at the Mississippi
River, Beale Street became a legendary name in the 1920s, when
musicians, millionaires, and gangsters mingled to flout Prohibition,
shop at the sharpest stores in Memphis, and hear the blues.

Beale Street was a fashionable area in the years before the Civil
War, with stately homes built by wealthy cotton planters lining its
length. But yellow fever epidemics in the postwar years gave the
riverfront an unhealthy reputation, and the rich moved out to the
city's eastern area. The street became a bustling, mostly Jewish
commercial strip in the 1890s, and after the turn of the century was
known as the heart of the city's black neighborhood.

The was the street W. C. Handy saw when he arrived in Memphis,
the rip-roaring avenue he described in his "Beale Street Blues." But
the street began to fade in the 1950s and by the end of the sixties only
a few struggling businesses and a couple of bars remained to signify
what had been. The story was part of an all-too-familiar urban cycle in
this country. But Memphis decided to go against the tide and bring
Beale Street back to life. Starting in the late seventies, the street
became the focus of a major civic restoration project that built on its
storied past to turn it into a tourist attraction.

This is a sanitized Beale Street, to be sure. Stores sell memorabilia
of Elvis Presley, the patron saint of Memphis, and a police museum
occupies a building near its center. But the sound of the blues and
Rufus King's celebrated "Memphis Sound" in popular music pour
again from its places of entertainment. A statue of Handy, trumpet in
hand, looks down on the street from a park near Third Street, in
front of the house he lived in. Schwab's, the dry goods store that has
been a Beale Street fixture through all of its changes since 1876, is
still doing business under the slogan: "If you can't find it here, you're
better off without it."

A miniature version of the Washington Monument at the western
end of the street is a memorial to Tom Lee, a black man who pulled

Beale Street

thirty-two people out of the river when an excursion boat sank in 1925. Lee happened to be passing the *M. F. Norman* in his skiff when it started to capsize. Turning back, he started taking passengers aboard and ferrying them to shore. He made four trips and saved almost half of the total number who had been on the boat. The city provided him with a home and a pension for the rest of his life, and after his death this thirty-foot-high shaft was raised in 1954 to honor his memory.

Another old landmark, of a vastly different nature, is the Beale Street Baptist Church at the corner of Forth Street. It was built right after the Civil War, the first Negro Missionary Baptist Church in the country. Ulysses S. Grant delivered an address from its pulpit on a triumphal postwar tour of the South. The Daisy Theater, in which the top black acts in the country once played, has reopened and again is putting on musical shows. Historical markers on every corner outline the history of the street, recall the personalities who walked its pavement, and point out many of its surviving landmarks.

It's all a little hokey now, and much of the street's distinctly black character has been lost. But a little bit of the old Beale Street is better than none at all.

> **Location:** Beale St. is just south of downtown Memphis, 2 blocks from the city's landmark Peabody Hotel.
> **Hours:** Schwab's, at 163 Beale St., is open Monday to Saturday, 9-5, and a museum of the street occupies its basement.
> **Admission charge:** None.
> **Telephone:** (901) 523-9782.

Other attractions: The Beale Street Information Center
has details on current attractions and hours of all the clubs,
theaters, and museums in the area.
Telephone: (901) 526-0110.

Lorraine Motel

It was a bad time of year to call a garbage collectors' strike. The
rule is that such strikes are most effective in summer, when garbage
stacks up on huge, reeking piles, building public support for a quick
settlement. But the Memphis garbagemen went out in February,
1968, and the city's administration refused to budge on demands for
more pay, improved safety conditions, and an end to verbal racial
abuse from white supervisors.

So the walkout dragged on with no end in sight when Dr. Martin
Luther King, Jr., was invited to town. The strike had turned into a
power struggle between Mayor Henry Loeb and the city's NAACP,
and it was thought that King might be able to break the stalemate.
With the major civil rights victories won in the South, King had
turned his attention to breaking down patterns of housing segregation in northern cities. He called the reaction to his appearance in
Chicago more hostile than anything he had encountered in the South.
He also had become an outspoken opponent of the Vietnam War.
The trip to Memphis would return him to more familiar turf on an
economic issue that blended with the old civil rights campaigns of the
past.

As was his practice whenever possible, he checked into a black-
owned inn, the Lorraine Motel, just south of downtown. Its open
configuration, with balconies facing out onto Mulberry Street, made
any kind of security a nightmare, but King did not attach a high
priority to security.

He led a large downtown march on April 3, wearing a strikers'
badge that read: "I am a man." That night, he rallied spirits by
delivering a variation on what had become a favorite theme of his: the
leader who had been to the mountain and has seen the Promised
Land, even though he may not live to reach it. The following day,
that speech would become an eerie epitaph.

While standing on the balcony in front of Room 306 of the motel,
King was struck in the throat by a rifle shot fired by sniper James Earl
Ray, and he died hours later. The assassination of the thirty-eight-
year-old leader of the civil rights movement is now seen as a
watershed in American history. Racial riots broke out in many cities
in both North and South afterwards. His violent death seemed to
fulfil the worst fears of the nation's black people. Those who had
challenged his program of nonviolence were horribly vindicated, and
their voices grew to greater prominence in the years ahead. Separa-
tism and force replaced integration and idealism as the preferred
course for many leaders. The echoes of Ray's shot have never really
stopped resonating.

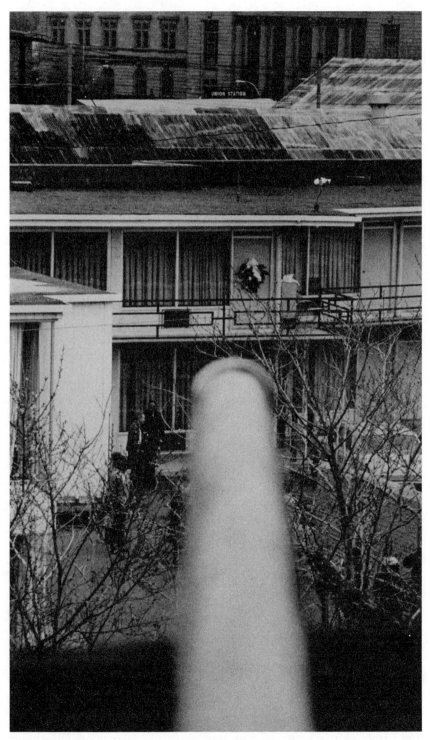

A rifle barrel view of the Lorraine Motel

The Lorraine shut down in 1988, and the state of Tennessee committed $8.8 million to turning it into a national civil rights museum and memorial to King. It is scheduled to open in 1991, although opposition has surfaced to elements of the plan viewed as overly commercial and inconsistent with King's own philosophy.

> **Location:** The Lorraine Motel, at 406 Mulberry St., is located about 1 mile south of downtown. Take 2d St. south to Linden, the cut over 1 block west to Mulberry and follow it south.
>
> **Exhibits:** Currently, the building is not open to visitors, and a wire fence surrounds it. The site of the assassination, visible from the street, has been glassed in and covered with floral wreaths.

Nashoba

One of the strangest experiments in attacking the institution of slavery was put into effect on a plantation near the Wolf River, which is now within the Memphis city limits. Frances Wright was a wealthy young Scot who toured the United States in 1818 and wrote a glowing account of the democratic society she saw there. Since few Europeans were writing anything complimentary about America in those days, she became a celebrity and was warmly welcomed on her return trip six years later.

Her initial enthusiasm was tempered when she saw the extent of slavery and its contrast with the tenets of democracy. She decided to deal with the problem at its source. She bought Nashoba Plantation and purchased a group of black slaves for the purpose of educating and "upraising" them in preparation for a life of freedom. Impressed by a famed utopian community in New Harmony, Indiana, she brought in one of its supervisors to run the experiment for her.

Unfortunately, her chosen disciple had an agenda that went beyond education. A firm believer in free love and communal living, the reports he turned in on these activities alienated the American sponsors of the experiment, and they withdrew their support. Wright was forced to sell Nashoba in 1827, and its residents were shipped off to live in the West Indies.

> **Location:** The site of Nashoba was immediately south of the point at which U.S. 70 crosses the Wolf River, just east of I-40.

Nashville

Fisk University, Meharry Medical School

In the early days of Reconstruction, newly freed black slaves understandably wanted to put the years of slavery behind them.

Memories of those times were bitter, and leaders of the black community encouraged obliteration of all aspects of the experience. Among them were the songs of slavery, including the religious songs that became known as spirituals.

The black poet James Weldon Johnson, writing half a century later, considered it remarkable that Christianity should have been so earnestly embraced by slaves, in view of "the vast gulf between the Christianity that was preached and the Christianity practiced by those who preached." He felt the sustaining influence was the Old Testament chronicle of the Jews. "This story at once caught and fired the imaginations of the Negro bards, and they sang their hungry listeners into a firm faith that as God saved Daniel in the lion's den, so would He save them; as God delivered Israel out of bondage in Egypt, so would He deliver them."

These songs were unknown to the American public outside the South. But in the late 1860s, an effort began among a few academics to set down the words and melodies before they passed into oblivion. Leadership of this project was taken by newly founded Fisk University in Nashville. In its first year of operation, a group called the Jubilee Singers was formed there, dedicated to preserving African-American music. The school opened in 1866 and was named for Gen. Clinton B. Fisk, head of the Freedmen's Bureau in the state. But funds to build a campus were scarce. Administrators of the struggling school decided the Jubilee Singers and their songs might be the key to saving Fisk.

With the encouragement of the famed Brooklyn clergyman Henry Ward Beecher, a tour of northern cities was organized in 1871. The Jubilee Singers, seven women and four men, were so enthusiastically received that the tour was extended to the British Isles and Germany. The concerts raised $150,000 for the university. Equally important, it established the music of American blacks as worthy of preservation, scholarly study, and inclusion at the highest levels of culture.

Black musicians of later generations would dismiss them as "Europeanizers" of the culture, with their crisp diction and structured form. But the Fisk tour was successfully repeated by other black schools, and the Jubilee Singers became the symbol of the spiritual to the world. Jubilee Hall, erected in 1873 with the funds raised by the first tour, is a National Historic Site. Originally a classroom, it is now a women's dormitory, with the wood for its massive front doors shipped here from Sierra Leone. A portrait of Queen Victoria, commissioned by the monarch after she heard the singers and presented to the school, hangs in a ground-floor room.

Another historic structure on the campus is the Van Vechten Art Gallery, built in 1888 as a physical education center. It was renovated in the 1950s and now houses the Alfred Stieglitz art collection, willed to the University by his wife, painter Georgia O'Keeffe.

Adjoining the Fisk campus is Meharry, the largest predominantly black medical school in the country. By the 1950s, Meharry was credited with graduating more than half of the black physicians in the United States. That number was substantially lowered after segrega-

tion ended admission bars at many schools, and Meharry now enrolls
a substantial minority of white students. The school was founded in
1876 as repayment for a kind deed. As a teenager, Samuel Meharry
was on family business in Kentucky when his wagon became mired in
mud on a back road. Seeing a slave cabin nearby, Meharry went for
assistance. Its occupants helped pull his wagon free and put him up
for the night. The youngster had no money, but promised to pay off
the debt when he could. Years later, as a successful Indiana
businessman with longtime abolitionist sympathies, Meharry was
approached by Dr. John W. Braden, who proposed the establishment
of a medical school at Central Tennessee College. Meharry gave him
$500 immediately and over the years donated $30,000 to the school,
which was eventually named in his honor. Meharry was given full
accreditation in 1923, and is regarded as being in the forefront of the
country's medical training and research facilities.

> **Location:** Fisk and Meharry are located north of down-
> town Nashville, by way of I-40 to the eastbound Jefferson
> St. exit. Since Jubilee Hall is now a dormitory, inquiries
> should be made in advance about visiting times.
> **Telephone:** (615) 329-8500.
> **Other attractions:** The art gallery is on 17th Ave. North.
> **Hours:** Tuesday to Friday, 10-5, and Saturday and Sun-
> day, 1-5.
> **Admission charge:** $2.50.
> **Telephone:** (615) 329-8543.
> **Handicapped access:** Yes.

The Southeast

Florida

•

Georgia

•

North Carolina

•

South Carolina

•

Virginia

•

Washington, D.C.

•

West Virginia

The Southeast

FLORIDA

1. Bethune-Cookman College, *Daytona Beach*
2. American Beach, *Jacksonville*
3. Kingsley Plantation, *Jacksonville*
4. Black Archives History and Research Foundation, *Miami*
5. Olustee State Historic Site, *Olustee*
6. Castillo de San Marcos National Monument, *St. Augustine*
7. Fort Gadsden, *Sumatra*

GEORGIA

8. APEX Museum, *Atlanta*
9. Atlanta Life Insurance Headquarters, *Atlanta*
10. Atlanta University Center, *Atlanta*
11. Hammonds House, *Atlanta*
12. Herndon Home, *Atlanta*
13. Martin Luther King, Jr., National Historic Site, *Atlanta*
14. Bragg Smith Monument, *Columbus*
15. St. Andrew's Episcopal Church, *Darien*
16. Uncle Remus Museum, *Eatonton*
17. Harriet Tubman Historical and Cultural Museum, *Macon*
18. First African Baptist Church, First Bryan Baptist Church, *Savannah*
19. King-Tisdell Cottage, *Savannah*

NORTH CAROLINA

20. Biltmore Estate, Young Men's Institute, *Asheville*
21. North Carolina Mutual Life Insurance Company, *Durham*
22. Stagville Preservation Center, *Durham*
23. Fayetteville State University, *Fayetteville*
24. Lunch Counter Sit-ins, North Carolina Agricultural and Technological State University, *Greensboro*
25. Yellow Tavern, Presbyterian Church, *Milton*
26. Pea Island Coast Guard Station, North Carolina Aquarium, *Roanoke Island*
27. Livingstone College, *Salisbury*
28. Charlotte Hawkins Brown Memorial, *Sedalia*

SOUTH CAROLINA

29. Robert Smalls House, Baptist Tabernacle Church, *Beaufort*
30. Avery Research Center for African-American History and Culture, *Charleston*
31. Catfish Row, DuBose Heyward House, *Charleston*
32. Denmark Vesey House, *Charleston*
33. Old Slave Mart Museum, *Charleston*
34. Mann-Simons Cottage, *Columbia*
35. Penn School, *Frogmore*
36. Prince George Winyah Church, *Georgetown*
37. Battery Wagner, *Morris Island*
38. Stono River Slave Rebellion, *Rantowles*

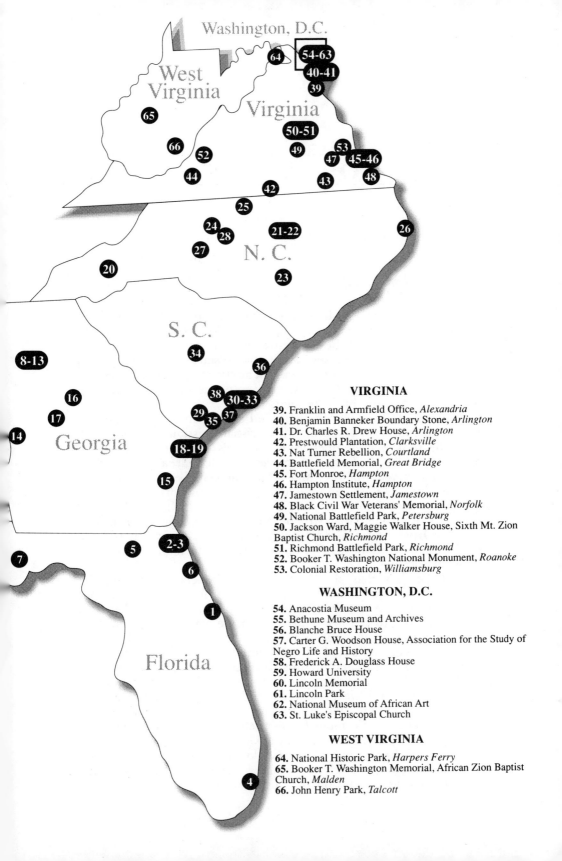

Washington, D.C.

West Virginia

Virginia

64

54–63

40–41

39

50–51

49

53

47

45–46

48

43

42

25

24

28

21–22

27

52

66

65

44

20

23

N. C.

26

S. C.

34

8–13

36

16

38

30–33

17

29

37

35

14

Georgia

18–19

15

5

2–3

6

7

1

Florida

4

VIRGINIA

39. Franklin and Armfield Office, *Alexandria*
40. Benjamin Banneker Boundary Stone, *Arlington*
41. Dr. Charles R. Drew House, *Arlington*
42. Prestwould Plantation, *Clarksville*
43. Nat Turner Rebellion, *Courtland*
44. Battlefield Memorial, *Great Bridge*
45. Fort Monroe, *Hampton*
46. Hampton Institute, *Hampton*
47. Jamestown Settlement, *Jamestown*
48. Black Civil War Veterans' Memorial, *Norfolk*
49. National Battlefield Park, *Petersburg*
50. Jackson Ward, Maggie Walker House, Sixth Mt. Zion Baptist Church, *Richmond*
51. Richmond Battlefield Park, *Richmond*
52. Booker T. Washington National Monument, *Roanoke*
53. Colonial Restoration, *Williamsburg*

WASHINGTON, D.C.

54. Anacostia Museum
55. Bethune Museum and Archives
56. Blanche Bruce House
57. Carter G. Woodson House, Association for the Study of Negro Life and History
58. Frederick A. Douglass House
59. Howard University
60. Lincoln Memorial
61. Lincoln Park
62. National Museum of African Art
63. St. Luke's Episcopal Church

WEST VIRGINIA

64. National Historic Park, *Harpers Ferry*
65. Booker T. Washington Memorial, African Zion Baptist Church, *Malden*
66. John Henry Park, *Talcott*

F L O R I D A

Daytona Beach

Bethune-Cookman College

She started the school, she said, on dreams and a dollar and a half. Even in her wildest dreams, though, Mary McLeod Bethune could not have foreseen what the future had in store for her. Growing up on a South Carolina farm, she wasn't able to start her own education until she was eleven. But she became an advisor to presidents, and the little Florida school she founded grew into one of the nation's top training grounds for black teachers.

She attended Chicago's Moody Bible Institute on a scholarship, but when her application to become a Christian missionary was turned down, she took her energies instead to this oceanside community. Daytona Beach in 1904 was a young resort. The railroad had reached it only sixteen years before, and its magnificent beach was already bursting with new hotels and the homes of wealthy northerners. One-third of the population was black, almost all which was employed by the resorts. It was here that Mrs. Bethune established her Normal and Industrial Institute for Girls, with an enrollment of five. It was the first black institution in Florida to offer education beyond the elementary grades.

Her hope was that she would find a benefactor among the millionaires who vacationed there. She rode a bicycle up to the front door of James Gamble, the Cincinnati soap tycoon, and talked him into coming out to see her school. When he arrived, he found her sitting on a rickety chair behind a crate. "Where is this school you want me to see," he asked. "In my mind...and in my soul," she responded. Gamble wound up supporting the school in its early years. But Mrs. Bethune and her students supplemented those gifts by selling ice cream and sweet potato pies to railroad gangs and managed to accumulate enough money to buy the city dump, which was reclaimed as the new campus for her school. The first building was called Faith Hall, and many of the workmen took part of their pay in tuition credits after it merged with Cookman Institute, a male school, in 1922. Although the school was now coeducational, it remained fixed on its original mission of training teachers.

In 1930, Mrs. Bethune was invited to Washington by President Herbert Hoover to serve on the Child Health and Protection Conference. For the next twenty-five years of her life, through three administrations, she was deeply involved at the federal level in the push for equality. She served on several presidential boards and advisory groups and helped to found the National Council of Negro Women in 1935. (For further discussion of her activities, see the entry on the Bethune Museum and Archives, Washington, D.C.)

> **Location:** Bethune-Cookman College is on 2nd Ave., just west of the business district.
> **Exhibits:** The home in which Mrs. Bethune lived after 1920 is preserved on the campus as she left it.
> **Hours:** By appointment.
> **Admission charge:** None.
> **Telephone:** (904) 255-1401.

Jacksonville

American Beach

While Florida developed as the country's great resort playground, black people found themselves walled off from the ocean unless they happened to work in the hotels. The resorts were restricted and so were all but a few of the public beaches.

The Afro-American Life Insurance Company purchased some oceanfront land in the northeastern corner of the state in the 1920s and developed it as a black resort colony. The twenty-acre tract was laid out with electrically lit streets and modern homes. Many original property owners still have homes in the area and the beach is being restored.

> **Location:** The resort is on Amelia Island, about 40 miles northeast of Jacksonville, along Florida A1A, between Fernandina Beach and the Amelia Island Plantations.

Kingsley Plantation

This was the greatest slave-trading plantation in Florida in the early years of the nineteenth century. Zephaniah Kingsley came to Fort George Island, near the mouth of the St. Johns River, in 1817, when it was still ruled by Spain. The island was fortified by the Spanish as early as 1567 and an unsuccessful invasion of Florida by colonists from Georgia came this way in 1736. It did not become American territory until 1821.

The African slave trade had been cut off by federal law in 1808. But by using Florida as his base and with Spain unable to police the territory effectively, Kingsley managed to evade the restrictions and brought in slaves on his own fleet of ships. There are indications he

Main house, Kingsley Plantation

continued doing this even after Florida passed under American jurisdiction.

On one of these voyages, he married Anna Madegigine Jai, daughter of a Senegalese tribal leader. A tall, dignified woman of regal bearing she supervised the domestic life of the plantation. The main house and slave quarters are still standing on the site.

> **Location:** Kingsley Plantation is about 25 miles northwest of Jacksonville. Access is by ferryboat from Florida A1A, or by way of I-95 to eastbound Florida 105 (Hecksher Dr.) to Fort George Island.
> **Exhibits:** Besides the Kingsley House and its slave quarters, the Don Juan McQueen House, dating from 1792, is also on the site. This was the home of John H. McIntosh when he proclaimed a short-lived Florida Republic in 1812.
> **Hours:** Daily, 8-5.
> **Admission charge:** None.
> **Telephone:** (904) 251-2473.

Miami

Black Archives History and Research Foundation

The gateway to the Caribbean and South America, Miami has developed what is probably the most diverse, multi-ethnic black community in the United States. Blacks from the former British, French and Spanish colonies of the West Indies have flocked here in search of economic opportunity and political freedom. The result is a dynamic mixture that is constantly redefining its cultural position in this polyglot metropolis. The archives is trying to research the roots of black involvement in south Florida. Its exhibits emphasize the continuity of this association and it conducts an ongoing series of trips through the area to places connected with the experience of blacks in Miami.

> **Location:** Archives headquarters is at 5400 N.W. 22d Ave., north from the N.W. 22d Ave. exit of Florida 112 (Robert Frost Expy.).
> **Hours:** Monday to Friday, 10-5.
> **Admission Charge:** None.
> **Telephone:** (305) 638-5729.

Olustee

Olustee State Historic Site

In February 1864, twelve regiments of Union troops marched out of Jacksonville into Florida's interior. Their ambitious goal was to cut off a base of southern supplies, recruit blacks for the northern army, and return Florida to the Union. They accomplished none of these things and instead were decisively defeated near the town of Olustee.

The Eighth U.S. Colored Troops, poorly trained and led and unprepared for an offensive, took the brunt of the punishment. With Confederate sharpshooters securely protected by fieldworks, the Eighth lost more than three hundred men, over half of its number, in the battle. The combat-toughened Fifty-fourth Massachusetts Volunteers held its position tenaciously, however, and Sgt. Stephen A. Swails, cited for bravery in the battle, was made its first black commissioned officer shortly afterwards.

The engagement accomplished nothing and the federal force retreated to Jacksonville, where it stayed for the rest of the war.

> **Location:** Olustee State Historic Site is 42 miles west of Jacksonville and 3 miles east of the town of Olustee on U.S. 90.
> **Exhibits:** There is a museum and a walking tour around the battleground.
> **Hours:** Daily, 9-5. Museum, Thursday to Sunday only.
> **Admission charge:** None.
> **Telephone:** (904) 752-3866.

Castillo de San Marcos

St. Augustine

Castillo de San Marcos National Monument

The oldest city in what would become the United States, St. Augustine was founded in 1513. It would remain under the Spanish flag for three centuries, almost twice as long as it has been part of American territory. Always an irritant to the colonists in the Carolinas and Georgia, the town was under constant threat of British attack from the sea. It responded by constructing the massive fortress of San Marcos, starting in 1672.

As long as Florida was under Spanish control, San Marcos was a beacon of hope to black slaves. Spain encouraged black rebellions in the British colonies and offered protection to those who could make their way south. Many such refugees were settled just north of St. Augustine in an outpost called Fort Moosa and used in raids against British settlements. It was occupied as late as 1759, but four years later Florida was ceded to Britain for a twenty-one-year period. The British relinquished control after the Revolutionary War, but during its period of rule, Fort Moosa was destroyed.

America eventually won control of Florida in 1821 and inherited a large number of former slaves who had become free under the Spanish or were living with the Seminole tribes. Using any pretext to enslave these freedmen, the Americans quickly touched off a war with the Seminoles. Resentful at attempts to grab Indian-owned land in the state's interior, the tribes were further infuriated when the wife of one of their leaders, Osceola, was taken off by slavers because she was partly black. The Seminole War raged for seven years, from 1835 to 1842, resulting in thousands of casualties on both sides and a humiliating defeat for Gen. Zachary Taylor by Chief Billy Bowlegs at Okeechobee. Even the treacherous seizure of Osceola under a flag of truce didn't end the conflict, although it touched off revulsion against the army in the northern states. Osceola was imprisoned in St. Augustine before being taken off to South Carolina where he died.

> **Location:** The site of Fort Moosa is still under excavation and is not open to the public. The place of Osceola's capture is marked by a small memorial near Moultrie, 6 miles south of St. Augustine on U.S. 1. In Castillo de San Marcos, a new display relates the history of black freedmen under Spanish rule. The National Monument is in the city, on Florida A1A, Avenida Menendez, just north of the Bridge of Lions.
> **Exhibits:** Besides the displays on black history, Castillo de San Marcos is one of the oldest military structures in America, a compendium of Florida history for 200 years.
> **Hours:** Daily, 9-5:15.
> **Admission charge:** Adults, $1; Senior citizens and children under 16, free.
> **Telephone:** (904) 829-6506.

Sumatra

Fort Gadsden

When the War of 1812 erupted on the southern frontier, it quickly turned into a conflict between the Creek tribes and the American settlers. Andrew Jackson was placed in charge of the federal army sent into the Alabama Territory and defeated the Creeks at Horseshoe Bend. Afterwards, with an army at his disposal on the Florida border, he could turn his attention to two other irritants.

One was the port of Pensacola, nominally under Spanish control but suspected by the Americans of permitting a British fleet to use it as a base. Jackson marched in, took the city, and threw out the Spanish commander, the first steps in the events that led inevitably to American ownership of Florida.

The second problem was Fort Gadsden. The British had set it up in 1814 to recruit runaway slaves and Seminoles to fight against the Americans. They abandoned it when the war ended, but their allies continued to man it and use it as a refuge for escaping slaves from Georgia. Variously known as British Fort or Fort Negro, the place was attacked by Jackson's forces in 1816 as part of the First Seminole War. The general's specific instructions to his commanders were: "Blow it up. Return the Negroes to their rightful owners." Of the 334 defenders of the fort, all but sixty were killed in the fight.

Location: The site of the fort, now a state park, is 6 miles south of Sumatra on Florida 65, or about 26 miles north of Apalachicola, by way of U.S. 98 and Florida 65.

G E O R G I A

Atlanta

APEX Museum

Situated on Auburn Avenue, but not a part of the National Historic District, the title of the museum is an acronym for African-American Panoramic Experience. The facility concentrates on local black history, especially as it relates to Auburn Avenue, and features exhibits by Atlantans and national artists.

APEX Museum

Location: The museum is at 135 Auburn Ave., adjacent to
the western portion of the Dr. Martin Luther King, Jr.,
Historic District.
Hours: Tuesday to Friday, 10-5; Saturday, 11-6.
Admission charge: Donation requested.
Telephone: (404) 521-2739.

Atlanta Life Insurance Headquarters

For sixty years this was the home office of the country's second
largest black-owned life insurance company. It is now a part of the
western portion of Dr. Martin Luther King, Jr., Historic District, in
the midst of the city's largest black business center. The building was
put up in 1920 by the company's founder, Alonzo Herndon, who also
erected the Herndon Building, an office center one block east, in
1926.

Location: Atlanta Life is at 148 Auburn Ave., across the
street from the APEX Museum (see above).
Exhibits: Historical displays about the company and its
founder are in the lobby.
Hours: Monday to Thursday, 8-4:30.
Admission charge: None.
Telephone: (404) 659-2100.

Atlanta University Center

A few months after the Civil War ended, the American Missionary
Association sent a boxcar to this city, which was still mostly in ruins,
and began holding classes for freed slaves on the railroad tracks.
These classes grew into Atlanta University, the first black institution
of higher education in the Deep South.

In turn, Atlanta University became the core for a group of four
other schools—-Clark, Morris Brown, Morehouse, and Spelman—
which aligned themselves with it over the course of the next sixty-five
years. Today they form the most extraordinary black educational
complex in the country, having adjoining midtown campuses and a
reputation for academic excellence.

The best way to explore these schools is to simply get out and walk.
Driving is difficult along the narrow streets and parking impossible. If
you've visited the Herndon Home (see below) on University Place, at
the northeastern end of the complex, the best idea is to leave the car
there.

The first campus you come to is Morris Brown, which moved to this
site at the end of University Place in 1932 from its original location
elsewhere in Atlanta. It occupies the first Atlanta University campus
and has a number of fine nineteenth-century buildings that provide
an evocative setting. The university was established by the African
Methodist Episcopal Church in 1885 and is recognized for its
theology program.

Atlanta University today

Take the pedestrian walkway over Martin Luther King, Jr., Drive and angle to your right across the Atlanta University campus to Chestnut Street. This is the main collegiate thoroughfare in the area, with many shops, fraternity houses and university landmarks, including the Library and Administration Building, situated along its length. Across Fair Street is Clark College. Look for Stone Hall, the oldest building in the entire complex, dating from 1882 and originally part of the Atlanta University campus.

To the immediate west is Morehouse College, a men's school which won a certain notoriety in the late 1980s as the setting for the movie *School Daze* made by alumnus Spike Lee. Noted for upholding rigorous academic standards and instilling in its students a sense of mission to the black community, the school was shaped by its longtime president Benjamin Mays. He told his faculty that their job was to "prepare the sons of Mississippi sharecroppers for Harvard, and I will tolerate no lesser standard." Dr. Martin Luther King, Jr., completed his undergraduate work here. When a Morehouse man was accepted to the graduate program in chemical engineering at the University of California, he was told by Mays: "You realize that if you fail no Morehouse man will be accepted there again." The graduate told the *Wall Street Journal* in a 1987 article, "Until that moment, I never knew what pressure was."

Just to the south, at the end of Chestnut Street, is Spelman College, a women's school which was used as the model for the fictitious Hillman College in the popular TV series *A Different World*. The producer of that show, actor Bill Cosby, gave Spelman a $20 million gift in 1988, the largest single donation to any historically black school in history. It is regarded as the female counterpart of Morehouse and has a strong academic program as well as a sense of obligation to the black community. The school was handsomely supported by John D. Rockefeller in its early years and was renamed for his wife's family in 1884, three years after its founding as Atlanta Baptist Female Seminary. Sisters Chapel, named in honor of Rockefeller's mother and aunt, has been a campus landmark since its dedication in 1935. It is where the body of Dr. King lay in state before his funeral in 1968. Its campus, with oaks, elms, and magnolias towering above a grassy oval, is an especially lovely spot.

> **Location:** Atlanta University Center is immediately west of downtown, by way of Martin Luther King, Jr., Dr.

Hammonds House

This was the home of Dr. O. T. Hammonds, a supporter and connoisseur of black art. He collected outstanding examples of Haitian folk art and the works of Romare Bearden, who depicted urban life in the northern cities in the style of Social Realism and became one of the best-known collagists in the world. The home is now a national center for black visual arts, with ongoing exhibitions and programs.

> **Location:** The Hammonds House is at 503 Peeples St., just a few blocks west of the Morehouse College campus (see above.)
> **Hours:** Tuesday to Friday, 10-6, and weekends, 1-5.
> **Admission charge:** None.
> **Telephone:** (404) 752-8215.

Herndon Home

Many success stories of black business in the nineteenth century began with a barber shop. That was one trade in which slaves were trained that could be put to practical use after emancipation. Alonzo Herndon started life as a slave near Social Circle, Georgia, and opened a barber shop when he moved to Atlanta. He managed to accumulate enough capital to set up the Atlanta Life Insurance Company in 1905. With a rapidly growing black middle class in this prosperous city, Herndon's company soon made him the wealthiest black businessman in the country.

In 1910 he built a mansion near Atlanta University, where his wife Adrienne taught drama. Unfortunately, she died before the home was completed and his second wife, Jessie Gillespie Herndon, presided over the mansion. She eventually became vice president of the company and lived in the home until 1947. His son, Norris, succeeded Herndon as the head of the company. A collector with highly cultivated tastes in furniture and Venetian glass, he turned the house into a showcase of art treasures. After his death in 1977, the

Herndon Home

house was turned over to the Herndon Foundation and opened to the public, with the family belongings kept intact.

> **Location:** The home is at 587 University Pl., just north of Martin Luther King Dr. at Vine St., and immediately east of the Morris Brown campus of the Atlanta University Center.
> **Exhibits:** Artwork and furnishings collected by the Herndon family.
> **Hours:** Tuesday to Saturday, 10-4. Tours begin on the hour.
> **Admission charge:** None.
> **Telephone:** (404) 581-9813.

Martin Luther King, Jr., National Historic Site

To understand the forces that shaped a great man, it helps to see the places he knew as a child. In most cases, this is impossible. Change is an American constant and by the time a person achieves greatness the settings of childhood have usually disappeared.

On Atlanta's Auburn Avenue, however, the National Park Service had a unique opportunity. This was the street on which Dr. Martin Luther King, Jr., grew up, a middle-class slice of black Atlanta which had been nicknamed generations before "Sweet Auburn." The literary-minded will recognize the allusion to Oliver Goldsmith's poem, "The Deserted Village." Unlike that Auburn, however,

"Behold," a tribute to Martin Luther King, Jr., was unveiled near his crypt in 1990

Auburn Avenue still clung to life when the area around it became a part of the National Park System in 1980.

The historic site preserves not only the house in which Dr. King was born, the church at which his grandfather and father were pastors, and his gravesite, but the neighborhood texture in which his earthly voyage was charted. He was born here in 1929 and lived on Auburn Avenue until 1941. Many of the houses and businesses he knew then are still in place and still in private hands. A total of sixty-seven structures lie within the historic district, one-fifth restored with federal funding. The Park Service describes itself as the steward for the rest of the neighborhood.

Dr. King returned to Auburn Avenue in 1960. His work in Montgomery, Alabama (see Dexter Avenue-King Memorial Baptist Church entry in that chapter) had taken him to the forefront of the civil rights struggle. With insufficient time to devote to his ministry there, he resigned and came home to join his father as co-pastor of the Ebenezer Baptist Church. That arrangement permitted him to head the Atlanta-based Southern Christian Leadership Conference and direct its program. It was after returning to Atlanta that he led the boycott in Birmingham, Alabama, the historic march on Washington in 1963, and the voting rights march from Selma to Montgomery two years later.

It was also to Auburn Avenue that he was brought in April 1968, after his assassination in Memphis. He was first buried in Southview Cemetery, but his body was returned here and his memorial tomb dedicated in 1977.

> **Location:** The historic district is immediately east of downtown Atlanta, with Auburn Ave. 2 blocks south of Peachtree Center. From I-85/95 northbound, take the Edgewood/Auburn exit and turn right. From the southbound freeway, take the Butler St. exit and continue south to Auburn Ave., then turn left. There are 2 sections to the district. West of the freeway is the residential area, containing the King birthplace and tomb and Ebenezer Baptist Church. East of the freeway is the black business district, containing several historically significant offices and churches.
>
> **Exhibits:** The birthplace, at 501 Auburn, has been restored to its appearance in Dr. King's childhood. The 14-room house was built in 1895 and purchased by his grandfather, Rev. A.D. Williams, in 1909. The tomb, 1 block west, is part of the Center for Non-Violent Social Change, which contains a museum of Dr. King's life and work. The Ebenezer Baptist Church, 1 more block to the west, was built in 1922. This is where funeral services for Dr. King were conducted and where his mother was shot to death by a distraught youth in 1974. Walking maps of the historic district are available at the National Park Service kiosk in Community Center Plaza, directly opposite the gravesite on Auburn Ave.
>
> **Hours:** Tours of the birthplace are given on the half hour, 10-6, Memorial Day to Labor Day; 10-5, the rest of the year. Capacity is limited on each tour, so there may be a wait. The best strategy is to get a ticket first and then see the rest of the area until the time for your tour comes around. The museum is open daily, 9-5. The church is open Monday to Friday, 9:30-12 and 1:30-4:30, and Saturday by appointment.
>
> **Admission charge:** None.
>
> **Telephone:** Birthplace (404) 331-3920; museum (404) 524-1956; church (404) 688-7263.
>
> **Handicapped access:** Yes.

Columbus

Bragg Smith Monument

Even in the midst of segregation, individual acts of heroism were sometimes strong enough to break down the color bar. Smith was an employee of the Public Works Department working with a black construction crew in 1933 when the superintendent of the city agency was trapped in a collapsed trench. Smith lost his life in the attempt to save him.

Columbus erected a memorial to Smith, believed to be the first civic memorial in the country to honor a black man. Porterdale Cemetery, in which it stands, however, is designated on the maps of that time simply as "Colored Cemetery."

> **Location:** Porterdale Cemetery is located southeast of downtown, at 4th St. and 7th Ave.

Darien

St. Andrew's Episcopal Church

It was an incident in this little coastal town that set in motion the chain of events leading to the Fifty-fourth Massachusetts Regiment's costly attack on Battery Wagner (see entry on Morris Island, South Carolina.) Having recently been assigned to duty in Georgia's Sea Islands, the Fifty-fourth was sent on a raid to this nearby community with other black units. Its commander, Col. Robert Gould Shaw, was incensed at the wanton destruction he saw being carried out here by black troops, under direct orders from their officers to loot and burn. "Southerners must be made to feel that this is a real war and that they are to be swept away by the hand of God like the Jews of old," he was told by another colonel.

Shaw reported the incident to Washington and demanded that his troops be allowed to fight, instead of being relegated to punitive raids. He was taken at his word and the deadly engagement at Battery Wagner soon followed.

A marker on this church, rebuilt in 1872, nine years after its destruction, recalls the torching of this town by federal troops.

> **Location:** Darien is located 16 miles north of Brunswick, on U.S. 17.

Eatonton

Uncle Remus Museum

When the Walt Disney Studio turned the stories of Georgia writer Joel Chandler Harris into a movie in 1947, the NAACP and other black organizations protested the film. They claimed that the Uncle Remus character depicted in *Song of the South* perpetuated black stereotypes. The movie has been reissued several times since then and seems to have won acceptance as a piece of harmless folklore.

Animated version of the Uncle Remus tales by Joel Chandler Harris

The work of Harris, which appeared in the 1890s, was the first contact much of the country had with black storytelling. Written in dialect, many of the stories are based on legends that folklorists have traced back to Africa and which were handed down in the oral tradition through generations of slavery. It was not Harris's intent to romanticize the antebellum South. As a journalist with the Atlanta Constitition, he was an advocate of the New South, urging his readers repeatedly to put such sentimentality behind them and give African Americans fair treatment. He grew up around the town of Eatonton and was working for the weekly paper here when Gen. William Sherman's troops came through on their march to the sea. Much of Uncle Remus's character is based on George Terrell, an elderly black man who sold cookies on market days in Eatonton. Harris recalled listening to his stories, many of which furnished the foundation of his books.

Location: Eatonton is about 80 miles southeast of Atlanta by way of I-20 and southbound U.S. 129 and 441. There is a monument to Harris on the east side of the courthouse square. The museum, 3 blocks south in Turner Park, is set up to resemble the slave cabin in which Harris first heard the stories.
Exhibits: There are displays of the Uncle Remus characters and Harris's books.
Hours: Monday to Saturday, 10-12 and 1-5, and Sunday, 2-5. Closed Tuesday from Labor Day to May.
Admission charge: $.75.
Telephone: None.

The original First African Baptist Church

Macon

Harriet Tubman Historical and Cultural Museum

A massive wall mural depicting the voyage through time of black people from ancient Africa to contemporary America dominates this cultural center. It also features exhibits of black crafts.

> **Location:** The museum is at 340 Walnut St., on the northern edge of downtown.
> **Hours:** Monday to Friday, 10-5, and Saturday, 2-5.
> **Admission charge:** Donation requested.
> **Telephone:** (912) 743-8544.

Savannah

First African Baptist Church, First Bryan Baptist Church

Both institutions trace their roots back to the start of the African-American Baptist church in Georgia. George Liele, the servant of a British officer, began holding services for a black congregation while the city was occupied during the American Revolution in 1779. Three years later, when American forces retook Savannah, Liele evacuated to Jamaica and established the black Baptist church on that island. His work in Georgia was carried on by his assistant, Andrew Bryan.

Bryan began preaching at a nearby plantation and by 1788 had a congregation of forty-five members. In 1797 they were able to buy a lot in Savannah, which is still the location of the church. The original First African church outgrew these quarters and moved, however, in 1832. When dissension developed in the rapidly growing church, a splinter group decided to return to the former site and formed the First Bryan Baptist Church.

> **Location:** The First African Baptist Church is located on Franklin Sq., at 23 Montgomery St., in the northeastern corner of the historic district. The structure erected here in 1832 still stands. The First Bryan Baptist Church is a few blocks north, at 565 W. Bryan St., on the other side of Broad St.
> **Exhibits:** There is a memorial to Liele in the First Bryan Baptist Church and a black Baptist historical museum in the First African Baptist Church.
> **Hours:** By appointment.
> **Telephone:** First African Baptist Church, (912) 964-2941; First Bryan Baptist Church (912) 232-5526.

King-Tisdell Cottage

This gingerbread Victorian cottage has been restored to reflect a typical black middle-class residence on the Georgia coast of the 1890s. The furnishings are consistent with the time and setting, and parts of the home serve as a museum of local black history. The house also functions as a cultural center and sponsors tours of black Savannah.

> **Location:** The cottage is at 514 E. Huntingdon St., a few blocks west of Forsyth Park and the historic district.
> **Hours:** Monday to Friday, 10:30-4:30, and weekends, 1-4.
> **Admission charge:** Adults, $1.50; children 12 and under, $1.
> **Telephone:** (912) 234-8000.

NORTH CAROLINA

Asheville

Biltmore Estate, Young Men's Institute

This city at the edge of the Great Smoky Mountains had been a summer resort for southerners fleeing the heat of the coast for sixty years before George Vanderbilt arrived. But with his acquisition of the Biltmore Estate in 1889, the place changed forever.

Vanderbilt rearranged the community, restoring old crafts and pioneering reforestation techniques that would soon be used across the country. His holdings amounted to 130,000 acres (much of which was donated to the federal government and is now Pisgah National Forest), and at its center he built Biltmore, a French Renaissance chateau. It took five years to complete this 250-room palace surrounded by thirty-five acres of gardens. Some artisans were imported from Europe to work on it, but the majority were local black craftsmen.

As a token of gratitude for their efforts, Vanderbilt built an 18,000-square-foot recreation center in Asheville and sold it for a nominal sum to a group of black businessmen to offer vocational training. The Young Men's Institute is now a cultural center of the black community.

> **Location:** The southern edge of Asheville at the U.S. 25 exit of I-40. The Young Men's Institute is downtown, at 39 S. Market St. Take the southbound U.S. 25 exit from I-240 and turn left at the first intersection to reach Market.
> **Exhibits:** Self-guided tours of Biltmore take several hours to absorb the wealth of detail in the home and gardens.
> **Hours:** Biltmore and the Institute are open daily, 9-5.
> **Admission charge:** Biltmore, Adults, $19.95; 12-17, $15; 11 and under, free with paying parent. The Institute is free.
> **Telephone:** Biltmore (704) 255-1776; the Institute (704) 252-4614.

The Biltmore House

Durham

North Carolina Mutual Life Insurance Company

This city was one of the first examples of the New South that rose from the ashes of the Civil War. An industrial town built on tobacco, it had a population of less than one hundred at the end of the war. But within a few years, it had become a manufacturing boom town and a place where blacks could find work for decent wages.

A group of black businessmen saw an opportunity in the formation of this middle class and in 1898 they started the North Carolina Mutual Life Insurance Company Achieving financial success despite formidable barriers, the company at one time was the largest black-owned business in America and still grosses more than one billion dollars annually. Its home offices were declared a National Historic Site in 1975.

Location: Downtown Durham at 114-116 W. Parish St.
Hours: Lobby is open during normal business hours.
Telephone: (919) 682-9201.

Stagville Preservation Center

This is part of a state-run archeological and historical study of the old plantation culture. On the grounds of the Bennehan plantation, built in 1787, the center attempts to preserve a picture of what daily life was like on one of these enterprises in the heart of tobacco country. The Horton Grove area of Stagville concentrates on slave life and presents exhibits of folk arts and crafts.

> **Location:** Northeast of the city by way of Roxboro Road (U.S. 501) to Old Oxford Hwy.
> **Exhibits:** The center, spread over 71 acres, is a project to showcase advances in preservation techniques, as well as living history.
> **Hours:** Daily, 9-4.
> **Admission charge:** None.
> **Telephone:** (919) 620-0120.

Fayetteville

Fayetteville State University

Educational reform began taking hold in New England in the late 1830s. Led by Horace Mann, the movement emphasized the necessity of training teachers how to teach properly and of establishing a professional norm. New state-funded institutions for this purpose were called normal schools.

The concept was slow in reaching the South because in those years any ideas originating in New England were not well received there. But in 1877 North Carolina's Gov. Zebulon Vance promoted the idea of turning a small black school in Fayetteville into the state's first normal college. The school, then known as Howard School, in honor of the former head of the state's Freedmens Bureau, had been started ten years before upon the request of seven local black families who had purchased a lot for that purpose. Fayetteville State Colored Normal School became the first such facility in the south for either black or white teachers.

The present campus dates from 1908. Tablets on the grounds pay tribute to two of its former principals: Dr. E. E. Smith, who headed the school for fifty years (1883 to 1933) and was also U. S. Minister to Liberia, and Charles W. Chesnutt, one of the first American writers of fiction to write about black concerns from a black perspective. His collection of short stories, *The Conjure Woman,* published in 1899, is among his best works. He was awarded the Spingarn Medal by the NAACP in 1928. The school library is also named for Chesnutt.

> **Location:** Northwestern part of Fayetteville, at 1200 Murchison Rd.
> **Telephone:** (919) 486-1295.

The original participants in the Greensboro lunch counter sit-ins re-enact the scene at a thirtieth anniversary observance. From left to right: Joseph McNeill, Jibreel Khazan (Ezell Blair), Franklin McCain, and David Richmond.

Greensboro

Lunch Counter Sit-ins, North Carolina Agricultural and Technological State University

By 1960, the civil rights movement in the South seemed to have reached a lull. The early excitement over the bus boycott in Montgomery and school integration in many cities was in the process of being resolved. White southerners believed that they had weathered the initial shock of change; now things could get back to normal and the region would deal with its problems in its own way.

But on February 1, four young men from North Carolina A&T State College walked into the Woolworth store on South Elm Street in Greensboro and sat down at its lunch counter. And with that act, the civil rights revolution switched into high gear and started rolling towards its greatest triumphs.

The south in those years was a patchwork of local customs regarding blacks. In most chain stores, it was all right for blacks to shop but there was a blanket prohibition against sitting down for a meal. Northern-based corporate management usually deplored such things but stated that it could not defy regional tradition.

But a store like Woolworth was also vulnerable. Because it had outlets all over the country, it was susceptible to national pressures. That played an important part in the thinking of the lunch counter sit-ins.

The four men were all freshmen. Three of them, Ezell Blair, David Richmond, and Joseph A. McNeill, were from North Carolina and the fourth, Franklin E. McCain, was from Washington, D. C. Their ideas for a dramatic gesture to bring national attention to the demeaning Jim Crow laws grew out of late-night bull sessions in their dormitory. At the last moment, they conferred with local officials of the NAACP and the Congress on Racial Equality, but the initiative and strategy was their own.

They took their seats at 4:30 P.M. The white waitress (who would serve them again thirty years later at an anniversary re-enactment of the protest) was under the impression that they had made a mistake. She informed they could not be served. But they refused to move. Store managers were sent for, who requested that they get up. Instead, the students took out their books and began to study. There was just one hour until closing time, so nothing more was done. The managers hoped the men would leave when the store closed and that would be the end of it.

The next day they returned with sixteen allies. Each of them made a purchase elsewhere in the store and sat down at the counter. They argued that if they could be served in one part of the store, it was absurd to refuse them service in another. By the third day, the counter was completely filled with seventy students from the campus. The demonstration also spread to the counter at the nearby Kress store. At the end of the week, all Greensboro chain-store lunch counters were closed and negotiations were begun to end discrimination in the city.

But it was too late for Jim Crow. The next week, sit-ins were being held throughout North Carolina, and by March they were taking place in every southern state.

In each instance, leadership was taken by young people of the community. And all of them employed the techniques of passive resistance, even in the face of violent provocation. Reaction spread all over the country. As anticipated, Woolworth came under tremendous pressure by northern demonstrators who staged their own sympathy sit-ins at the chain's outlets. A new wave of student activism had begun to swell and a new organization, the Student Nonviolent Coordinating Committee, suddenly became a major force in the civil rights struggle. White students also became engaged and started heading south to participate in demonstrations. Energized by the vigor of youth, the movement picked up a momentum that became unstoppable, and within a few more years brought about the Civil Rights Act, the Voting Rights Act, flowing directly into the Vietnam War protests.

Historian and journalist Lerone Bennett, Jr., referred to the Greensboro sit-ins as the Bastille of the civil rights movement. It was the act that ignited a revolution.

> **Location:** Woolworth is still doing business in downtown Greensboro on S. Elm St., the main north-south thoroughfare in the city. A historic plaque is now fixed to the store

exterior. North Carolina A&T State University is a few blocks away, on E. Market St.

Exhibits: There is an African Heritage Museum on the college campus with some fine examples of basket work.

Hours: Monday to Friday, 9-4.

Admission charge: None.

Telephone: (919) 334-7500.

Milton

Yellow Tavern, Presbyterian Church

Like many southern states in the years before the Civil War, North Carolina passed a succession of laws aimed at making life as hard as possible for black freedmen and slaves. The most onerous was an 1827 statute that forbade the immigration of any free black or mulatto into the state.

Two years later, sixty residents of this town on the Virginia border journeyed to Raleigh to seek an exemption for one of their black fellow citizens. Tom Day was threatening to leave Milton because the law made his marriage illegal and his departure would have been an economic calamity to the town.

Day was a furniture maker and his factory in the Yellow Tavern, which he had purchased in 1823, sent Milton products throughout the south and employed many local white craftsmen. His mahogany pieces are prized today by collectors. The state legislature, having heard Day described as "a first-rate workman, a remarkably sober and steady and industrious man, a high-minded good and valuable citizen, possessing a handsome property" voted an exemption from the immigration act for his wife.

Day also won another exemption from the Presbyterian Church. In return for carving mahogany pews, he wanted the right to come down from the gallery, to which blacks were restricted, and sit with the rest of the congregation. The elders reluctantly agreed. Only after Day's death was it discovered that he'd enjoyed a subtle revenge. The pews turned out to be not mahogany at all, but walnut.

> **Location:** Milton is on North Carolina 57, about 10 miles southeast of Danville, Virginia and 50 miles northwest of Durham, by way of U.S. 501.
>
> **Exhibits:** The Yellow Tavern is now a private home, but a marker identifies it as a National Historic Landmark. Day's pews may still be seen in the Presbyterian Church. Inquire at the parsonage next door.

Roanoke Island

Pea Island Coast Guard Station, North Carolina Aquarium

This lifesaving unit, the only all-black Coast Guard facility in the country, was on neighboring Pea Island. It was in operation for seventy-two years, after being founded by onetime slave, Capt. Richard Etheridge. But after its closing in 1952, the wind and waves of the Outer Banks wiped away any trace of its existence.

On nearby Roanoke Island, however, the North Carolina Aquarium has an exhibit on the Pea Island station as part of its displays on the state's coastal history and ecology.

> **Location:** The aquarium is on U.S. 64, just east of the bridge from the mainland. Pea Island is about 15 miles southeast, along North Carolina 12.
> **Exhibits:** Most of Pea Island, including the site of the rescue station, is now part of a national wildlife refuge, which is a winter haven for the Greater Snow Geese. The aquarium features exhibits on the variety of sea life in the area, along with historical displays. It is just a few miles from the site of Fort Raleigh, established in 1585 as the first British colony in North America. Its settlers disappeared, however, while the supply ship returned to England and they were never found.
> **Hours:** Pea Island Refuge, open daily during daylight hours. Aquarium, Monday to Friday, 9-5, and weekends, 1-5.
> **Admission charge:** None.
> **Telephone:** Pea Island (919) 987-2394; aquarium, (919) 473-3493.
> **Handicapped access:** Aquarium, yes.

Salisbury

Livingstone College

More than five thousand Union soldiers died at the Confederate prison camp outside this city. Among them was Robert Livingstone, son of the famed missionary and explorer, David Livingstone. He had enlisted under an assumed name to pursue his father's anti-slavery ethos by more direct means. In 1881, when Zion Wesley Institute, an African Methodist Episcopal church school moved here from nearby Concord, its name was changed to Livingstone College.

Its founder was Joseph C. Price, who was celebrated for his skills as a platform speaker. His tomb is located on the campus, in the Poets and Dreamers Garden, which is patterned on themes drawn from the

Charlotte Hawkins Brown

Bible and Shakespeare. The school's Heritage Hall contains African-American art exhibits and artwork relating to the AME church.

> **Location:** West of downtown, at 701 W. Monroe St. Take the central Salisbury exit from I-85.
> **Hours:** Heritage Hall is open Monday to Saturday, 10-4, during the school year.
> **Admission charge:** None.
> **Telephone:** (704) 683-5500.

Sedalia

Charlotte Hawkins Brown Memorial

She had moved to New England as a child and was educated there at a normal school. But in 1901, Charlotte Hawkins Brown returned to her home state of North Carolina to teach rural black children in the town of Sedalia.

That church school closed after one year, but Dr. Brown had seen enough in that time to realize that she had found her calling. She returned to Massachusetts to raise money and came back to Sedalia in 1902 to open the Palmer Institute, a preparatory school for young black women named after her friend and advisor, Alice Freeman Palmer, the first woman president of Wellesley college.

It started off following the Booker T. Washington model, emphasizing manual education and practical vocational training. But it soon elevated academic excellence and cultural studies to greater importance. It was fully accredited as a secondary school when very few southern black institutions were given that recognition.

The school was virtually a triumph of an individual personality. Dr. Brown ran Palmer Institute for fifty years and was nationally respected as a social worker and religious leader. Her credo was that graduates would be "educationally efficient, religiously sincere and culturally secure."

Dr. Brown died in 1961 and the school survived for only ten years afterwards. But in 1987, the campus became North Carolina's first historic memorial honoring a black person.

> **Location:** Sedalia is located about 15 miles east of Greensboro, by way of I-85.
> **Exhibits:** Tours of the campus and Dr. Brown's residence, Canary Cottage, are combined with displays on the history of the education of African Americans in North Carolina.
> **Hours:** Tuesday to Saturday, 10-4, and Sunday, 1-4.
> **Admission charge:** None.
> **Telephone:** (919) 449-6515.

SOUTH CAROLINA

Beaufort

Robert Smalls House, Baptist Tabernacle Church

Robert Smalls began his service in the Civil War as a pilot on the Confederate steamer *Planter*, based in Charleston Harbor. The southern states recoiled from using blacks in combat. That would have meant arming them, reawakening fears of a slave insurrection that had haunted the South for centuries. But many, such as Smalls, were used in support positions behind the lines.

But Smalls had thoughts of his own about his role in the war. He saw his position on the *Planter* as a ticket to freedom. On the morning of May 13, 1862, while the ship's white officers were ashore, Smalls, with his wife and three children (whom he had smuggled onboard), and twelve black crewmen sailed the *Planter* into the hands of the Union naval force blockading Charleston.

In recognition of this well-publicized achievement, he was given the rank of pilot in the U.S. Navy aboard the *Planter*. The following year he relieved the ship's captain when the latter panicked under enemy fire. Smith brought the *Planter* to safety. He was then promoted to captain of that ship, the only black to hold that rank in the war.

A heroic figure among South Carolina's newly freed blacks, he was elected to the state senate in 1868 and went on to Congress in 1875. He served five terms, longer than any other black congressman in the Reconstruction era, and while there, carried on a losing rear-guard action against the rising tide of Jim Crow laws in the South.

His home in Beaufort was declared a National Historic Landmark in 1973 and the Baptist Tabernacle Church also contains a memorial to him.

> **Location:** Beaufort is about 75 miles southwest of Charleston by way of U.S. 17 and U.S. 21. Its historic district, in the heart of town, contains one of the South's largest groupings of antebellum homes and churches.
> **Exhibits:** Within the district are the Smalls House, at 511 Prince St., and the Baptist Tabernacle Church, at 907 Craven St.
> **Hours:** The Smalls House is not open to the public. The church interior is open by appointment.

Robert Smalls

Telephone: (803) 524-0376.

Charleston

Avery Research Center for African-American History and Culture

This facility, a part of the College of Charleston, is the country's largest research center devoted to the Gullah culture. This group of blacks inhabits the barrier islands of the entire southern Atlantic seaboard, but their greatest influence have been on South Carolina. Even the distinctive speech patterns and drawl of white Charlestonians have been traced back to the Gullah dialect.

Until late in this century, the Gullah dialect was almost unintelligible to outsiders. Even blacks from upcountry South Carolina were mystified when they heard it. It combined fragments of West African languages mixed in with West Indian dialects and archaic forms of English that disappeared from the language in other areas two hundred years ago.

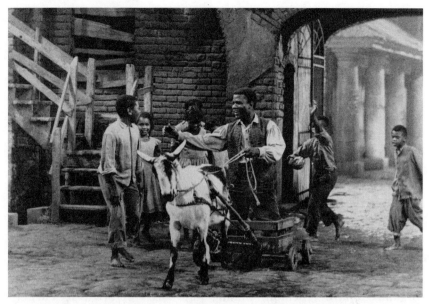

Sidney Poitier in "Porgy and Bess," the opera based on life in Charleston's Catfish Row

Many local educators and writers have made an effort to preserve the distinctive dialect, and Avery Center is a reflection of their work.

Location: 67 George St., north of the historic district and just off U.S. 52 (E. Bay St.).
Exhibits: Displays of material relating to the Gullahs and other African-American cultures.
Hours: Monday to Friday, 10-1 and 2-4:30.
Admission charge: None.
Telephone: (803) 792-5742.
Handicapped access: Yes.

Catfish Row, DuBose Heyward House

The first depiction of the African-American experience to reach much of the world was the opera *Porgy and Bess.* Productions of the show toured Europe and Asia repeatedly in the years after World War II, and it was frequently chosen as the American representative in pioneering cultural exchange programs with the Soviet bloc.

The show does not give the cheeriest picture of black life in America, but the beauty of its music, drama of its story line, and talents of the all-black casts who toured with it were regarded as ample compensations. The opera is based on a novel by white Charlestonian DuBose Heyward that appeared in 1925. Ten years later, when George Gershwin turned it into a musical production, he spent several months in the Charleston area, drawing inspiration from the music he heard here. He adapted many Gullah street cries for his

score. The name of Porgy, the lead character, is derived from a
Gullah vendor's word for a small local fish.

> **Location:** Heyward wrote the novel while living at 76
> Church St., and the house was made a National Historic
> Landmark in 1971. It is not open to the public. The
> inspiration for Catfish Row was known historically as
> Cabbage Row. But the fictional name was too strong to
> resist, and it is Catfish Row today. While the book placed it
> off E. Bay St., it is located near 91 Church St.

Denmark Vesey House

Denmark Vesey's plan called for a general black uprising and the
seizing of Charleston on the second Sunday in July 1822. But he
never lived that long. The scheme, which apparently involved more
than one thousand slaves, was betrayed to the authorities by a black
servant and Vesey, along with thirty-four other conspirators, was
hanged on July 2. It was one of the best-documented cases of an
organized slave rebellion, coming nine years before Nat Turner's
celebrated uprising in Virginia.

Vesey, like Turner, was a minister when he started making his
plans. Born in the West Indies, he was brought to Charleston as a
youth. An epileptic, he was regarded as having low value as a slave
and his owner happily accepted Vesey's payment for his freedom after
Vesey won a lottery.

Vesey used his Methodist church in the city as a meeting place for
the conspirators, who also included four white men. But the state
militia was called out to round them up and 150 were put on trial. A
total of seventy-nine persons involved in the plan were either put to
death or transported out of the state. As a result, South Carolina
passed a series of harsh new laws restricting the number of blacks
allowed to gather at one time and imposing strict curfews. In
addition, slaves were no longer permitted to purchase their freedom
except by special act of the state legislature.

> **Location:** The Vesey House, his residence during the time
> of the planned rebellion, at 56 Bull St., was declared a
> National Historic Landmark in 1976. It is not open to the
> public.

Old Slave Mart Museum

According to historians, this building wasn't actually the slave
market at all. That was located right up on the wharves for ease of
access. This structure, a few blocks inland, was used primarily as a
warehouse in which newly arrived blacks were kept prior to sale.

South Carolina was the southern state whose economy was tied
most closely to slaveholding because of its labor-intensive sugar, rice,
and tobacco plantations. From earliest colonial times, black slaves

The Old Slave Mart Museum

outnumbered white residents, a balance that didn't tilt the other way until the 1930 census. As a result, Charleston was among the most active American slave ports with traders putting in here directly from Gambia and the Gold Coast. The museum features displays of African-American crafts and historical artifacts of the slave trade.

> **Location:** The Old Slave Mart is on Chalmers St., just off Church St., in the historic district.
> **Hours:** The Old Slave Mart is undergoing renovation and will reopen in 1992.

Columbia

Mann-Simons Cottage

This home in South Carolina's capital was built in 1850 by a freedwoman, Celia Mann, and remained in her family for the next 120 years. It was restored in 1977 by the county Historic Preserva-

Penn School

tion Commission and has been turned into a museum of African-American culture.

> **Location:** 1403 Richland St., on the northern edge of the downtown area.
> **Exhibits:** Displays relating to the black history and culture of the Carolinas and Georgia.
> **Hours:** Tuesday to Friday, 10-4, and Saturday, 10-2.
> **Admission charge:** Donation requested.
> **Telephone:** (803) 252-1450.

Frogmore

Penn School

Among the more idealistic abolitionists, the education of freed slaves was regarded as the most urgent order of business after the Civil War. Some of them did not even want to wait that long to begin their mission. They followed right on the heels of northern troops in occupied parts of the South.

When the South Carolina sea islands were taken by the Union in 1862, two Quakers from Philadelphia arrived in a matter of weeks to open the first of these schools. Laura Towne and Ellen Murray would stay on to run the Penn Normal Institute on St. Helena Island for forty years. The women made pioneering efforts in providing health care for the islanders, as well as training in agriculture and home economy. The school sponsored the first farming co-op in the state, and at its peak had workshops for tanning, basketry, carpentry, and shoe repairing. The school is now a National Historic Landmark and its buildings house a museum of its history.

> **Location:** Frogmore is 7 miles east of Beaufort, across the St. Helena Causeway (U.S. 21). The school is just south of town on Lands End Rd.
> **Exhibits:** Displays on the history of the school and local Gullah culture.
> **Hours:** Monday to Friday, 9-5.
> **Admission charge:** Donation requested.
> **Telephone:** (803) 838-2432.

Georgetown

Prince George Winyah Church

This red brick church, named for the monarch in whose reign it was built (1746) and the bay on which the town is situated, was financed by a three-year sin tax on imported liquor. Of note here are the stained glass windows behind the altar. They came from Waccamaw Neck, across the inlet, and originally were part of St. Mary's Chapel for Negroes. This deserted chapel was located on a plantation owned by the DuPont family, who donated the windows to the church.

> **Location:** Georgetown is about 65 miles northeast of Charleston by way of U.S. 17. The church is in the heart of town, at Highmarket St. and Broad St.
> **Hours:** Monday to Friday, 9-5.
> **Telephone:** (803) 546-4358.

Morris Island

Battery Wagner

On July 18, 1863, the men of the Fifty-fourth Massachusetts Colored Infantry charged valiantly against the entrenched guns of this Confederate fort that guarded the approach to Charleston Harbor. A previous infantry assault had been beaten back and an artillery barrage had done little damage. Still, the Fifty-fourth, led by Col. Robert Gould Shaw, managed to reach the parapet of the fort, but could not dislodge the enemy. In the attempt, it lost more than 1,500 men, many of them horribly mangled after being hit by artillery shells at close range. Shaw was killed and Sgt. William H. Carney, who was twice wounded in the engagement and led the final

W. H. Carney

charge after picking up the colors from the fallen standard-bearer, was awarded the Congressional Medal of Honor.

The battle was dramatized in the 1988 film *Glory*. Since its release, the Charleston Visitor Information Center reports that it has received hundreds of inquiries about visiting the site. Unfortunately, nothing remains of the fort and there is no public transportation to Morris Island, which is visible from Fort Sumter National Monument and the resort of Folly Island.

Rantowles

Stono River Slave Rebellion

Spain, always eager to disrupt the British colonies to the north of its Florida colony, managed to get a message through to the slaves of South Carolina in 1739. Any who made their way to St. Augustine would be given their freedom. The news resulted in the largest slave rebellion of the colonial period.

Led by a man known only as Cato, a group of about one hundred managed to break into a storehouse to obtain weapons and then killed twenty-one whites as they made their way south to freedom. The lieutenant governor of the colony narrowly escaped capture and managed to alert the militia. Within five hours, the band was overtaken at the Stono River and forty-four were executed. The colony quickly enacted legislation making it illegal to teach a slave how to read.

> **Location:** Rantowles is about 12 miles west of Charleston on U.S. 17. An historical marker near the town commemorates the rebellion and was made a National Historic Landmark in 1974.

V I R G I N I A

Alexandria

Franklin and Armfield Office

Virginia's tobacco plantations began failing early in the nineteenth century. At just about the same time, the cotton gin was opening up vast new lands for that crop in the Deep South, requiring an expansion of the slave labor pool to work them. After 1808, though, it was illegal to import new slaves from Africa. This combination of circumstances changed the nature of slavery in Virginia. The state became the center of slave breeding and trading for the rest of the South.

In the 1830s, when the trade was at its peak, the black population of the state dropped from 517,000 to 499,000, although demographers estimate the natural increase would have been about 24 percent. That means about eleven thousand blacks a year were being exported to the cotton states, primarily young men who were torn from their families.

"How can an honorable mind, a patriot and lover of his country," said Thomas Jefferson Randolph to the state legislature in 1832, "bear to see this ancient dominion converted into one grand menagerie, where men are to be reared for market like oxen for the shambles?"

The center of this trade was the offices of Franklin and Armfield. From 1828 to 1836, according to its records, it was the largest slave-trading firm in the South. What makes this even more ironic was that during this entire period, Alexandria was part of the District of Columbia, as it had been since 1789. It was not returned to Virginia until 1847. So the largest slave trade in America was carried on within its very capital.

> **Location:** The offices, which are still intact, are at 1315 Duke St., in the western edge of the downtown area. The building, declared a National Historic Landmark in 1978, is not open to the public.

Arlington

Benjamin Banneker Boundary Stone

One of the most erudite men in early America, Benjamin Banneker was a farmer, clockmaker, astronomer, mathematician, writer of almanacs. But his greatest achievement was saving and surveying the District of Columbia.

Banneker was born of free parents on a small tobacco farm outside Baltimore in 1731. He received an eighth-grade education in an integrated school and then settled down to work the family farm. But he was fascinated by mathematics and produced a mechanical wooden clock that struck the hours, a marvel of its time. He discovered the study of astronomy at the age of fifty and was so fascinated by it that he spent nights wrapped in blankets outdoors observing the heavens. He noted some errors in the books he had been given and accurately predicted the solar eclipse of 1789. This work brought Banneker to the attention of the scientific community, including Thomas Jefferson. The future president, impressed by Banneker's mathematical proficiency, had him appointed to the three-man team that was planning the future American capital city, Columbia.

Pierre Charles l'Enfant was in charge of the master plan. Irked by criticism of his design, though, he quit, picked up his complex plans, and returned to France. Banneker, however, had committed the entire scheme to memory. With the team's remaining member, Charles Ellicott, he managed to reconstruct the master plan and complete the surveying work to l'Enfant's design. While still working on this project, he published an almanac, the first such work authored by a black man in America. It appeared in 1791 and was published annually for ten years thereafter. Jefferson was impressed and sent one of the books to the French Academy of Sciences. Another was presented as an argument for the education of blacks during a debate in Britain's House of Commons.

At his death in 1806, Banneker was regarded as the best-known black man in America. After decades of obscurity, his achievements were restored to life in a 1972 biography. The author of that work, Silvio A. Bedini stated: "Never had the tangible memorabilia of an important man's life vanished so completely as had Banneker's." In 1980 the U.S. Post Office issued a commemorative stamp in his honor.

The boundary stone marking the original southwestern border of the District of Columbia, before the Virginia portion was returned to that state, was renamed as a memorial for Banneker in 1976 and declared a National Historic Landmark. Ironically, a traffic circle named in his honor in the District of Columbia is tucked off in a corner of the huge l'Enfant Plaza.

Location: The stone is at the corner of 18th St. and Van Buren St.

Title page of Benjamin Banneker's almanac

Dr. Charles R. Drew, developer of the blood bank

Dr. Charles R. Drew House

The concept of the blood bank, storing and preserving donated blood until it is needed for transfusions during surgery, has become such a routine function of health care that it's hard to grasp how recent a medical development it is. Until the eve of World War II, it was a theoretical concept only. But Dr. Charles R. Drew gave the idea its first clinical application and showed that it could work successfully.

Drew, a native of Washington, D.C., was a star athlete at Amherst and won the Mossman Trophy in 1926 as the man who brought the most credit to the school. He went on to McGill University and entered medical school, where he earned a Master of Surgery degree. He then returned to Howard University to teach. Awarded a Rockefeller scholarship to Columbia University, he began researching the practicality of storing plasma. For his doctoral thesis, he set up the country's first blood bank and was soon recognized as the leading expert in the field. With war imminent, England chose him to set up a national blood bank system there, and he was asked to do the same for the American Red Cross.

He returned to Howard shortly after Pearl Harbor to head the school's department of surgery. He died in 1950 in an automobile accident. His Arlington home was made a National Historic Landmark in 1976.

> **Location:** The Drew House is at 2505 1st St. S. Dr. Drew lived there from 1920 to 1939. It is not open to the public.

Clarksville

Prestwould Plantation

In 1795 Sir Peyton Skipwirth built this manor house in one of the rare stone mansions on the Virginia frontier at that time. The land was originally held by William Byrd II in 1730, but, according to legend, his son lost its title to the Skipwirths at the end of a three-day card game.

In recent years, however, the home has attracted greater scholarly attention because of the discovery of what may be the largest collection of slave writings in America, detailing life at Prestwould from a hitherto unknown black perspective. An original two-family slave house stands on the property.

> **Location:** The plantation is 3 miles north of Clarksville on U.S. 15, and about 85 miles southwest of Petersburg by way of I-85 and U.S. 58.
> **Exhibits:** There are plans to add exhibits relating to the slave writings to existing displays on the home's furnishings and gardens.
> **Hours:** Daily, 12:30-4, May to September; weekends only, October. By appointment, the rest of the year.
> **Admission charge:** Adults, $4.50; senior citizens, $3.50; children 6-12, $1.50; children under 6, free.
> **Telephone:** (804) 374-8672.

Courtland

Nat Turner Rebellion

One of the enduring myths about slavery in the South is that it was accepted passively with minimal resistance by those who were in chains. How bad could it have been, goes the argument, if the slaves themselves were content? In recent years, however, historians have turned up evidence that slave revolts were far more numerous than had previously been thought. It was to the interest of the slave owners to suppress news of such rebellions and eradicate them from the record. But diaries, the minutes of legislative meetings called to confront the problem, and plantation records are slowly yielding a different story. During the three hundred years of slavery, revolt was

The capture of Nat Turner

a constant fear among the owners and, in fact, the number of uprisings seems to have been in the hundreds.

But none was as fearsome as Nat Turner's. During the three August days in 1831 when his band cut through Southhampton County, fifty-five whites were killed and the county seat, Jerusalem (now known as Courtland), was in a state of siege. The rebellion sent a bolt of fear throughout Virginia and the entire South. For weeks afterwards rumors of Turner's approach sent citizens in places hundreds of miles from the actual site running in terror.

Turner was about thirty at the time of this uprising. He said later in the confession he dictated to a white lawyer while in prison that his mother wanted to murder him at birth, because she did not want her child reared in slavery. At an early age he began to astonish people with prophecies and knowledge of things that had happened before his birth. He mastered reading easily and became a charismatic figure in the slave community. An avid reader of Christian works, he was dumbfounded by the terrible discrepancies between the teachings of his religion and the reality of his life. It was at this time that he began seeing visions and hearing voices, which told him to watch for a sign.

Throughout the summer of 1831, the visions intensified. One urged him to free his fellows and go into Jerusalem. The identical names of the Virginia town and the holy city of the Bible seemed too strong for coincidence. On August 21, a Sunday, Turner struck. Starting with the slaying of his owner and family, Turner set off across the county, gathering recruits as he went. Every plantation house on the route was attacked and its occupants killed. The only whites spared were an impoverished farmer and his family. Turner's vengeance was directed only at the slaveowners.

By Monday evening, Turner and his force of sixty men were within three miles of Jerusalem and the county was in a panic. Plantation owners, rather than joining a militia, insisted that they had to stay home to protect their own land and families. At this point, however, Turner split his force, allowing a group of them to visit friends on a nearby plantation. This group was attacked by a larger force of whites and routed. When Turner appeared with the main body of blacks, the whites retreated towards town. But Turner felt his losses had been too great and instead of pressing on, he fell back. That gave the state the time it needed to get reinforcements to the scene.

By daybreak on Tuesday, enough troops were on hand to scatter Turner's forces at another engagement. By then, three thousand federal soldiers and state militia were in Jerusalem and a general massacre of those suspected of following Turner began. Those captured were tried and nineteen were hanged. Turner eluded his pursuers for two months before being captured, taken to Jerusalem, and executed.

The uprising polarized Virginia, with those arguing for more brutal restrictions on blacks almost balanced by those who argued for an end to slavery. Ultimately, the antislavery group lost by a sixty-five to fifty-eight vote in the legislature. The majority then pushed through laws that made it illegal to teach slaves to read or write or to hold religious meetings without a white minister in attendance.

Almost a century and a half later, these events were dramatized by novelist William Styron in his best-seller, *The Confession of Nat Turner*. But the most direct effect of Turner's uprising was to shatter the myth that slaves in the more enlightened southern states, such as Virginia, accepted their own enslavement.

> **Location:** Courtland is about 55 miles west of Norfolk, on U.S. 58. There is scant evidence or acknowledgement of the rebellion in the area. But if you turn south on Virginia 35, just west of the town, and follow it south, you will be heading through the midst of the plantation country that Turner and his followers terrorized.

Great Bridge

Battlefield Memorial

During the Revolutionary War period, the last British governor of Virginia, Lord Dunmore, saw that his best practical chance of preventing American rebels from taking over the colony was to win over its black population to his side. There were 270,000 slaves in Virginia in 1775, almost half of the total population. As early as April of that year, as rebels and redcoats clashed far to the north at Lexington and Concord, Dunmore threatened to "proclaim liberty to the slaves and reduce Williamsburg to ashes," if the rebellion did not end. In November, he followed through on the first part of the

Lord Dunmore recruited slaves to fight with the British

threat, declaring all slaves in the colony free. It was the first time he had shown much concern for slaves, however, and while several hundred blacks did flock to his base in Norfolk, the great majority ignored him.

On December 9, about seven hundred colonials advanced northwards to the bridge across the Albemarle and Chesapeake Canal, held by a force of about five hundred British regulars, loyalists, and blacks. After several hours of firing in this first battle on Virginia soil the British retreated and evacuated Norfolk. William Flora, a freedman who fought on the colonial side, helped defend the bridge at a critical time of the battle. Reportedly, a slave also deliberately gave the British force the wrong information, making the commander believe the colonial force was far smaller than it really was.

Great Bridge had its effects. A few weeks after the battle, George Washington reversed his opposition to accepting blacks into the colonial army and agreed to take in those who had already tried to enlist and had been turned away. And in the midst of the war, in 1778, the colonial legislature outlawed the importation of slaves to Virginia, thirty years in advance of such legislation at the federal level.

Fort Monroe

Location: Great Bridge is about 20 miles south of Norfolk. The site of the battle is marked on the Great Bridge cutoff from Virginia 168.

Hampton

Fort Monroe

There has been a fort on this point of land, protecting the approach to the James River and the interior of Virginia, since 1609, when the settlers at Jamestown erected Fort Algernoune to guard against the Spanish. It was rebuilt several times, strengthened to assist in the siege of Yorktown at the end of the Revolution, and, starting in 1819, expanded and renamed for President James Monroe. Although that expansion took twenty-eight years and was completed after its namesake was long in his grave, by the start of the Civil War the fort was a formidable military installation.

It was easily defended from Confederate assaults, serving as a Union naval base deep in southern territory. It also became a goal for escaped slaves seeking safety. In the first weeks of the war, there was no set policy on how such slaves were to be treated. One northern commander returned some to their owner, touching off a storm of outrage and demands for his court martial among abolitionists.

Benjamin Butler would have none of this. A Massachusetts politician, Butler had been commissioned as a general when the war began and sent to Maryland. An ardent antislavery man given to dramatic gestures and high-handed actions, Butler had no doubts about the purpose of the war. But his sentiments did not go over well in his first posting, so he was sent instead to the quieter base of Fort Monroe.

In late May 1861, three fugitive slaves made their way to his lines. Their owner soon appeared demanding their return. Under terms of the Fugitive Slave Act, Butler was bound to give them up. Instead, the former lawyer declared them contraband of war, legally taken from an owner in rebellion against federal authority.

"The fugitive slave act does not affect a foreign country, which Virginia claims to be," said Butler, "and she must reckon it as one of the infelicities of her position that in so far as this, at least, she was taken at her word." This position was approved by the War Department as a brilliant solution to the problem. Although it still balked at the idea of declaring a war against slavery, there was evidence that many of the refugees had been employed building Confederate entrenchments. As such, they could be regarded as legitimate spoils of war. From then on, as the word spread, blacks streamed into the old fort.

They were not allowed combat roles at first, but Butler used them in building roads and fortifications. Eventually, many of them were organized into the Army of the James and saw plentiful action in the Richmond campaign. Others served aboard the *U.S.S. Minnesota*, manning a gun carriage in a sweep along the North Carolina coast. "No gun in the fleet was more steadily served than theirs," Butler reported, "and no men more composed than they when danger was supposed to be imminent."

Historian Bruce Catton wrote that Butler's action was the first crack in the policy to keep the slavery issue out of the war and led inexorably to the recognition of the rights of slaves and the Emancipation Proclamation.

> **Location:** The fort is 3 miles south of downtown Hampton, off I-64 at the eastbound Virginia 143 exit.
> **Exhibits:** The Casemate Museum contains historical displays about the fort and the role it played in the Civil War. Included is the cell in which Jefferson Davis was imprisoned after the war on charges of conspiring against the life of President Lincoln.
> **Hours:** Daily, 10:30-5.
> **Admission charge:** None.
> **Telephone:** (804) 727-3973.

Hampton Institute

The great oak tree is hundreds of years old. It was already fully grown and regarded as ancient when Mrs. Mary Peake, a freedwoman, began holding classes beneath its boughs for the children of escaped slaves who came streaming into nearby Fort Monroe (see above.) The fort commander, Gen. Benjamin Butler, put the adults to

Hampton Institute

work in the war effort. He gave full approval to a program of education for the children on the grounds of the federal hospital under the auspices of the American Missionary Association.

These classes under the Emancipation Oak were the acorns from which Hampton Institute, one of the preeminent historically black universities, grew. Mrs. Peake's classes evolved into the Butler School. Then, in 1868, Gen. Samuel Armstrong, head of the eastern district of the Freedmen's Bureau, bought the site, installed himself as principal, rounded up fifteen students and two teaching assistants, and opened Hampton for business in the old hospital.

Armstrong had commanded two regiments of black troops during the war and was convinced the best hope for equality was through education. He was also no slouch when it came to raising money. Told that only $2,000 was on hand to build a new dormitory, Armstrong told the workers to "dig the hole and pile the bricks and lumber around. We'll make it look so interesting that people will be only too glad to give us the money." He also borrowed a technique from Nashville's Fisk University and gathered some of the school's top musicians to tour the North and "sing up" money for a building. Ivy-covered Virginia Hall is still a beloved campus landmark.

Armstrong was also adept at getting prominent northerners to sit on Hampton's board of trustees. Two presidents, James Garfield and William Howard Taft, as well as steel magnate Andrew Carnegie, served in that capacity and facilitated fund-raising efforts. For most of its early history, Hampton depended on that. It charged no tuition to its largely penniless students, depending on them to go out and serve the black community with what they had learned there. This is where Booker T. Washington came, walking across the entire width of Virginia, to get an education. This was far from uncommon. One student walked all the way from Florida to get here. Much of Hampton's philosophy of practical education and community service were taken by Washington to Tuskegee when he left the Hampton faculty in 1881 to establish that school.

A century later, Hampton has an enrollment of 4,100 students, the largest in its history, on its lovely campus along Hampton Creek, and regards itself as the most selective of the country's black schools.

> **Location:** Eastern end of Queen St., off exit 68 of I-64.
> **Exhibits:** Besides the Emancipation Oak, right at the school's main gate, and Virginia Hall, the school is known for its excellent museum of African Art and African-American history, in the Academy Building.
> **Hours:** The museum is open Monday to Friday, 8-5, and weekends, 12-4.
> **Admission charge:** None.
> **Telephone:** (804) 727-5000.

Jamestown

Jamestown Settlement

The first English colonists to settle permanently in North America landed here in 1607, followed in twelve years by the first boatload of black servants. The 1619 date cannot really be fixed as the beginning of black slavery in America. The practice had been going on in the Spanish and Portugese colonies in the West Indies and South America for more than a century. And these first arrivals were indentured servants who would be allowed to work for their freedom until they repaid their passage to the colony. That was common practice for both black and white laborers.

Two of these servants, Anthony and Isabella, were married and in 1625 became the parents of the first black child born in North America, William. Anthony Johnson (there is some debate whether this is the same Anthony mentioned above) had become so prosperous after working off his indenturement that by 1651 he was granted two hundred acres of land and owned five servants himself. More ominous, however, was the assertion of several landowners by 1653 that servants were now bound to them for life, the first such claim made in the colony in regard to persons other than prisoners.

Slaves arriving in Virginia

Within another few years, slavery had been legally sanctioned. A slave trade with Africa through the West Indies was formalized. By the end of the century, monopoly rights on the trade were removed and it was thrown open to the general public.

Location: Jamestown Settlement is adjacent to Colonial National Historical Park, which preserves the original site of the 1607 colony. Both are located at the western end of Colonial Pkwy., off the Virginia 199 exit of I-64, about 30 miles northwest of Hampton.

Exhibits: Jamestown Settlement is a living history recreation of the colony. An exhibit that opened in 1990 in Jamestown Gallery stresses the role of blacks during the first century of Virginia's existence. The national park shows the archeological work done on the site and the outline of the settlement. Markers on a self-guided walking tour help the visitor reconstruct its appearance. The only aboveground evidence remaining, however, is the ruin of a church tower. The capital was moved to Williamsburg in 1699 and by the middle of the eighteenth century, the site had been abandoned.

Hours: Both places are open daily, 9-5.
Admission charge: Jamestown Settlement, adults, $7;
children 6-12, $3.50. National park, $5 per vehicle.
Telephone: Jamestown Settlement, (804) 229-1607; national park, (804) 229-1733.
Handicapped access: Yes.

Norfolk

Black Civil War Veterans' Memorial

Norfolk fell to Union forces in May 1862 and never again was part of the Confederacy. It became a center for black refugees from the countryside, and a recent study estimates that there were seventy thousand former slaves in Norfolk when the war ended.

Norfolk was rich recruiting ground once the U.S. Army made a commitment to accept blacks. In Elmwood Cemetery stands what is believed to be the only memorial to black soldiers of the Civil War. Their gravestones stand behind a granite monument, topped by a black version of Billy Yank. Later, black veterans of the Spanish-American War were also buried in this area.

Location: Elmwood Cemetery is located on Princess Anne Rd. just north of the central business district. The cemetery is open daily during daylight hours.

Petersburg

National Battlefield Park

The Civil War has been described as a conflict that began in the eighteenth century and ended in the twentieth. At its start, it was fought by small, mobile forces, engaging in set battles over fixed terrain. It ended as a foretaste of World War I, with enormous armies entrenched, battling for advances that were measured in yards and inflicting horrendous casualties upon each other and the civilian population. This was typified by the Battle of Petersburg, a ten-month siege that slowly wore down the Confederate Army, but only at a terrible cost in Union casualties.

Gen. U. S. Grant arrived at Petersburg in June 1864, hoping that its fall would cut off rail supplies to Richmond and also cripple Gen. Robert E. Lee's army as a fighting force. Lee in turn hoped to prolong the siege as long as possible, feeling the north would grow tired of the endless casualties and accept a peace settlement.

Northern strategists sought a way for a quick resolution and hit upon the plan that led to the Battle of the Crater. A unit from Pennsylvania, made up mostly of coal miners from the Pittsburgh area, began digging a tunnel towards an exposed Confederate fort. The plan was to discharge explosives below the fort and then attack through this gap in the southern lines.

Thirty-two black infantry regiments and two cavalry units were involved in the siege and it was decided to send several black units into the gap caused by the explosion. It took a month to dig the tunnel and the blast, on July 30, worked to perfection, blowing the fort to smithereens. But in one of his major blunders, Grant changed his plan at the last moment, pulling back the black units, apparently, because he did not trust the combat capabilities of these troops. Unprepared white units made the attack and, instead of circling the one-hundred-seventy by sixty-foot crater, stumbled into it. The hole was thirty feet deep and as they tried to scramble out the other end, they were picked off by Confederate sharpshooters. Grant finally sent the black units into the battle, but by then the lead troops had panicked and were trying to retreat. The northern forces were trapped in the hole and slaughtered by counterattacking Confederates. There were reports that some blacks were bayoneted by northern whites. Of the four thousand casualties in the engagement, 1,234 were sustained by the black units. Sgt. Decatur Dorsey of the Maryland Thirty-ninth Colored Troops was awarded the Congressional Medal of Honor for his actions during the day. The siege, however, would drag on for eight more months. It was the longest in American military history and would end only a week before the final southern surrender.

Location: The Battlefield Park is on the northeastern edge of Petersburg, accessible from Virginia 36.
Exhibits: A self-guided loop tour takes you around the major points on the battlefield, including the Crater. The visitor center, near the park entrance, furnishes an overall perspective.
Hours: The park is open daily, 8-dark; the visitor center, 8-7 in summer; 8-5 the rest of the year.
Admission charges: The park charges $3 per automobile, $1 for those biking or walking, and children under 16 and senior citizens are admitted free.
Telephone: (804) 732-3531.
Handicapped access: Yes.

Richmond

Jackson Ward, Maggie Walker House, Sixth Mt. Zion Baptist Church

Within a generation of the Civil War, this district northwest of downtown had become the preeminent black neighborhood of the Confederacy's former capital. It runs from the campus of Virginia Union University, which was started in Richmond in a jail that

The Maggie Walker House. Reproduced by permission of the National Park Service.

formerly held runaway slaves, almost to the edge of the central business district. The area has undergone renovation since being declared a National Historic District in 1978 and many families have lived in its fine Greek Revival homes for generations.

The ward, which hasn't been a political subdivision for more than sixty years, nurtured many black institutions in its early years. Among the most powerful was the St. Luke Penny Savings Bank, which became the first bank in America to be headed by a woman. Maggie Lena Walker was born in Richmond in 1867 and after finishing high school worked as a secretary for the Order of St. Luke, a statewide black fraternal organization. As she traveled to its branches, she developed the concept of starting an insurance and banking company through the organization to serve the needs of black businessmen who could not get coverage or credit from white firms. The bank, founded in 1903, eventually became the Consolidated Bank and Trust Company. In the years after the turn of the century it was the largest black-owned bank in the country and still ranks tenth on that list. Her home in the Jackson Ward has been restored to its appearance during the last years of her life in the 1930s.

The best-known native of the neighborhood was probably Bill "Bojangles" Robinson, whose dancing defined the artistry of tap for two generations of Americans. In later years, tap was celebrated as an authentic African-American art form, Robinson helped shape it in its early years. He was born here in 1878 as Luther Robinson, and later claimed he never took a lesson in his life; his dancing just flowed out of the music he heard around him. In later life, he complained that too many dancers were concerned with acrobatics rather than delineating the flow of the music, which he felt was the most important purpose of dance. He started off on the minstrel circuit and became a Broadway star in the 1920s in a succession of reviews designed to show off his abilities. He inspired a host of imitators, including Fred Astaire, who borrowed liberally from Robinson and always acknowledged the debt. His greatest popularity came in his movie roles, where he showed off his famed staircase routine and co-starred with Shirley Temple in several pictures. His nickname, which he carried for forty years and said meant "easy going and happy-go-lucky," far outlived the man, who died in 1949. The song "Mr. Bojangles" became a national hit twenty years after his death, and helped define the work of Sammy Davis, Jr., his successor as the country's most beloved black entertainer.

Another landmark in the area is Sixth Mt. Zion Baptist Church, home of one of the best known black ministers of his time, Rev. John Jasper. A former slave who found himself with seventy-three cents in his pocket when the war ended, he decided to start this church in a Richmond shanty. Within ten years, it had become the city's largest black church. His sermon of 1879, "The Sun Do Move and the Earth Am Square," won him national fame. It argued that God couldn't have made the sun stand still in answer to the prayer of Joshua if it hadn't been moving to begin with. It may have been bad astronomy but it impressed theologians who liked a good argument.

Location: The Jackson Ward is bordered by 4th St., Marshall St., Smith St., and I-95. The most impressive homes are along Marshall St. and Clay St. The Maggie Walker House is at 110 1/2 Leigh St., two blocks north of Marshall. The Mt. Zion Church is at the corner of Duval St. and St. John's St.

Exhibits: The Walker House has many original furnishings. In the Mt. Zion Church is a bust of Rev. Jasper, sculpted by local artist Edward V. Valentine, who also did the city's monument to Jefferson Davis.

Hours: Walker House is open Wednesday to Sunday, 9-5. Inquire in advance for the church.

Admission charge: None.

Telephone: Walker House, (804) 780-1380; Mt. Zion Church, (804) 648-7511.

Richmond National Battlefield Park

As the autumn of 1864 began, the main bodies of the two great opposing armies were entrenched opposite each other near Petersburg (see National Battlefield Park entry above). But some northern generals still hoped that a decisive thrust in the Richmond area could lead to the breakthrough that would take the Confederate capital and shorten the war.

Gen. Benjamin Butler decided that the most vulnerable point in the southern defenses around Richmond was at Fort Harrison, southeast of the city, on New Market Heights. He conceived a plan to attack the fort and he wanted black troops to carry it out. Since the earliest days of the war (see entry for Fort Monroe, under Hampton, Virginia), Butler was convinced the conflict was about black freedom. He was disgusted at the way many northern commanders hesitated at using black troops in combat. Just two months before, Gen. U. S. Grant himself had replaced specially trained black soldiers for the battle at the Crater at Petersburg and had suffered a debacle when the substitutes failed to execute the attack properly. Butler wanted vindication. Although it had been shown repeatedly by this time in the war that black soldiers were an effective fighting force, he wanted to end all doubts.

Nine black regiments were included in the attacking force, most of them former slaves from Maryland, Virginia, and North Carolina. They were ferried secretly across the James River and at dawn on September 29, began their charge up the heights to the fort. By the end of this day, thirteen of these men would perform acts of bravery that would win them the Congressional Medal of Honor. Charging up a thirty-five degree incline, hacking their way past two barriers of felled trees, and vaulting over the exterior works of the fort, the troops swept on in an unstoppable wave. The southerners, who had started the day by hurling taunts at them, turned around and ran.

So many white officers were killed in the wild dash to the top that several units ended up being led by black sergeants. No fewer than nine of these noncommissioned officers won Medals of Honor for their heroism in rallying their men.

Butler, riding up the path of this charge immediately afterwards, found 543 dead and wounded black troops between the base of the hill and the fort. "As I guided my horse this way and that way that his hoof might not profane their dead bodies," he wrote later, "I swore to myself an oath, which I hope and believe I have kept sacredly, that they and their race should be cared for and protected by me to the extent of my power as long as I lived."

The taking of Fort Harrison, as Butler had hoped, left the road to Richmond open temporarily. But by the time the federal troops could pursue this advantage, the Confederates had regrouped at Fort Gilmer and managed to beat back a northern assault. The following day, the Confederates countered with a massive attack on Fort Harrison. In a battle that ended up as hand-to-hand combat on the outer breastworks of the fort, the southern line finally broke and black troopers holding the heights were left in control of the fort.

The battles in this area, which collectively are known as Clafflin's Farm, did not shorten the war significantly. They did force Lee to redraw his defensive line around Richmond to the north's slight advantage. Until the war ended, however, Clafflin's Farm remained the only time these defenses were breached.

> **Location:** Richmond Battlefield Park virtually encircles Virginia's capital and was the site of two separate campaigns: Gen. George McLellan's offensive of 1862 and U.S. Grant's siege of 1864-65. Chimborazo Visitor Center, at 3215 E. Broad St. in the city, provides an overview of both campaigns and their major engagements. Fort Harrison Visitor Center concentrates on the battles of late September 1864. It is located 10 miles southeast of Richmond by way of Virginia 5 and Battlefield Park Rd.
> **Exhibits:** Both visitor centers contain historical exhibits and artifacts. They are the starting points for self-guided loop trails to the major points of interest on the battleground.
> **Hours:** Chimborazo, daily, 9-5; Fort Harrison, daily, 9-5, June to August.
> **Admission charge:** None.
> **Telephone:** (804) 226-1981.

Roanoke

Booker T. Washington National Monument

When he wrote his autobiography, Booker T. Washington called it *Up from Slavery*. This two-hundred-acre tobacco farm in the Virginia

Booker T. Washington's birthplace

Piedmont is where that ascent began. His name first appeared on an inventory of the farm's slaves when he was five years old, and a value of four-hundred dollars was placed on him.

The farm, owned by James Burroughs, was Washington's home for the first nine years of his life until the Civil War ended and he was freed. With his mother, he moved on to Malden, West Virginia to join his stepfather (see entry on Booker T. Washington Memorial, Malden, West Virginia). He didn't return until 1908, when he was president of Tuskegee University and a nationally known figure. On that trip he pointed out many landmarks of his boyhood. Those identifications furnished the basis for the restoration when the farm became a national monument as part of the centennial celebration of Washington's birth in 1957.

The Burroughs farm appears now approximately as it looked when Washington was born. It has been set up to illustrate how such a small, self-sufficient operation functioned in the final years of slavery.

> **Location:** The national monument is located 22 miles southeast of Roanoke by way of I-581, Virginia 116, and northbound Virginia 122.
>
> **Exhibits:** This is a living history museum, with staffers recreating the roles of craft workers and occupants of the

A coachman guides his horses near the Governor's Palace in Williamsburg

Burroughs farm in the 1850s. A visitor center provides information on the historical context of the farm, and a nature trail offers visitors a self-guided loop through countryside that has been restored to its nineteenth-century appearance.

Hours: Daily, 8:30-5.

Admission charge: Adults, $1; senior citizens and children under 16, free.

Telephone: (703) 721-2094.

Williamsburg

Colonial Restoration

The showplace of America's historical restorations, Williamsburg from the first made an effort to show the role of African Americans in Virginia's colonial capital. For many years, that involved recreating the roles of servants and custodians, including the white-wigged major domo of the House of Burgesses. But in the 1980s, the

Williamsburg Corporation approved an expanded examination of the part blacks played in the life of this city before the state capital was transferred to Richmond in 1780. Called "The Other Half," this living history demonstration by black actors is put on at intervals throughout the restoration.

Location: Williamsburg is about 50 miles southeast of Richmond by way of I-64 and the Colonial Pkwy.

Exhibits: When John D. Rockefeller, Jr., became interested in this area in 1926, virtually nothing remained to remind a visitor of Williamsburg's glorious past. But now the historic area contains almost 100 buildings in a one-by-one-half mile area, filled with crafts demonstrations, living history, and the most thorough and painstaking restorations intended to recapture the texture of a past era anywhere in the country.

Hours: The visitor center, at which tickets for the historic buildings are sold and shuttle buses leave for the restored area, is open 8:30-8, March to December; 8:30-6, January and February.

Admission charge: Adults, $19; children 6-12, $12.50; children under 6, free. Weekly and monthly passes available.

Handicapped access: Yes.

WASHINGTON, D. C.

Anacostia Museum

Another member of the Smithsonian family, this is regarded as a neighborhood museum. Its intent is to illustrate African-American culture in this area, which has long been identified as a black neighborhood of Washington. It is also a research center and schedules ongoing programs relating to the black community.

> **Location:** The museum is in Fort Stanton Park, at 1901 Fort Pl. SE. From the 11th St. Bridge, go straight on Dr. Martin Luther King, Jr., Ave., then left on Morris Rd. This turns into Erie St. and leads into the museum.
> **Hours:** Daily, 10-5.
> **Admission charge:** None.
> **Telephone:** (202) 287-3369.

Bethune Museum and Archives

The first U.S. President to seek Mary McLeod Bethune's counsel was Herbert Hoover. He asked her to serve on a White House conference on child health in 1930 and for the next twenty-two years she was a frequent visitor to the seat of the nation's power.

Franklin D. Roosevelt named her director of black affairs in the National Youth Administration, the highest government post a black woman had held at the time. Even more important were her unofficial contacts with FDR. She became a trusted advisor on minority affairs and a good friend of Eleanor Roosevelt, meeting with the president and his wife frequently on an informal basis to put forth her ideas on black voting rights, the abolition of the poll tax and a federal anti-lynching law. After the president's death, Mrs. Roosevelt sent Bethune one of his favorite canes. She said later: "I swagger it sublimely. It gives me strength and courage and nothing to fear."

She served as a special emissary during the conference that formed the United Nations, and in 1952 she capped off her government service as President Harry Truman's personal representative at inauguration ceremonies in Liberia.

During her years of public service she established a residence in Washington. That home became the Bethune Museum and Archives in 1979. This is an independent organization dedicated to continuing the work of the founder of the National Council of Negro Women

The Mary McLeod Bethune Memorial in Lincoln Park

with exhibits and programs emphasizing the contributions of black women to American life.

> **Location**: The Bethune Museum is at 1318 Vermont Ave. NW., near Logan Circle.
> **Exhibits**: Memorabilia of Mrs. Bethune and changing exhibits on black women.
> **Hours**: Monday to Friday, 10-4.
> **Admission charge**: None.
> **Telephone**: (202) 332-1233.

Blanche Bruce House

Only two black men served in the U.S. Senate in the nineteenth century and both were from Mississippi. During the Reconstruction era, twenty African Americans were elected to the House of Representatives by southern states. At that time, however, senators were appointed by state legislatures and only in Mississippi was the political decision made to send black senators. Hiram Revels was the first, appointed in 1870 to the seat once held by Jefferson Davis. Even the most bitter opponents of Reconstruction admitted that he was a "man of some education and culture." He served only one year, however, before resigning to become president of the newly formed Alcorn University.

In 1875, Blanche Bruce followed him to the Senate. He was only thirty-four at the time, a man of considerable wealth, who had come to Mississippi in 1868 and amassed significant land holdings. Becom-

Sen. Blanche Bruce

ing active in Republican politics, he was tax assessor and sheriff of Bolivar County before being nominated to the Senate. During his single term he was active in defending minority rights, including those of Chinese and Indians, and, like Revels, backed the return of the franchise to those southern whites whose vote had been taken away because of their service in the Confederate army.

The success of that very policy returned control of the state legislature to white Democrats and Bruce, with no chance at a second term in office, never returned to Mississippi. He lived on in Washington, named to a succession of government jobs by Republican administrations. He was Registrar of the U.S. Treasury on two occasions and held that position under President William McKinley at his death in 1898. His Washington home was declared a National Historic Landmark in 1975.

The last black congressman of that era survived him in office by only three years. It would be another twenty-eight years until Oscar DePriest, of Chicago, became the first black congressman from a northern state. And not until 1966, with the election of Edward Brooke of Massachusetts, did a third black man sit in the U.S. Senate.

Location: The Bruce House is at 909 M St. NW. It is not open to the public.

Carter G. Woodson

Carter G. Woodson House, Association for the Study of Negro Life and History

In 1916, when Carter Woodson began to publish the *Journal of Negro History*, the field was virtually a blank page. The tools of modern historiography were applied to other areas, and while some pioneering work had been done, black history was largely uncharted as a field of scholarship.

Woodson had worked in the Virginia coal mines as a teenager and couldn't attend high school until he was twenty. But he went on to win degrees from the University of Chicago and Harvard and came to Washington in 1909 as a public school teacher and principal. His concern as a teacher was that his students were getting absolutely no idea of the role black people played in American life through the textbooks used in the schools. Moreover, no programs existed to offer instruction in such studies. While still a teacher, he organized the Association for Negro Life and History, running it out of the ground floor of his home, which he owned from 1915 until his death in 1950.

Leaving teaching to dedicate himself to publishing the *Journal* and original scholarly works, Woodson also campaigned for observance of a week in which schools would concentrate on black history. He

Frederick A. Douglass House

wanted it held in February so that it would fall near the birthdays of Abraham Lincoln and Frederick Douglass. The first Black History Week was observed in 1926 and has now been extended through the entire month. He founded the *Negro History Bulletin* in 1937 to provide materials for teaching the subject at elementary and secondary-school levels. His own scholarship in the field is regarded as the basis for contemporary black history.

> **Location**: The Woodson House, which was also the former headquarters of the Association for the Study of Negro Life and History, is at 1538 9th St. NW. Now officially known as the Association for the Study of Afro-American Life and History, the organization's offices have relocated to 1401 14th St. NW. The Woodson House was declared a National Historic Landmark in 1976. It is currently occupied by the Visions Foundation, publisher of *American Visions* magazine and is not open to the public.
> **Telephone**: (202) 667-2822.

Frederick A. Douglass House

For much of the nineteenth century, Frederick A. Douglass was the nation's black conscience. He agitated endlessly for abolition of slavery before the Civil War and demanded that the country fulfill its promises to the slaves it freed afterward. He was born in Maryland and after escaping to the north based himself in Rochester, New York, where he published his newspaper, *North Star*. The appearance of his autobiography in 1845 meant that he had to flee the country, because its admission that he was an escaped slave made him a target for bounty hunters. British admirers purchased his freedom and he was able to return the following year. A powerful physical presence, with his beard and white hair giving him the demeanor of a biblical prophet, Douglass wrote and spoke tirelessly, becoming the dominant black voice in the North as the nation careened towards war. His Independence Day address of 1852, in which he asked what that holiday of freedom could possibly mean to him as a black man, is a masterpiece of eloquence. After the Emancipation Proclamation, he was instrumental in recruiting black troops for the Army, including his two sons.

He moved to Washington in 1872 and five years later bought Cedar Hill, a twenty-room home on the east side of the Anacostia River. The Republican party, which he supported as the best hope for blacks, appointed him to several posts in the District during his residence there. He was made U.S. Marshal in 1877 and four years later became Recorder of Deeds. Bitterly disappointed by the failure to protect the rights of blacks in the post-Reconstruction South, he lashed out in an Emancipation Day anniversary address in 1888 and accused the federal government of having abandoned them. Still, he supported Benjamin Harrison's successful presidential campaign that year and was rewarded by being named consul-general to Haiti and Santo Domingo. Disillusioned by the predatory practices of American businessmen in the islands, he resigned in 1891 and spent the last four years of his life at Cedar Hill, writing and agitating for black rights.

His second wife, Helen Pitts Douglass, arranged for the home to be preserved as a memorial to him. With the assistance of the National Association of Colored Women's Clubs, the home was first opened to visitors in 1916. Since 1962 it has been a part of the National Park Service.

> **Location**: The Douglass House, at 1411 W St. SE, is reached from central Washington by taking I-395 to the 11th St. Bridge, then straight ahead on Dr. Martin Luther King, Jr., Ave. and left on W.
> **Exhibits**: The house has been kept as it appeared during Douglass's eighteen-year residence. There is also a museum of his life and work. His study, a detached structure behind the main house which he referred to as "The Growlery," has also been preserved.
> **Hours**: Daily, 9-4.
> **Admission charge**: None.
> **Telephone**: (202) 426-5961.

Howard University

Of all the historically black universities in the country, this is the one whose name is probably familiar to most Americans. That's because Howard exists in a fishbowl, next door to the most intensive concentration of media in the world. Whatever happens at Howard is immediately flashed across the wire services, commented upon by syndicated columnists, and placed on the network news as emblematic of what is happening among black college students around the country.

That isn't necessarily the case. Simply because of its location in the capital, Howard draws the sort of student who tends to be politically involved and an activist. As far back as the 1930s, Howard students were making headlines by demonstrating at the segregated restaurant of the House of Representatives. In 1989, they made more news by demonstrating when Lee Atwater, President George Bush's campaign manager, was named to the school's Board of Trustees after running what the students considered a racist campaign.

Howard didn't start off as a black institution, however. Although founded in 1867 by the Freedmen's Bureau and named for the head of that agency, Gen. Oliver O. Howard, its charter called for the education of all youth, regardless of race. Its first students were white girls, the daughters of faculty members. But as the coils of segregation tightened throughout the South, Howard became the alternative to growing numbers of black students who would have been shut out of a higher education. By the turn of the century, the school was 88 percent black.

The university's law school is regarded as the cradle of the civil rights movement. Most of the attorneys involved in that struggle received their training and shaped the legal theories that shattered segregation in Howard's classrooms.

> **Location:** Howard's hilltop campus, one of Washington's highest points, is at 2400 6th St. NW, just east of U.S. 29 (Georgia Ave.).
>
> **Exhibits:** Founders Library houses one of the largest African-American research centers in existence, Moorland-Spingarn Research Center, an outstanding resource in the field of black history. The Gallery of Fine Arts contains the Alain Locke African Collection, named for the first black man to win a Rhodes Scholarship. The General Howard House is one of four original buildings still on campus and a National Historic Landmark. For visiting hours call in advance.
>
> **Telephone:** (202) 806-6100.

Lincoln Memorial

The shrine to America's sixteenth president has also been the focus of some of the most dramatic and memorable events in the capital's black experience.

On its steps, on Easter Sunday, 1939, Marian Anderson gave her famous concert after being denied the facilities of Constitution Hall. Regarded as one of the world's greatest contraltos, the Philadelphia-born Anderson had made her New York debut four years earlier and her performance had been hailed as "music-making that probed too

The Poor People's March on Washington in 1968 culminating at the Lincoln Memorial

deep for words." But when concert promoters in the country's segregated capital city applied to use Constitution Hall, they were told by its owners, the Daughters of the American Revolution, that they must abide by "local custom" and were denied access. The concert at the Lincoln Memorial became a major political event and the outcry resulting from the affair resulted in the desegregation of most of Washington's public facilities in the following months. Anderson continued as a major operatic attraction for many years and appeared at Constitution Hall in 1953 for the first of six concerts she would hold there. Five years later, she was named as a U.S. delegate to the United Nations.

The Mall in front of the Lincoln Memorial was the site of the most electrifying event in Dr. Martin Luther King, Jr's., career. It supplied the backdrop for the climax of the 1963 March on Washington and his "I have a dream" speech, which dramatized for all time the black quest for equality and dignity.

Five years later, the same area was the site of Resurrection City, the massive encampment built during the Poor People's March on Washington, which was being planned by Dr. King at the time of his death. It was carried on by his longtime associate, Rev. Ralph Abernathy, and the location continued to be a favorite rallying place for his organization, the Southern Christian Leadership Conference.

Location: The Lincoln Memorial is at the western end of the Mall, in a direct line with the Washington Monument and U.S. Capitol. Nearby is the Vietnam Veteran's Memorial, the most popular attraction in Washington throughout the 1980s, with its statue depicting the reality of integrated armed forces.

Exhibits: The Memorial was approved by an Act of Congress in 1867, but it took 44 years before financing was secured and another 11 years until the completed structure was dedicated, on Memorial Day, 1922. The shrine, which depicts a seated Lincoln, was sculpted by Daniel Chester French. The text of the Gettysburg Address and Second Inaugural Address are carved into the side walls.

Hours: The Memorial is always open.

Admission charge: None.

Lincoln Park

The first memorial to Abraham Lincoln in Washington, the statue in this park was unveiled on the eleventh anniversary of his death, April 14, 1876. A five-dollar donation came in from a black woman in Ohio a few weeks after his assassination and in an accompanying letter she suggested that freed slaves send whatever they could to help build it. As money began to arrive, Congress set aside a parcel of land east of the Capitol and Thomas Bell was commissioned to create the statue of Lincoln breaking the chains of slavery.

For ninety-eight years, Abe had the park to himself. But in 1974, a second statue was unveiled in Lincoln Park, to honor the memory of Mary McLeod Bethune. The educator and civil rights advisor was born the year before the Lincoln statue was unveiled. She was the founder of Bethune-Cookman University and worked with three U.S. Presidents on matters relating to the black community. (For more information on Bethune, see the entries on Bethune-Cookman College, Daytona Beach, Florida, and the Bethune Museum and Archives above.)

The memorial was the first monument to a black person on public land in the capital. It bears this inscription: "I leave you love. I leave you hope. I leave you the challenge in developing confidence in one another. I leave you a thirst for education. I leave you respect for the use of power. I leave you faith. I leave you racial dignity."

Location: Lincoln Park is on E. Capitol St. between E. 11th St. and E. 13th St.

National Museum of African Art

Part of the Smithsonian Institution, this handsome hall, situated in an underground pavilion, replaced a series of nine townhouses in the Capitol Hill area. It houses a collection of six thousand objects of sub-Saharan African art and also shows the influence of African art on the work of major European artists. Its collection of bronze, ivory, and wood sculpted figures is regarded as the country's primary source of research in the field.

Entrance to the National Museum of African Art

Location: The museum is part of a complex which includes the centers for Asian and Near Eastern art. It is located beneath the Enid A. Haupt gardens, near the center of the Smithsonian grouping behind the Castle, at 950 Independence Ave. SW.
Hours: Daily, 10-5:30.
Admission charge: None.
Telephone: (202) 357-1300.

St. Luke's Episcopal Church

For fifty-five years, the pulpit of this church was occupied by Alexander Crummell, who used it to advance his ideas of creating a black intellectual elite in the United States and liberating black Africa. Crummell, who served here from 1879 to 1894, founded the American Negro Academy to further the first part of his concept. The church was made a National Historic Landmark in 1976.

Location: St. Luke's is located at 15th St. and Church St. NW, between P St. and Q St. It is open by appointment.
Telephone: (202) 667-4394.

W E S T V I R G I N I A

Harpers Ferry

National Historic Park

This was George Washington's personal choice for the location of a federal armory. He was familiar with the site from his travels in the West. It was close to the newly planned capital in the District of Columbia, had access to waterpower on the Potomac River, and the surrounding hills made it secure. So the armory was established by act of Congress in 1794 and in seven years was turning out its first firearms, weapons that Lewis and Clark would carry with them on their exploration of the Northwest.

The geography of Harpers Ferry also appealed to John Brown. Just south of the Mason-Dixon line in what was then the slave state of Virginia, it seemed the perfect place to touch off the black insurrection that would bring on civil war. Brown belonged to the activist wing of the abolitionists. He believed that the only way to end the intolerable evil of slavery was to take up arms against it. His hope was that one violent act would hasten the inevitable conflict.

After months of preparation, Brown's force of twenty-one men, including five blacks, attacked after dark on October 16, 1859, and quickly seized the armory. The first victim of the raid was cut down in the first few moments. He was Heyward Shepherd, a freedman, the baggagemaster of the railroad station. The rest of Brown's plan began to unravel almost at once. Instead of rallying to their banner, the townsfolk took up arms against the "army of liberation." Brown's battered force was driven to the armory fire engine and guardhouse to make a stand. Two of his sons were killed in the battle and Brown, pinned down in the armory, had to abandon his escape plan, which called for carrying on guerilla warfare from the hills. On October 18, federal troops arrived from Washington and marines commanded by Gen. Robert E. Lee and Gen. J. E. B. Stuart stormed the fort and captured him.

Brown's act split the abolitionist movement, with some activists rallying to his support and others, most notably Frederick Douglass, breaking with him. In just forty-five days, Brown was tried, convicted of murder, treason, and conspiracy, and hanged in nearby Charles Town.

John Brown's Fort at Harpers Ferry

Within two years of the raid, the armory was burned to the ground by retreating Union troops to keep it from falling into the hands of the Confederate army. With the loss of the armory, Harpers Ferry settled back to the obscurity of a remote mountain town. But it still functioned powerfully as a symbol. West Virginia itself was created through events that were set in motion by the raid. Storer College, a school for freed slaves, was established there within months of the Civil War's end. One of the key early meetings of the group that became the National Association for the Advacement of Colored People (NAACP) was held here, by design, in 1906. And troops marched into battle for years afterwards singing about "John Brown's Body."

Location: Harpers Ferry is about 70 miles northwest of Washington, D.C., by way of I-270 and U.S. 340.
Exhibits: The entire town is a museum of the pre-Civil War era. The National Park Service has constantly expanded its holdings and is slowly recreating the appearance of Harpers Ferry in 1859. Guides assume living history roles of the townsfolk of that period. There are also scenic lookouts over the junction of the Potomac and Shenandoah Rivers.
Hours: The park is open daily, 8-5.
Admission charge: None.
Telephone: (304) 535-6223.

Malden

Booker T. Washington Memorial, African Zion Baptist Church

The first salt works in the Kanawha River Valley was established here, and by 1850 there were thirty furnaces in the area. The industry declined after the Civil War, but there was still enough work to attract the family of Booker T. Washington, who moved here from Virginia after emancipation (see entry on Booker T. Washington National Monument, Roanoke, Virginia.)

While working here Washington was encouraged to pursue a higher education by Viola Ruffner, the wife of his employer. He returned to teach briefly after getting his degree and always regarded Malden as his hometown. Washington is credited with starting the first Sunday school class at African Zion Baptist Church, where he worshiped.

> **Location:** Malden is on the eastern outskirts of Charleston, on the north bank of the Kanawha by way of U.S. 60. The Washington Memorial, erected in 1963, is on the main highway. The Church is at 4100 Malden Dr. Call in advance to enter.
> **Telephone:** (304) 768-2635.

Talcott

John Henry Park

West Virginia gave America a song about John Brown's body. But the state produced an equally famous tune about the legendary hammer of John Henry, the greatest steel-driving man the railroad ever saw.

There is no conclusive evidence that the man celebrated in the folk song ever existed, or that he actually worked here on the Big Bend Tunnel of the Chesapeake and Ohio Railroad in the 1870s. Two scholarly inquiries conducted by historians and folklorists in the 1920s, in which actual participants on the tunnel project were interviewed, seemed to indicate that there was a kernel of truth in the legends. Steam drills were coming into widespread use then and there was a likelihood that a test could have been set up for one, matching it against the best steel-driver on the job. A few men who were then in their seventies, even claimed to have known John Henry, a powerfully built former slave who could drive steel into the rock for the setting of explosive charges like no one else.

The familiar song pits the strength in his arms against the power of the mechanical steam drill. It has always struck a responsive chord with Americans, who choose to believe that no machine can replace

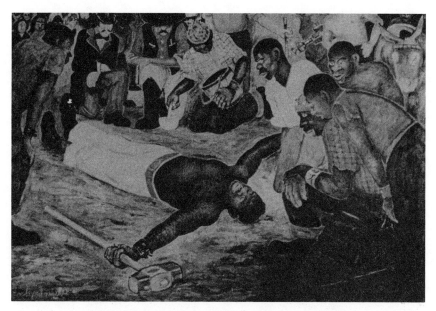

John Henry: "He died with his hammer in his hand"

human skill. John Henry, by holding onto his dignity in the face of the mechanical challenge, became the champion of the individual laborer. In the song, the steam drill clogs up and John Henry wins the race. An examination of the rock at Big Bend Tunnel indicates that it is the sort of soft sandstone that would present a drill with just that difficulty. But none of the witnesses recalled him "dying with his hammer in his hand." A more likely explanation, according to historians, is that he was killed in a subsequent accident with explosives, a common occurrence in the old rail tunnels, and was buried secretly within the rock of Big Bend.

> **Location:** Talcott and the Big Bend Tunnel are in the southeastern corner of the state, on West Virginia 12 and 3, about 35 miles southeast of Beckley. A statue of John Henry stands in a park near the tunnel entrance.

5

The West

Arizona	New Mexico
•	•
California	Oklahoma
•	•
Colorado	Oregon
•	•
Hawaii	South Dakota
•	•
Kansas	Texas
•	•
Montana	Utah
•	•
Nebraska	Washington

The West

ARIZONA

1. Fort Bowie National Historic Site, *Bowie*
2. Old Fort Museum, *Fort Apache*
3. Coronado National Memorial, *Sierra Vista*
4. Fort Huachuca, *Sierra Vista*
5. John Swain Grave, Boot Hill, *Tombstone*

CALIFORNIA

6. Allensworth State Park, *Allensworth*
7. Beckwourth Pass, *Beckwourth*
8. California Afro-American Museum, *Los Angeles*
9. El Pueblo de Los Angeles State Historic Park, *Los Angeles*
10. Ebony Museum of Art, *Oakland*
11. Northern California Center for Afro-American History and Life, *Oakland*
12. St. Andrew's African Methodist Episcopal Church, *Sacramento*
13. Liedesdorff Street, *San Francisco*

COLORADO

14. Barney Ford Hill, *Breckenridge*
15. Clara Brown's Chair, *Central City*
16. Black American West Museum and Heritage Center, *Denver*
17. El Pueblo Museum, *Pueblo*
18. Beecher Island Battlefield, *Wray*

HAWAII

19. USS Arizona Memorial, *Pearl Harbor*

KANSAS

20. Carver Homestead, *Beeler*
21. Fort Scott National Historic Site, *Fort Scott*
22. Fort Leavenworth, *Leavenworth*
23. Black Frontier Settlement, *Nicodemus*
24. John Brown Memorial State Park, *Osawatomie*
25. Sumner Elementary School, *Topeka*

MONTANA

26. Fort Shaw, *Fort Shaw*
27. State Capitol, State Historical Museum, *Helena*
28. Fort Missoula, *Missoula*

NEBRASKA

29. Mayhew Cabin, John Brown's Caves, *Nebraska City*
30. Great Plains Black Museum, *Omaha*

NEW MEXICO

31. Pancho Villa State Park, *Columbus*
32. Fort Stanton, Lincoln Courthouse Museum, *Lincoln*
33. Hawikuh Pueblo, *Zuni*

OKLAHOMA

34. Black communities, *Boley, Langston*
35. Five Civilized Tribes Museum, *Muskogee*
36. 101 Ranch, *Ponca City*

OREGON

37. Fort Clatsop National Memorial, *Astoria*

SOUTH DAKOTA

38. Holy Rosary Mission, *Pine Ridge*

TEXAS

39. Fort Davis National Historic Site, *Fort Davis*
40. Fort Concho, *San Angelo*
41. Institute of Texas Cultures, *San Antonio*

UTAH

42. Brigham Young Monument, Pioneer Trail State Park, *Salt Lake City*

WASHINGTON

43. George Washington Park, Chehalis County Museum, *Centralia-Chehalis*
44. Douglass-Truth Library, *Seattle*
45. Mt. Zion Baptist Church, *Seattle*
46. George Bush Exhibits in Henderson House Museum, *Tumwater*

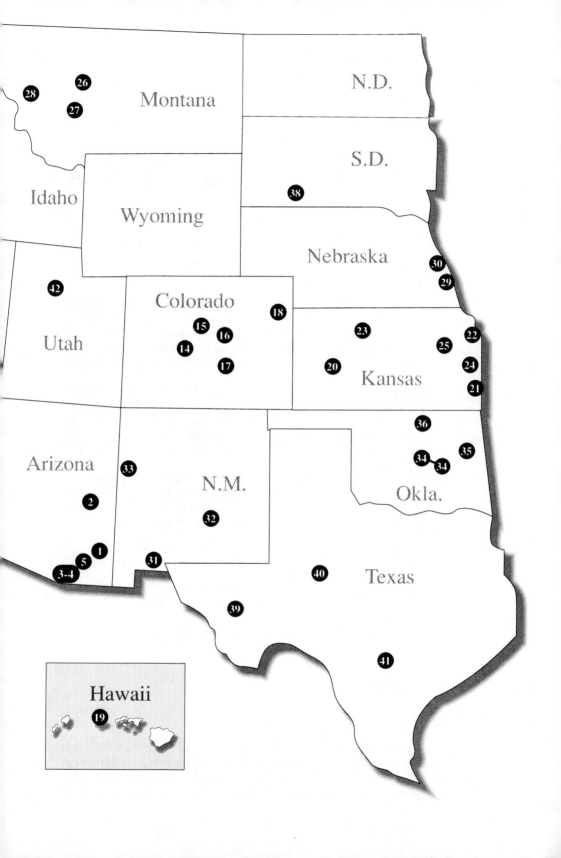

A R I Z O N A

Bowie

Fort Bowie National Historic Site

Although this outpost at the entrance to Apache Pass is now in ruins, it gives an evocative picture of an isolated cavalry post during the Indian Wars in Arizona. Fort Bowie was established in 1862 and closed thirty-two years later. During the early 1880s it was the base for the campaign against Geronimo and his raiders in southeastern Arizona.

Both the Ninth and Tenth cavalries, the all-black "Buffalo Soldier" units, were stationed here during this period. While their stays at other outposts in the territory were longer, this was regarded as the most hazardous. So many troopers and civilians were killed in the area that stagecoach drivers had to be given triple pay to make the run through the pass.

After the defeat of Cochise in 1874, the surrounding area was designated as a reservation for the Chiricahua Apache. The closing of this tract and the removal of the band to the San Carlos reservation in the late 1870s led directly to the rebellion of Geronimo.

> **Location:** The fort is 15 miles southeast of Bowie and I-10, by way of Apache Pass Rd., a marked side road, and a 1-mile footpath.
> **Exhibits:** Only the adobe walls of the fort and about 30 other buildings remain on the summit of a hill.
> **Hours:** Dawn to dusk.
> **Admission charge:** None.

Fort Apache

Old Fort Museum

The name itself has passed into the language of American folklore, symbolizing a remote and dangerous outpost. This fort also figured in the Geronimo campaign, and the Tenth Cavalry returned here after overseas service in the Spanish-American War. It was from this base

Corral, Fort Apache, 1877

that they embarked on their famed raid into Mexico in 1916 in pursuit of the bandit Pancho Villa. (See the entry on Pancho Villa State Park in Columbus, New Mexico.)

It was converted into a government school shortly afterwards and part of the onetime fort is now a cultural center for the San Carlos Apaches.

> **Location:** On Arizona 73, in the heart of the San Carlos Reservation, 21 miles east of U.S. 60 from Carrizo and 93 miles south of I-40, from the Holbrook exit.
> **Exhibits:** There are displays and photos relating to the Buffalo Soldiers in the cultural center museum.
> **Hours:** Monday to Friday, 8-5.
> **Admission charge:** Donation requested.
> **Telephone:** (602) 338-4625.

Sierra Vista

Coronado National Memorial

Through this pass in the Huachuca Mountains, the first party of Europeans entered what would become the southwestern United States. The year was 1540 and the leader of the expedition was Francisco Vasquez de Coronado, directed by the Spanish viceroy to find the fabled Seven Cities of Gold. He found the Grand Canyon, the pueblos of the Rio Grande Valley, and the plains of Kansas, but no gold.

Preceding Coronado through this pass by one year was one of the men who had first carried the reports of these illusory riches. He has come down to us through history as Estevanico or Esteban, a black man. He was the first person who was not a native American who is recorded to have entered the southwest.

His story is one of the most fantastic tales in early American history. He was a slave, part of the Cabeza de Vaca expedition which left Florida in 1528, and was shipwrecked on the Texas Gulf Coast. For six years, Estevanico, de Vaca and two other Spaniards were held captive by tribes in the area. Finally managing to escape, they headed west and wandered for two more years before reaching Spanish settlements in Mexico in 1536. They were received as heroes, a welcome that grew even more enthusiastic when they relayed stories heard from the Apaches about fantastic riches in the cities of the northern Rio Grande Valley.

The authorities, in wild excitement, immediately began planning an expedition to find this treasure. The three exhausted Spanish explorers declined to participate, saying that they had been through enough. Estevanico, however, eagerly accepted the invitation. He was given his freedom and, since he had heard the reports firsthand, was placed in charge of part of this expedition, which was headed by a priest, Fray Marcos de Niza.

They set out on March 7, 1539. Two weeks later Fray Marcos decided to remain in a frontier settlement to observe Easter. Estevanico, who was not a Christian, was sent on ahead and instructed to report back on his findings. Sometime in May he arrived at the Huachucas and entered what would become Arizona. Ignoring demands to stop from Fray Marcos, which may never have reached him, he pushed into the unknown, heading steadily north and east along the route that is now known as the Coronado Trail, U.S. 666. By the end of the month he had passed into New Mexico and the grim fate awaiting him there. (See the entry on the Hawikuh Pueblo in Zuni, New Mexico.)

> **Location:** The Memorial is 22 miles south of Sierra Vista, by way of Arizona 92 and a park road.
>
> **Exhibits:** There is a visitors' center, which presents a historical and ecological introduction to the area, as well as a short trail with markers relating to the Estevanico and Coronado expeditions. There are also stirring views over the surrounding country.
>
> **Hours:** The visitors' center is open daily, 8-5.
>
> **Admission charge:** None.
>
> **Telephone:** (602) 458-5024.

Fort Huachuca

This is the only Arizona outpost of the Indian Wars that is still active as a military base. It also figured prominently in the history of the Ninth and Tenth Cavalry, the all-black "Buffalo Soldiers," during their posting in the Southwest. These segregated units had been formed immediately after the Civil War following a furious debate within the military about the role of black soldiers in the army. They first went into battle in Kansas in the late 1860s in a campaign against the Cheyenne. For the next twenty-five years they saw action in the most hazardous stations, in Texas, New Mexico, Arizona, and even the northern wilds of Montana. (See entries under each of those states.) Battling institutional racism on military bases, southern hostility in Texas, blizzards in Montana, and some of the most accomplished riders and fighters in the world as their enemies, the Buffalo Soldiers eventually won both renown and respect.

Then they were all but forgotten. When the tale of how the west was won was retold in America's popular culture, it became a story in which the good guys all wore white hats and had white skin. The record of the Ninth and Tenth was all but obliterated, some historians say by deliberate policy, and has only begun to be revived in the last generation.

At Fort Huachuca, established in 1877 as one of a string of outposts during the Apache campaigns, there are exhibits on black military history in the West. The fort was again home to the Tenth Cavalry from 1910 to 1931. During World War II it housed black soldiers for a final time, as the Ninety-second Division, which won twelve thousand decorations and citations in North Africa and Europe, trained here. The fort is now the base of the U.S. Communications Command.

> **Location:** The city of Sierra Vista has grown up right outside the gates of the fort, which covers 73,500 acres in southeastern Arizona. It is about 25 miles south of I-10, by way of Arizona 83.
> **Exhibits:** Many of the nineteenth-century fort buildings still stand, and the Museum has displays on the role of the U.S. Army in the development of the Southwest.
> **Hours:** Monday to Friday, 9-4, and weekends, 1-4.
> **Admission charge:** None.
> **Telephone:** (602) 538-7111.

Tombstone

John Swain Grave, Boot Hill

It is called the town that was "too tough to die," and during its 1880s heyday as a rip-roaring mining camp, its citizens were indeed some of the toughest individuals in the country. From its founder Ed

Boot Hill Cemetery

Schiefflin (who was told that if he went looking for gold in the area he'd find his tombstone, instead) to Wyatt Earp, Doc Holliday, and John Slaughter.

Among the toughest was John Swain. He came to Tombstone on a cattle drive from Texas with the Slaughter family. He had formerly been a slave and still worked for Slaughter as a cowhand. Swain was almost the embodiment of the town's motto. He lived on to the age of ninety-nine, and his funeral in 1945 was a civic event, one of the last links to the frontier town that had become a legend.

Both Swain and another of Slaughter's black cowpunchers, known as Old Bat, were respected for their courage. One chronicler of old Tombstone relates that when two miners were ambushed by Apaches, the town was hesitant to organize a party to retrieve their bodies. Old Bat went out alone and brought back the dead on muleback. From all accounts, Slaughter was loyal to these two longtime hands and supported both of them into their old age.

> **Location:** Tombstone is on U.S. 80, about 25 miles south of I-10 from the Benson exit.
> **Exhibits:** Swain's grave is in Row 11 of Boot Hill Cemetery, the resting place of some of the town's most famous and notorious characters. Excellent displays about Tombstone's lively past are contained at the Courthouse Museum.
> **Hours:** Boot Hill, daily, 8-6. Courthouse, Thursday to Monday, 8-5.

Admission charge: Boot Hill, donation requested. Courthouse, adults, $1; 17 and under, free.
Telephone: (602) 457-3311.

C A L I F O R N I A

Allensworth

Allensworth State Park

California is a state that has stood, throughout its existence, for new beginnings. "Out here in this matchless Southern California, there would seem to be no limits to your opportunities, your possibilities." The words could have been spoken by any of a hundred promoters for the area. But they happen to be he words of W. E. B. Du Bois, writing about what he had observed among black people he had visited in the Los Angeles area in 1913.

Three years before that, another group of black newcomers to the state had been seized by the same hopes. Under the leadership of Col. Allen Allensworth they had come to settle an all-black town in the state's Central Valley, north of Bakersfield. Allensworth was a compelling leader. Born into slavery in Kentucky, he became a well-known jockey and rode frequently in big races at Louisville. He entered the Navy in the Civil War and afterwards became a chaplain in the all-black Twenty-fourth Infantry Regiment. The look at the West which that experience gave him convinced him that the future of black people was in that area, away from the racial animosities of the older part of the country.

Allensworth could not survive economically in the changeover to massive agricultural holdings in the area. But the town site is now a state park, saluting the legacy of its settlers and founder.

> **Location:** Allensworth is about 165 miles north of downtown Los Angeles, by way of I-5, California 99, and westbound Tulare County road J22. The closest town is Earlimart, about 10 miles east.
> **Exhibits:** The school and Col. Allensworth's home have been restored and there is a museum of the town's history. A campground is adjacent.
> **Hours:** Daily, 10-3.
> **Admission charge:** None.
> **Telephone:** (805) 849-3433.

Jim Beckwourth

Beckwourth

Beckwourth Pass

When some of his old prospecting associates heard that Jim Beckwourth had been the subject of a biography, they were struck with curiousity. Knowing that Beckwourth had a reputation for stretching the truth a bit, they sent one of the men into town to buy the book. Not having much literary experience, he picked up a Bible, instead. Opening it at random when he got back to camp, the miners starting reading the story of Samson tying torches to the tails of foxes and burning the crops of the Philistines. "There," one of them shouted. "I'd know one of Jim Beckwourth's lies anywhere."

The story is told by historian Bernard DeVoto in his study of the early western frontier *Across the Wide Missouri.* Beckwourth figured prominently in those years as a trapper, explorer, Crow war chief, and miner. Contemporary historian Francis Parkman described him as "a ruffian of the first stamp, bloody and treacherous, without honor or honesty." But Parkman was a proper Bostonian and

Beckwourth was probably no worse than his peers, in a time and place in which honor was a shortcut to the grave.

He was the most prominent of the few black mountain men of that era, one of the founders of the town of Pueblo, Colorado (see the entry for El Pueblo Museum there). He left his name on the map, however, in California, where he is credited with discovering a major shortcut through the Sierras to the goldfields. It is still called Beckwourth Pass and the town at its western end is Beckwourth.

> **Location:** Beckwourth Pass is traversed by California 70, running west from U.S. 395, about 25 miles north of Reno, Nev. It crosses the mountains at an elevation of 5,212 feet, about 2,000 feet lower in height than the more heavily used Donner Pass to the south.

Los Angeles

California Afro-American Museum

This facility concentrates on exhibitions about the history, art and culture of black Americans, with special reference to southern California. There is a museum store, library, and workshops. One of its best-received recent shows was "Black Angelenos, 1850-1950," an examination of the African-American presence in the city during the period of its growth from a tiny village to one of the largest urban concentrations in the country.

> **Location:** The museum is at 600 State Dr., in Exposition Park, southwest of downtown along I-110, the Harbor Fwy.
> **Hours:** Daily, 10-5.
> **Admission charge:** None.
> **Telephone:** (213) 744-7432.

El Pueblo de Los Angeles State Historic Park

When the Spanish authorities in Mexico began to recruit settlers for a new farming community in Alta California, they concentrated their efforts on a poor area of Sinaloa. The purpose of the new colony was to heighten the Spanish presence in the area and to raise food for nearby military garrisons. The offer of free land sounded good to the inhabitants of the village of Rosario and a band of forty-four settlers arrived in the area late in the summer of 1781. Census figures show that two-thirds of Rosario's inhabitants then were listed as mulattoes. According to a study conducted in 1988 by Lonnie G. Bunch III, curator of history at the Los Angeles Afro-American Museum, twenty-six of these first settlers were either black or of mixed ancestry.

Eventually, the racial identification dwindled away. By 1850, when Los Angeles had a population of 1,598, only twelve were noted as being black. But many descendants of the original settlers were among those who had become prominent in the city and acquired vast land grants. Bunch suggests that Pio Pico, the last Mexican governor of California and a man of enormous wealth and political influence, was the grandson of a mulatto settler, and in photographs "Pico is shown to be dark with broad features that suggest his Afro-Spanish origins."

One of the city's major thoroughfares, Pico Boulevard, is named for him. He also built one of its first great hotels, the Pico House, in 1870. This is part of the Pueblo de Los Angeles restoration.

> **Location:** The Pueblo occupies 44 acres at the heart of downtown Los Angeles, two blocks north and across the Santa Ana Fwy. from City Hall. The Pico House is at 500 N. Main St., which bisects the area.
> **Exhibits:** The Pico House is undergoing restoration, but other structures, some dating from the early nineteenth century, are open. Also nearby is Olvera Street and its famous Mexican outdoor market.
> **Hours:** The visitor center in the Sepulveda House, at 622 N. Main St., is open Monday to Friday, 10-3, and Saturday, 10-4:30.
> **Admission charge:** None.
> **Telephone:** (213) 628-1274.

Oakland

Ebony Museum of Art

This facility is situated in a restored Victorian home in one of the city's atmospheric older neighborhoods. It specializes in African and African-American art as well as memorabilia of the black experience in the East Bay area.

> **Location:** The museum is at 1034 14th St., just north of the downtown area.
> **Hours:** Tuesday to Saturday, 11-6.
> **Admission charge:** None.
> **Telephone:** (415) 763-0141.

Northern California Center for Afro-American History and Life

The emphasis at this facility, opened in 1965, is on the history of blacks in the East Bay area. There is a small museum, a collection of photographs and artifacts, and a research library of works pertaining to the area.

Location: The Center is at 5606 San Pablo Ave., California 123, northeast of downtown.
Hours: Tuesday to Saturday, 12:30-5.
Admission charge: None.
Telephone: (415) 658-3158.

Sacramento

St. Andrew's African Methodist Episcopal Church

The first church of this denomination on the west coast, it was organized in the center of the Gold Rush country one year after the Forty-Niners arrived. By 1854, when it moved to its present location, the church was holding the first public school in California for black, native American, and Chinese children in its basement.

Location: 2131 8th St., west of the State Capitol.
Hours: By appointment.
Telephone: (916) 448-1428.

San Francisco

Leidesdorff Street

This narrow lane is almost lost amid the new towers of the city's Financial District. If it continued straight ahead on its course, it would smash right into the TransAmerica Pyramid, which many admirers of the old San Francisco think would be an excellent idea.

William Leidesdorff, for whom the street is named, is also a bit lost in the city's history. He arrived from the Virgin Islands in 1841, of black and Danish ancestry, as a ship's master. He maintained his ties to the sea, and started a small store with goods brought in from overseas trade. Soon he had opened a warehouse at the corner of California and Sansome, a block away from the location of today's Leidesdorff Street. He served as a consul to Mexico for a time and was on the first municipal council that met after the American takeover of California. He also is credited with launching the first steamboat on San Francisco Bay, although it sank after three months of service.

Leidesdorff died of what was described as brain fever in 1848, practically on the eve of San Francisco's explosive growth from Mexican village to supply center for the Gold Rush. His property holdings, which couldn't even cover his debts at his death, would have made him a millionaire. On the other hand, repressive racial laws that went into effect in the 1850s, would have made it illegal for him to hold public office. Leidesdorff is buried in the graveyard at the Mission Dolores.

Location: Leidesdorff St. is tucked away in the area bounded by Montgomery, Sansome, Clay, and Sacramento Streets. Mission Dolores is about 2 miles away, south of Market Street, on Dolores at 16th.

C O L O R A D O

Breckenridge

Barney Ford Hill

The town is famous as a ski resort today, but it had its beginnings as a mining camp during the 1859 gold rush. One of the prospectors who passed through then was Barney Ford, a mysterious black man, a fugitive slave who claimed to have run a station of the Underground Railroad in Chicago, worked with abolitionist John Brown, and made

Barney Ford

a fortune in Nicaragua. Ford stayed only a short while and moved on to Denver, saying that outlaws had cheated him of his claim. Soon he opened a smart hotel, the Inter-Ocean, which became one of Denver's finest and earned him another fortune. Stories persisted, however, that the source of his money was actually a gold strike he'd secretly made in Breckenridge. The area in which the funds were reputedly hidden became known as Barney Ford Hill, and despite his repeated denials that such a trove existed, local miners searched the site for years.

Ford eventually became active in the Republican party and fought vigorously to hold up Colorado's admission to the Union until black citizens were given the right to vote. The Fifteenth Amendment accomplished that, and he then became an ardent supporter of statehood.

> **Location:** Breckenridge is about 90 miles west of Denver, by way of I-70 and southbound Colorado 9. Barney Ford Hill is just to the southeast of this charming Victorian resort.

Central City

Clara Brown's Chair

The only thing it really was central to was the other mining camps in Gregory Gulch. When gold was discovered here in 1859, however, fortune seekers from all over the world converged on Central City and it became famous as "the richest square mile on earth." Journalist Horace Greeley visited the camp, and some local fun-lovers took him to a site that had been salted with gold dust from a shotgun. The famous editor was amazed to find gold so easily and his glowing reports added to the fever.

Many of Colorado's greatest fortunes were founded here, including those of both the state's first U.S. Senators and George Pullman, who would go on to invent the railroad sleeping car. By the turn of the century, though, the mines were played out and the town was in decline. Even the Opera House, built in 1878 as Central City's claim to culture, was decaying. There was some sentiment for turning it into a courthouse, but preservationists prevailed.

The Central City Opera House Association was formed in 1931 and came up with the idea of sponsoring a renovation of the theater by selling memorial chairs. Although these were Depression times, the idea was a success, and next year the opera house reopened with a performance of *Camille,* starring Lillian Gish. Since then, the Opera and Drama Festival has turned into an event that runs through July and August every year and turns Central City into the liveliest old mining town in the country.

If you look over the list of memorial chairs, you will find one dedicated to Aunt Clara Brown. A former slave who was freed in

Clara Brown

Missouri, she made her way to the gold fields and opened the first laundry in the Colorado Territory here. Her goal was to save enough money to buy freedom for the rest of her family. When they were emancipated by the Civil War, she brought them all to Central City and for the rest of her life dedicated herself to charitable works and nursing. When she died in 1877 she was buried with official honors from the Colorado Pioneers Association.

Fifty-five years later, when it came time for Central City to salute its illustrious citizens of the past, the town remembered Aunt Clara, and the chair was its tribute to her.

Location: Central City is about 40 miles west of Denver, by way of I-70 and northbound Colorado 119. The Opera House is on Eureka St.

Exhibits: Some of the greatest names in the theater performed on this stage, including Sarah Bernhardt, Edwin Booth, and Otis Skinner. Its murals and crystal chandeliers are noteworthy, as well as the original hickory memorial chairs.

Hours: Tours are given Tuesday to Sunday, 10-5, in July and August; Wednesday to Sunday, 11-5, the rest of the year. The schedule may vary with stage performances.

Admission charge: $3.50.
Telephone: (303) 582-5202.

Denver

Black American West Museum and Heritage Center

The lore of the Old West is so heavily wrapped up in myth and legend that it is almost impossible to separate historical fact from tall tale. Exaggeration and sly bragging were part of the tradition, one that would be carried forward by writers such as Mark Twain. But the role of blacks in the making of these legends has been pretty much ignored.

Nat Love, for example, was a tale-spinner of the first order. In his autobiography, a late nineteenth-century best-seller, he told about his origins as a slave and his life as a cowboy, Indian fighter, and gunslinger in the West. He claimed to be the orginal Deadwood Dick, winning the name at a shooting competition in the Dakota town in 1876. Like most of Love's tales, it is improbable but not altogether impossible, and never boring.

Writer Paul W. Stewart has dedicated himself to rescuing the stories of such black frontiersmen, and his museum is intended to set the record straight on their contributions to the legend of the West.

Location: The museum is at 3091 California St., just northeast of downtown.
Exhibits: The recently enlarged facility concentrates on the role of the black cowboy on the frontier.
Hours: Wednesday to Friday, 10-2; Saturday, 12-5; and Sunday, 2-5.
Admission charge: Adults, $2; senior citizens, $1.50; children under 12, $.50.
Telephone: (303) 292-2566.
Handicapped access: Yes.

Pueblo

El Pueblo Museum

Another legendary black figure of the West was mountain man Jim Beckwourth. He was an explorer, a fur trapper, a Crow war chief, and a feared adversary in the territories beyond the law. Like Nat Love (see above) he became famous in later life as the subject of a biography. (For a more complete discussion of Beckwourth, see the entry on the Beckwourth Pass in Beckwourth, California.)

Beckwourth arrived at the junction of the Arkansas River and the Raton Pass Trail in 1842 and, assisted by a few other independent

Cowboy Nat Love

trappers, erected a trading post. He called it El Pueblo, Spanish for The Town. The adobe construction was sixty yards square, and to historian Francis Parkman, who visited the place in 1846, was "nothing more than a square enclosure, surrounded by a wall of mud, miserably cracked and dilapidated" and inhabited by people "as mean and miserable as the place itself." He didn't have much good to say about Beckwourth personally, either.

A Christmas Day attack by the Utes in 1854 wiped out the settlement, and the present city dates from its rebuilding four years later, using material salvaged from Beckwourth's original post. The museum contains a full-scale reproduction of the old pueblo.

> **Location:** The El Pueblo Museum is at 905 S. Prairie Ave., just south of downtown and off I-25.
> **Exhibits:** Besides the reproduction of the original fort, there are displays on southern Colorado history and the iron and steel industry in this city.
> **Hours:** Tuesday to Friday, 10-5, and Saturday, 10-2, Memorial Day to Labor Day; Wednesday to Saturday, 10-3, the rest of the year.
> **Admission charge:** Adults, $2; children 6-16 and senior citizens, $1; children under 6, free.
> **Telephone:** (719) 564-5274.

Wray

Beecher Island Battlefield

It is a familiar image from Western movies. The small force is hopelessly outnumbered by hostile Indians, and just when the situation looks most desperate the cavalry comes, riding to the rescue. That is exactly how it happened at Beecher Island, a battle that broke the spirit of the Cheyenne in Colorado. The force that came riding up in the nick of time was the all-black Tenth Cavalry.

In 1868, a party of about fifty troopers and scouts were pursuing a band of Cheyenne up the Arikaree Valley from Fort Wallace, Kansas. Camping along the river in an area surrounded by high bluffs, they awoke to find themselves surrounded by an array of Cheyenne, Arapaho, and Oglala Sioux. Retreating to an island in the stream, they dug in to make a stand, under the command of Col. George Forsythe and Lt. Fred Beecher.

Fortunately for them, the Cheyenne leader, Roman Nose, was killed during the first charge. Without his leadership the various Indian allies, despite overwhelming numbers, could not coordinate an effective assault on the island. The troopers were reduced to using their fallen horses for meat and for fortifications. They held out for a full week, but with Beecher killed, almost everyone else wounded, and food and water exhausted, the men decided to make a desperate charge to escape. But four scouts who had slipped through the lines

Black cavalry units riding to the rescue at Beecher Island

had made it back to Fort Wallace and returned at the last second, bringing the men of the Tenth with them to save the battered force. The battle is regarded as a turning point in the Plains Indians campaign.

> **Location:** Beecher Island is about 17 miles south of Wray, in extreme eastern Colorado, by way of U.S. 385 and Colorado 53. The island itself was obliterated by a flood in 1934. A memorial has been erected on the riverbank.

H A W A I I

Pearl Harbor

USS Arizona Memorial

The Japanese attack on Pearl Harbor achieved complete surprise. The men stationed at the huge U.S. Navy base here had no inkling of what was coming shortly after dawn on December 7, 1941. But as bombs started to rain down upon the slumbering naval force, a few men simply reacted instinctively and did whatever they could to fight

Dorrie Miller

off the assault. Among them was Dorrie Miller, an African-American mess attendant on the battleship *Arizona*.

He was collecting laundry when the sirens started to blare. Like the overwhelming majority of black sailors, Miller was in a noncombatant post. The most segregated of all the military branches, the Navy directed its black recruits into support duties rather than training them for combat. Nonetheless, Miller rushed on deck and, after pulling an injured officer to safety, he took up an anti-aircraft gun, which he had never been trained to use, and brought down four Japanese planes before being ordered to abandon ship.

Five months later he was awarded the Navy Cross for "extraordinary courage" and sent on a tour of black areas of the country to raise support for war bonds. Then he was returned to the battle zone . . . as a messman. He was serving on the aircraft carrier *Liscome Bay* when it went down with all hands in the Pacific in 1943. Miller was twenty-four years old. In 1988 legislation was introduced in the U.S. House of Representatives to award him the Congressional Medal of Honor.

> **Location:** The *USS Arizona* Memorial at Pearl Harbor is about 10 miles west of downtown Honolulu, Oahu, by way of Hwy. H1 and the Kamehameha Hwy. Shuttle boats to the memorial leave from the visitors' center, on Kamehameha Hwy. at the gate to the base.
> **Exhibits:** The memorial spans the hull of the sunken ship. A film on the Pearl Harbor attack and the war in the Pacific is shown at the visitors' center.
> **Hours:** Daily, 8-3. Boats depart every half-hour.
> **Admission charge:** None.
> **Telephone:** (808) 422-2771.

K A N S A S

Beeler

Carver Homestead

For the first few decades of his life, George Washington Carver's course seemed to be westward with the growing nation. Born on a farm in southwestern Missouri, he made his way to Kansas for high school and then moved on to the western part of the state and a 160-acre homestead on the edge of the Great Plains.

He arrived in Beeler at the age of twenty-three, a young man still toying with the idea of becoming an artist, thwarted by bigotry in his aspirations for a higher education and looking for a place in life. Besides farming, his natural curiousity led him to conduct geological surveys in the area, and he predicted that oil would be found there. It took about forty years, but drillings proved him right.

Carver was long gone from Beeler by then, though. He sold the homestead in 1891, after two years on the land, and turned back east to Iowa, college, and the beginning of his great career in science. Many residents of the area helped contribute to a bust of Carver that still is on display at Tuskegee University, Alabama.

> **Location:** Beeler is in Ness County, in the west central part of the state, about 80 miles west of Great Bend. A historical marker, describing the site as the "homestead of a genius" is located on Kansas 96.

Fort Scott

Fort Scott National Historic Site

When the U.S. Army closed down Fort Scott in 1853 and sold off the buildings at auction, it was thought that history had passed the place by and a frontier era had ended. But history has a way of doubling back on itself, and within two years American troops had returned to the old fort for another two decades.

It was here that the First Kansas Colored Infantry was raised, and the fort was its base during the Civil War. (The Fifty-fourth

Fort Scott

Massachusetts may have received the "Glory" in the 1989 Academy-Award winning movie, but the Kansas unit was actually the first black unit to see action in the war.)

Fort Scott was built in 1843 to protect travelers on the Santa Fe Trail and to keep the peace between settlers and local tribes. It was also a jumping-off point for American troops heading for the Mexican War. But as tranquility settled over eastern Kansas, troops were sent to outposts further west. The peace was deceptive, however. Soon abolitionists and pro-slavery forces were killing each other in "Bleeding Kansas," and the troops were brought back to try and restore order.

On January 13, 1863, the Kansas Colored Volunteers were formally mustered here, about twelve weeks after first going into combat at Island Mound, Missouri and beating back a Confederate assault. They participated in five engagements and suffered more casualties than any other Kansas regiment.

> **Location:** Fort Scott is about 85 miles south of Kansas City by way of U.S. 69. It is adjacent to the business district of the town of Fort Scott.
> **Exhibits:** The fort has been restored to the way it looked in the 1840s. A museum explains its significance in the time of the western frontier, the Kansas violence, and the Civil War.
> **Hours:** Daily, 8-5.
> **Admission charge:** None.
> **Telephone:** (316) 223-0310.
> **Handicapped access:** Yes.

Leavenworth

Fort Leavenworth

At the close of the Civil War, the United States Army had 186,000 black combat troops in uniform and another 200,000 blacks in support units. There were 120 infantry regiments, seven cavalry regiments, and twenty-two artillery regiments. Their members had seen action in more than two hundred engagements.

But with the silence at Appomattox, the Army hadn't the faintest idea what to do with them. Resistance to integrating these units into the regular Army was massive, and yet there was a strong sense that they would be a valuable asset for the series of Indian wars that were beginning to take shape on the western plains.

The question was resolved in 1866 when Congress authorized the formation of two all-black cavalry regiments, the Ninth and Tenth, and two of infantry, the Twenty-fourth and Twenty-fifth. For the next generation these units, particularly the cavalry, would be in the middle of the hottest fighting on the frontier, and twelve of their members would win Congressional Medals of Honor.

Their first post was Fort Leavenworth, the oldest military base west of the Mississippi. They would stay here for less than a year before embarking on a journey that would take them throughout western Kansas and then to the desert outposts of Texas, New Mexico, and Arizona. They would charge up San Juan Hill in Cuba with Teddy Roosevelt and his Rough Riders during the Spanish-American War, and ride south of the border in pursuit of the Mexican bandit Pancho Villa in 1916. Their history is one of the glorious chapters of the Old West, and this is where it began.

> **Location:** The fort is on the northern edge of the city of Leavenworth, about 40 miles northwest of Kansas City by way of Interstate 70 and Kansas 7.
> **Exhibits:** Still an active military base and the home of the General Staff College of the Army, the fort contains an excellent museum, which outlines its history and the role it played on the western frontier. A self-guided tour of the post also begins here.
> **Hours:** Monday to Saturday, 10-4, and Sunday, 12-4.
> **Admission charge:** None.
> **Telephone:** (913) 651-7440.

Nicodemus

Black Frontier Settlement

Long before southern blacks began their historic migration to the industrial centers of the North, another area was briefly regarded as a

Pioneers at Nicodemus

haven for those wishing to escape economic and social oppression of the Old Confederacy. Between 1875 and 1881, an estimated sixty thousand blacks from the southern states headed for Kansas, drawn by the dream of their own land on the western frontier.

They were called the Exodusters, and their Moses was a man named Benjamin Singleton. He called himself Pap and he roamed the South, talking up the good life in Kansas within the three all-black colonies he was organizing there—Dunlap, Singleton, and Nicodemus. He is credited with bringing in seven thousand settlers from Tennessee alone. Singleton promised more than he could deliver. Those who had some tools and a little know-how could make it in the farming colonies. The majority, however, wound up in the urban black communities of Kansas City and Topeka.

Nicodemus is the only surviving colony. It was named for a legendary slave who foretold the coming of the Civil War. The first group of settlers arrived here in 1877, penniless and too late in the year to plant crops. They were reduced to living in dugouts and were bitterly resented by neighboring white settlers, who chased the man who sold Singleton the land out of the county.

This is harsh country for small farmers, and the Nicodemus colony never prospered. But it did create a community life, with churches and schools and even an art-club building. From its peak population of five hundred, it dwindled to less than two hundred by the 1910 census. Only a handful of families remain there today.

Location: Nicodemus is on U.S. 24, about 115 miles northwest of Grand Bend, and about 90 miles north of the George Washington Carver homestead in Beeler (see entry

John Brown depicted as a violent religious zealot in Kansas

above). There is a historical marker and roadside park on the highway.

Osawatomie

John Brown Memorial State Park

In the late 1850s Kansas became the stage for a dress rehearsal of the Civil War, a nightmarish succession of massacre and reprisal that made it known through the rest of the country as "Bleeding Kansas." The Missouri Compromise, which had arranged for one slave state and one free state to be admitted to the Union in tandem, had been repealed. Kansas was organized as a territory in 1854 with its neighbor on the north, Nebraska, and each would hold a vote on the slavery issue before becoming states. It was hoped in Washington that Kansas would vote for slavery and balance Nebraska's certain free-state vote.

But the abolitionists would have none of this. Calling themselves Free Staters, they poured into Kansas from the East, organizing communities to swing the coming vote their way. When slaveholders from Missouri saw what was happening, they, too, started planting settlements in the territory. The conflict drew extremists on both sides. Factions from one side would raid a community and kill a few opponents, and reprisal would be swift and sure.

John Brown, the most fiery of the abolitionists, settled in Osawatomie, bringing with him from Ohio a wagon full of guns. When pro-slavery forces passed a set of Black Laws, mandating the death penalty for anyone aiding a fugitive slave and making it illegal to spread antislavery opinions, the tinder was lit. A raid on the Free State town of Lawrence was answered by Brown with a strike near his home in which five pro-slavery men were taken out and executed at Potawatomi Creek. That unleashed open war all across Kansas. One of Brown's sons was gunned down a year later in retaliation, and part of Osawatomie burned by raiders from Kansas City.

Eventually, the antislavery forces won out through sheer weight of numbers and managed to repeal the onerous Black Laws, bringing Kansas into the Union as a free state. Brown had departed long before this, however, to plan his climactic raid in 1859 on the arsenal at Harpers Ferry, West Virginia. Osawatomie still celebrates his residence there with a John Brown Jamboree, four days of entertainment held annually in the last week of June.

> **Location:** Osawatomie is about 50 miles southwest of Kansas City by way of U.S. 169. John Brown Memorial Park is west of the center of town, at 10th St. and Main St.
> **Exhibits:** A statue of Brown, a memorial to men killed in the Osawatomie raid, and a log cabin in which Brown lived and which is thought to have sheltered fugitive slaves during the time of the Black Laws are on the site.
> **Hours:** Tuesday to Saturday, 11-5, and Sunday, 12-5.
> **Admission charge:** Donation requested.
> **Telephone:** (913) 755-4384.

Topeka

Sumner Elementary School

There were three black elementary schools in this capital of Kansas in 1951. They were not obviously inferior facilities, as in many southern states, lacking the amenities enjoyed by white students. But as far as Rev. Oliver Brown was concerned, they were not the schools he wanted his daughter, Linda, to attend. He wanted to enroll her in Sumner Elementary, closer to their home, and he had been turned down because of segregation laws. So almost 100 years after pro- and anti-slavery forces clashed in this state, Kansas would once again become the turning point in a national racial drama.

Actually, the case became known as Brown v. Board of Education because of the alphabet. It was part of a package of school segregation

Attorneys who argued the Brown v. Board of Education case before the Supreme Court. L. to R: George E. C. Hayes, Thurgood Marshall, and James Nabrit, Jr.

cases that the NAACP was carrying to the United States Supreme Court, and Brown's name just happened to be listed first. The NAACP had solicited cases in many parts of the country in a concerted effort to break down educational segregation. This had been one of the more promising cases. It had gone to the Federal appeals level, and in that decision the judges ruled that while the plaintiffs had made their case well, the court was still bound by Plessy v. Ferguson, the 1896 precedent establishing that segregated facilities were a legitimate use of state police powers.

The cases were twice argued before the high court by a team of lawyers headed by Thurgood Marshall, who would become the first black man to sit on that bench in the following decade. After the first hearing, however, Chief Justice Fred Vinson had died and was replaced by Earl Warren, a man with totally different views on the issue. Warren's appointment, in December, 1953, gave the anti-segregation forces a majority on the Court. But Warren knew the opinion would be bitterly controversial, and he wanted a unanimous vote. So for the next five months he lobbied behind the scenes to obtain a 9-0 result.

The announcement came on May 17, 1954. Using material presented by Marshall, which had concluded that the effects of separating black children from white resulted in "a feeling of inferiority," Warren wrote his decision. "We conclude that in the field of public education the doctrine of 'separate but equal' has no place. Separate educational facilities are inherently unequal. Therefore, we hold that the plaintiffs and other similarly situated for whom the actions have been brought are, by reason of the segregation complained of, deprived of the equal protection of the laws guaranteed by the Fourteenth Amendment."

The implications of that decision were immediately apparent. Segregation was doomed, not only in the schools but in the entire sweep of its power over daily life. Only a few people, Marshall among them, had an inkling of how terrible and bloody the battle would be before the Supreme Court's ruling that day truly became the law of the land. But American history had been altered forever, and Linda Brown was soon enrolled in Sumner Elementary School.

Location: Sumner Elementary is located at 330 S.W. Western Ave., south of downtown and west of Topeka Ave. (U.S. 75).

M O N T A N A

Fort Shaw

Fort Shaw

This outpost on the remote Montana frontier was opened in 1867. The all-black Twenty-fifth Infantry Regiment was posted here for a time, but it is of more significant note here because its namesake, Col. Robert Gould Shaw, was commander of the Fifty-fourth Massachusetts Volunteers.

Shaw had fallen three years before, leading the all-black Fifty-fourth into battle at Battery Wagner, South Carolina. The naming of a fort in his honor is an indication of the high esteem in which he was held after his death. While alive he was ridiculed for insisting that black troops could fight well under fire. The fort closed in 1890 and was used as an Indian school for twenty years afterwards.

> **Location:** Fort Shaw is about 30 miles west of Great Falls, by way of U.S. 89 and Montana 200. A historical marker was placed on its site.

Helena

State Capitol, State Historical Museum

There were two epic adventures in the earliest explorations of the American West: the southwestern journey of Coronado and the northwestern trek of Lewis and Clark. Preceding Coronado by a year, though, was the black guide Estevanico (see the entries on the Coronado National Monument in Sierra Vista, Arizona, and the Hawikuh Pueblo in Zuni, New Mexico). And accompanying the Lewis and Clark expedition was York, a black man who is variously described as a manservant, guide, and interpreter.

The party set out from St. Louis on May 14, 1804, with the mission to explore the headwaters of the Missouri River and the even lesser-known country beyond. The enormous tract had come into American hands in the previous year's Louisiana Purchase. Only a few French

York amazes the Indians on the Lewis and Clark Expedition in a painting by Charles Russell

trappers had ever entered these lands, and no other Europeans had done so in sixty years.

After spending the winter in a Mandan Indian village, the explorers reached the source of the Missouri, near Helena, fourteen months after setting out. Capt. William Clark was a Virginian, and it was he who had brought York on the expedition. But as the months wore on, York's role seemed to expand. The Indians were fascinated by him. They had limited experience with whites, but had never encountered a black man before. There were repeated instances of York having his face rubbed to see if the pigment would come off. After a dozen or so of these episodes, according to the expedition's journal, he finally lost all patience and drew a knife on an Indian who wanted to test it again in Idaho. But York proved to be an enormous asset to the party through his strength, marksmanship, and the generally amiable relations he had with the Indians. He accompanied the expedition all the way to the Pacific coast of Oregon, which was reached in December, 1805. At the conclusion of the long voyage back to St. Louis, he was given his freedom.

Montana dates its history to the Lewis and Clark expedition. Accordingly, the entire wall behind the speaker's desk in the State House of Representatives is covered by a 12-by-25 foot painting of the meeting between the expedition and the Flathead chiefs. York is prominently depicted in the work by Western artist Charles Russell. It is regarded as priceless.

In the nearby State Historical Museum is another Russell painting, showing York among the Mandans, and dioramas of the Lewis and

Clark expedition. The museum has artifacts of the state's black cowboys and army units that served here.

> **Location:** The State Capitol is at 6th and Montana, with its copper dome visible throughout the city. The Museum, at 225 N. Roberts St., is 1 block east and north of the Capitol.
> **Hours:** Tours of the Capitol on the hour, daily, 8-5, Memorial Day to Labor Day; Monday to Friday only, the rest of the year. Museum, Monday to Friday, 8-6, and weekends, 9-6, Memorial Day to Labor Day; Monday to Saturday, 9-5, the rest of the year.
> **Admission charge:** None.
> **Telephone:** (406) 444-2694.
> **Handicapped access:** Yes.

Missoula

Fort Missoula

The outpost was built in 1877 during the time of the Nez Percé uprising under Chief Joseph. It was home to the Twenty-fifth Infantry and from here the all-black regiment shipped out for the Spanish-American War in 1898. It was also the site of one of the more curious experiments on the frontier: an attempt to replace mounted patrol duty horses with bicycles. The Twenty-fifth was given the dubious honor of testing this theory, which did not prove practical in Montana's bumpy landscape.

> **Location:** Fort Missoula is 2 miles south of the city, by way of Reserve St. and South Ave.
> **Exhibits:** Twelve buildings remain from the historic fort, some of which have been renovated to show aspects of life here. Others house permanent exhibits. The bicycle corps material is part of the fort museum's collection.
> **Hours:** Tuesday to Saturday, 10-5, and Sunday, 12-5, Memorial Day to Labor Day; Tuesday to Sunday, 12-5, the rest of the year.
> **Admission charge:** Donation requested.
> **Telephone:** (406) 728-3476.

N E B R A S K A

Nebraska City

Mayhew Cabin, John Brown's Caves

This wide-open frontier town on the Missouri River was also one of
the westernmost stations of the Underground Railroad in the 1850s.
Fugitive slaves making their way north from Missouri and Kansas
Territories came through here and were hidden until they could be
taken across to Iowa, a free state, after dark and outfitted for the trip
to safety in Canada.

A popular tradition ascribes the running of this station to John
Brown, the abolitionist who lived, for a time, in Osawatomie, Kansas.
(See the entry on John Brown Memorial State Park there.) But in
recent years, credit for this stop on the railroad has been given to
Allen B. Mayhew. An underground passage connects the log cabin to
caves along the river, and when danger was signalled to the hidden
slaves they were instructed to make their way to the water. They are
still known as John Brown's Caves.

> **Location:** The cabin is at the eastern edge of town, on
> Nebraska 2, near 20th St.
> **Exhibits:** A small museum devoted to the role of the cabin
> in the Underground Railroad network.
> **Hours:** Daily, 10-5, April to October.
> **Admission charge:** $2.50.
> **Telephone:** (402) 873-3115.

Omaha

Great Plains Black Museum

The northern plains have never been an area with a significant
black population. There are barely sixty thousand African Americans
in the five states of Nebraska, North and South Dakota, Montana, and
Wyoming. Yet, if you look into the history of many of these
communities you come across people like Mary Fields, who ran a
stagecoach stop in Cascade, Montana, or Aunt Sally Campbell, who

mined for gold in Deadwood, South Dakota and is credited with being the first woman who was not an Indian to enter the Black Hills.

This museum is intended to clarify the historical record for this part of the country. Its special emphasis is on the achievements of black women. It contains photographs, artifacts, and other historical material on these all but forgotten pioneers.

> **Location:** The museum is at 2213 Lake St., north of downtown by way of U.S. 75 to the Lake St. exit. The museum building itself is a home designed by a prominent Nebraska architect, Thomas R. Kimball, in 1907.
>
> **Hours:** Monday to Friday, 10-4, and weekends, by appointment.
>
> **Admission charge:** Adults and children, $2.
>
> **Telephone:** (402) 345-2212.

N E W   M E X I C O

Columbus

Pancho Villa State Park

On March 9, 1916, the notorious Mexican bandit Pancho Villa and about 800 of his followers came galloping across the border and fell upon the town of Columbus. A small detachment of American troops had been posted in the vicinity, but they were widely scattered. There was no hint that Villa, who was in revolt from the government of Venustiano Carranza and infuriated that it had been recognized by the United States, was near.

Eighteen soldiers and residents of the town were gunned down in the raid. Villa quickly disappeared into the desert of Chihuahua, but outrage swept the United States, and within a week a punitive expedition was formed to pursue him.

Brigadier General John J. Pershing was placed in charge of this force. Within two years, he would become known as commander of the American armies in France. But in 1916 he was still a rather obscure cavalry officer.

He was already nicknamed Black Jack, because as a young lieutenant his first command was the all-black Tenth Cavalry. The day had passed when leadership of these black troops was avoided by ambitious officers. According to some western historians, George Custer wanted nothing to do with the black cavalry units, turning down a command with them. It was also widely felt that the Tenth's longtime commander, Gen. Benjamin H. Grierson, a brilliant and inventive officer, had been held back because of his close association with the black troops.

But by 1896, when Pershing began his stay with the Tenth, they had become recognized as a superior fighting force. He led them through the Spanish-American War, and when he took command of the Villa expedition he specifically asked that the Tenth, based at Fort Huachuca, Arizona, accompany him.

The expedition came to nothing, never making contact with Villa and skirmishing instead with Mexican government troops who were outraged at American soldiers coming across their borders. It was, however, the first American campaign to use airplanes and motorized land vehicles. Pershing managed to enhance his reputation as a

Gen. John J. Pershing

leader, which led directly to his appointment in World War I. For the rest of his career he never lost a chance to praise the Tenth and the spirit of the men he led there.

> **Location:** Columbus is 32 miles south of I-10, by way of New Mexico 11, from the Deming exit.
> **Exhibit:** Mementoes of the raid are displayed at a museum in the old Southern Pacific rail depot in town. An adjacent state park is on the site of Camp Furlong, Pershing's base for the punitive expedition.
> **Hours:** Daily, 10-4.
> **Admission charge:** None.
> **Telephone:** (505) 531-2711.

Lincoln

Fort Stanton, Lincoln Courthouse Museum

Of the eleven Congressional Medals of Honor awarded to members of the Ninth Cavalry, seven of them came during campaigns in New

Mexico. The most dangerous of these was the pursuit of Vittorio and his band of Mescalero Apache, who raided freely across southern New Mexico, Texas, and into Mexico during 1879. Two troopers based at Fort Stanton, Sgt. Thomas Boyne and Sgt. John Denny, won the nation's highest military award in these engagements. Denny, particularly, was cited for dashing three hundred yards under fire to pull a wounded comrade to safety.

> **Location:** The fort, located just south of U.S. 380, about 70 miles west of Roswell, was converted into a hospital in 1899. Artifacts from the post can be seen at the Old Lincoln County Courthouse, in Lincoln, 8 miles east on U.S. 380.
> **Exhibits:** The courthouse has outstanding displays on the history of this part of the state, with emphasis on the local range wars that involved Billy the Kid.
> **Hours:** Daily, 9-5.
> **Admission charge:** Donation requested.
> **Telephone:** (505) 653-4372.

Zuni

Hawikuh Pueblo

In the spring of 1539, the inhabitants of this pueblo were confounded by an almost unbelievable sight. A tall black man approached at the head of a small party, sending before him a sacred medicine rattle and demanding an audience with the chief. The man was Estevanico, a former slave and now the leader of an advance detachment of the first group of Europeans to explore the American southwest. (For a more complete description of his background, see the chapter on Arizona.)

The Zuni refused Estevanico's demand and told him to leave or be put to death. But he was not about to give up that easily. He was searching for the Seven Cities of Cibola, a legendary treasure trove which he believed was somewhere nearby. He proceeded to the pueblo and was immediately taken prisoner. Upon interrogation, he told the Zuni headmen that white men were coming right behind him, who "knew of things in the sky and would instruct them on divine matters."

According to Pedro de Castaneda, who later spoke to members of this expedition, the Zuni did not believe him. "If the people were white in the country from which he came, why would they send him, being black?" They concluded that he was a spy and killed him.

When word of his death reached Fray Marcos de Niza, leader of the main body of the expedition, he stopped short of Hawikuh. Instead, he viewed it from a distance and in the rays of the sun it looked golden to him. He claimed the land for Spain and hastily retreated to

Mexico. Within a year the soldiers of Coronado had returned to the scene of Estevanico's death, eager to possess the treasure for which he died.

"Such were the curses that were hurled at Fray Marcos," wrote Castaneda, "that I pray God may protect him. Hawikuh is a little crowded village, looking as if it had been all crumpled up together. There are haciendas (in Mexico) which make a better appearance."

Coronado conquered the village and continued his fruitless quest for Cibola. The place today is a ruin, part of the Zuni Reservation.

> **Location:** The Hawikuh ruins are 12 miles south of Zuni
> Pueblo, by way of an unpaved road running south from
> New Mexico 53. A mission here was burned by Apache or
> Navaho raiders in 1670 and never rebuilt. Zuni itself has a
> population of 5,500 and is one of the largest contemporary
> pueblos. It holds several religious ceremonies open to
> outsiders during the year, most notably the Shalako dance
> of late November and early December.

O K L A H O M A

Boley, Langston

Black communities

Several black towns were established in Oklahoma in the years before statehood. Of the few that survive, Boley is best known because of its annual Black Rodeo, held each Memorial Day weekend. Langston is the site of one of the first black land grant colleges, the legacy of even more ambitious dreams.

Boley began as a railroad promotion. The Fort Smith and Western line was laying tracks towards the territorial capital of Guthrie in 1903 and planting settlements along its way. This area was selected for a black community because of its proximity to the Creek land grants. The Creeks were one of the Five Civilized Tribes, transported here from their homes in the South when Oklahoma was Indian Territory. Although their lands were taken from them by force, the tribes remained southern in their outlook. Many of them owned slaves, and several of their members fought for the Confederacy.

After the Civil War, the largest number of freedmen were listed as members of the Creeks, and it was primarily this group that settled Boley, named for the roadmaster of the railroad. The central area of the town is a National Historic District.

The men who settled Langston in 1891 didn't want to stop with just a town. They had visions of organizing a black state around the community. Oklahoma was still a territory, made up primarily of Indian lands, and there seemed to be any number of possibilities for its future.

E. P. McCabe, assistant state auditor of Kansas, and Fort Smith attorney S. H. Scott felt that a way to escape the tightening coils of segregation would be to make part of the territory a separate state for black people. It is a dream that has recurred several times in American history, most recently in the 1960s. But Langston never found a sustained basis for prosperity and within a few years its founders had moved on to Guthrie. The town was named for John M. Langston, a Congressman from Virginia and former inspector-general for education in the Freedmen's Bureau, because part of the overall plan was to turn it into an educational center. The territorial legislature voted funds for a land grant college in 1897, and Langston

University is still there, fulfilling some part of the hopes of the town's founders.

> **Location:** Boley is on U.S. 62, about 60 miles east of Oklahoma City. Information on the Black Rodeo and local landmarks can be obtained through the Boley Chamber of Commerce, at 125 South Pecan.
> **Hours:** Daily, 8-5.
> **Telephone:** (918) 667-3341.

Langston is located about 40 miles northeast of Oklahoma City on Oklahoma 33. Information on Langston University is available at (405) 466-2231.

Muskogee

Five Civilized Tribes Museum

As indicated above, members of these tribes—Creek, Cherokee, Choctaw, Chickasaw, and Seminole—were southern in background and many of them owned slaves. After the Civil War, however, the freedmen were accepted as citizens of the tribes, and several families in eastern Oklahoma trace themselves back to these black and native American origins. The museum has exhibits on the freedmen who lived among these tribes.

> **Location:** The museum is 3 miles northwest of Muskogee, in Honor Heights Park. It is housed in an old Indian Agency building dating from 1875.
> **Exhibits:** Artifacts of the Five Tribes, art museum, and library.
> **Hours:** Monday to Saturday, 10-5, and Sunday, 1-5.
> **Admission charge:** Adults, $2; senior citizens, $1.75; students, $1.
> **Telephone:** (918) 683-1701.

Ponca City

101 Ranch

It was more of a showplace than a ranch, a spread where the legends and traditions of the Old West were allowed to live on long after the frontier had vanished. Established in 1879, it eventually grew to over 110,000 acres and was credited with several advances in cattle breeding and seed cultivation. But it became famous as the place that institutionalized the rodeo and put it on the road. The 101 Ranch Wild West Show toured America for more than twenty years

Bill Pickett, one of the biggest stars of the 101 Ranch

in the early years of the twentieth century, bringing the excitement of the west to a nation that hadn't yet grown jaded with such spectacles.

The staple of the show was the cowboy competitions: the riding and roping which had been part of informal get-togethers in ranching communities throughout the west. The 101 shows gave them a form and a stipulated set of events. One of the biggest stars was Bill Pickett, a black cowboy. In an era when black athletes were barred from most professional sports, Pickett was writing the rules for this one.

Zack Miller, owner of the 101 and mastermind of the touring shows, credited Pickett with inventing the art of bulldogging, which involved going hand-to-horn with a wild longhorn steer and wrestling it to the ground while racing the clock. It remains one of the most popular events in the rodeo. Pickett claimed to have devised this stunt out of necessity while working in west Texas, where the mesquite grew so thick it was impossible to throw a lariat. Pickett topped it off by bringing his steer down in a hurry by biting it on the nostrils. That usually gave him the winning advantage. While the show was touring in Mexico, Pickett bet that he could throw a bull and hold it down for seven-and-a-half minutes. By the time all the money was in, the pot totalled $25,000, and Miller had put up his show as collateral. Pickett not only brought the bull down but held it for a full fifteen minutes, just to make sure there would be no argument afterward.

The show played throughout Europe and in its time was as great an attraction as the Barnum and Bailey Circus. But rising costs and changing public tastes caught up to it and the show closed for good in 1931. By that time, mounting debts had also overcome the ranch, and the 101 was sold off to pay creditors in 1936.

Bill Pickett had died four years before from injuries suffered while roping a bronco at the age of seventy-two. He was buried on the ranch, under a marker erected by the Cherokee Strip Cowboy Association. Zack Miller wrote a poem to mark his passing:

If they check his brand, and I think they will,
It's a runnin' hoss they'll give to Bill.
And some good wild steers till he gets his fill.
With a great big crowd for him to thrill.

Location: The 101 Ranch was located south of Ponca City, on both sides of the present U.S. 177. Pickett's grave is near White Eagle, about 8 miles south of Ponca City.
Exhibits: Memorabilia from the 101 Ranch and its show is displayed in the Ponca City Cultural Center Museum, at 1000 E. Grand Ave.
Hours: Monday and Wednesday to Saturday, 10-5, and Sunday, 1-5.
Admission charge: $1.
Telephone: (405) 767-0427.

O R E G O N

Astoria

Fort Clatsop National Memorial

More than a year and a half after leaving St. Louis, the Lewis and Clark Expedition arrived at the Pacific Ocean near the mouth of the Columbia River. They had spent the previous winter in an Indian village along the Missouri River, in what is now North Dakota. But now there was no other human habitation available.

So a vote was taken on where a shelter should be built. This site was selected for its good hunting, access to the ocean for salt, and protection from the winds. The party's black member, York, who had started the trek as a manservant to co-leader William Clark, significantly was given a full vote in the proceedings. His courage and strength during adversity had won the respect of everyone in the

Fort Clatsop

expedition, and by this time his status was equal to that of anyone in the party.

When the expedition returned home the following summer, York was granted his freedom. Clark, who would become governor of Missouri, a slave-holding state, must have felt that once you gave a man a vote equal to your own it became difficult to justify enslaving him.

Location: Fort Clatsop is six miles south of Astoria, off U.S. 101.

Exhibits: A reconstruction of the fort stands on its original site, and living history demonstrations, in which staffers take the roles of members of the expedition to show what their life was like here, are held during the summer.

Hours: Daily, 8-6, mid-June to Labor Day; daily, 8-5, the rest of the year. Living history presentations are held only during the summer.

Admission charge: None.

Telephone: (503) 861-2471.

Handicapped access: Yes.

SOUTH   DAKOTA

Pine Ridge

Holy Rosary Mission

On a bitterly cold winter morning, two days before the end of 1890, the exhausted troopers of the Ninth Cavalry arrived here after an all-night ride of fifty miles. They were immediately told to ride to the nearby mission church, where a squadron of the Seventh Cavalry was pinned down by Sioux gunfire.

Fighting off weariness and freezing temperatures, the all-black unit came upon the battle, with Sioux holding the ridges and firing down on the trapped soldiers below. The Ninth managed to drive off the Sioux and rescue the Seventh. Corporal William O. Wilson was awarded the Congressional Medal of Honor for his actions during this fight.

It would be the eleventh and last such award this valiant outfit would win in the Indian campaigns over a twenty-year period. The other black unit, the Tenth Cavalry, would go on to win five more Medals of Honor in the Spanish-American War. After that, no black soldier or sailor would be given the nation's highest military decoration for more than half a century, until the Korean War. Segregated units received the French Croix de Guerre in World War I, and many more blacks were decorated during World War II. But for fifty-three years, a combination of military policy that assigned blacks to noncombat roles and bias among officers who sought candidates for this award denied the Medal of Honor to blacks. (In contrast, eighteen of these decorations were awarded to black servicemen in Vietnam.)

The clash at the mission church came one day after the final climactic event of the Indian Wars, the massacre at Wounded Knee. Its very name has, in fact, become synonymous with the injustices done to native Americans. Over the next twenty-five years there would continue to be occasional, sporadic incidents in which a small band of Indians was confronted by military force. But the fight at the church was, to all purposes, the end of an era in the West and in black military history.

Location: Pine Ridge is in southwestern South Dakota, on U.S. 18, about 110 miles southeast of Rapid City on the

Pine Ridge Reservation. The church is five miles north of the town, near White Clay Creek. There are historical markers on the site.

T   E   X   A   S

Fort Davis

Fort Davis National Historic Site

The outpost was established in 1854 to protect travelers to El Paso on the long, hazardous trail through the hostile lands of west Texas. In the 1880s it played a major role in the history of the Tenth Cavalry, the black unit that served throughout the West in the years after the Civil War. It was the setting for both the Tenth's greatest victory and for the disgrace of the first black man ever to graduate from the U.S. Military Academy.

The Tenth arrived in Fort Davis in 1879, assigned to track down the wily Apache leader Vittorio and his band of raiders. These were some of the toughest fighters the Army had encountered, made even more formidable by their ability to slip across the border into Mexico and evade capture. On a few occasions, U.S. troops followed them across the Rio Grande, but Mexican protests made this a dangerous policy. Finally, the Tenth's commanding officer, Gen. Benjamin Grierson, persuaded the strategists to let Vittorio come to him, staking out the watering holes on his likely return route into Texas and trapping him. In two decisive engagements in the summer of 1880, the Tenth handed Vittorio two stinging defeats, at Quitman Canyon and Rattlesnake Springs. Prevented from heading north, Vittorio was forced to return south and was killed three months later in a fight with Mexican troops. The campaign cemented the reputation of Grierson and of the Tenth as a top fighting force.

Participating in these battles was the young Lt. Henry O. Flipper. Three years before, he had been the topic of a national debate as the first black graduate of West Point. The attitude generally held in the country was that an officer must be a "gentleman," and that Flipper's race disqualified him from that title. Flipper, the son of Georgia slaves, appointed to the Academy by a Reconstructionist Republican Congressman from his home state, was ostracized by his fellow cadets, reinforcing his determination to make it through the four-year grind.

He was assigned to the Tenth and served with distinction. But in 1882 he was charged with mishandling Army funds while serving as a commissary officer. He was court-martialed and dismissed from the

330

Henry O. Flipper

Army, his protests that he had been railroaded by a prejudiced colonel ignored.

The blow only seemed to stiffen Flipper's resolve to make something of himself. For the next fifty-eight years of his life, he had a remarkable career as a leading mining engineer in the Southwest, the first black man to attain recognition in that field. He dabbled in history, writing the first scholarly examination of the role of Estavenico in the exploration of the early Southwest (see the entries for Sierra Vista, Arizona, and Zuni, New Mexico). Eventually, he became associated with the future Secretary of the Interior, Albert Fall, and went to Washington as his assistant, and a top expert on Mexican government policy. Finally retiring to Atlanta, he finished his days writing history and trying to clear his name. He died in 1940 with the blemish still clouding his reputation.

As a postscript, ninety-four years after his dismissal, the Army re-examined the documents of his trial and concluded that the charges were not warranted. The record was changed to give him an honorable discharge, and in 1978 his body was reinterred in Thomasville, Georgia, with full military honors.

Rifle drill at Fort Concho

Location: Fort Davis is adjacent to the town of the same name, 207 miles southeast of El Paso by way of I-10 and Texas 118.
Exhibits: One of the most outstanding re-creations in the country of a frontier miliary post. There is a museum, restored quarters, and commissary and military ceremonies during the summer based on Army manuals of 1875.
Hours: Daily, 8-5.
Admission charge: $1 per person not to exceed $3 per family.
Telephone: (915) 426-3224.
Handicapped access: Yes.

San Angelo

Fort Concho

This is the best preserved of all the Texas frontier forts, with eleven original buildings still standing as they were when Concho closed down in 1889. It was the home of the Tenth Cavalry before its move to Fort Davis in 1879, so the fort that visitors see today, more than any other in the West, is little changed from the one on which they served.

Location: The fort is in the center of San Angelo, at 213 E. Ave. D. Town and post grew up at the intersection of the state's most heavily traveled cattle and stagecoach trails, which are now U.S. 87, 67, and 277.

Exhibits: Displays in original buildings tell the story of this fort's role on the frontier and the Indian wars.

Hours: Monday to Saturday, 9-5, and Sunday, 1-5.

Admission charge: $1.50.

Telephone: (915) 657-4441.

San Antonio

Institute of Texas Cultures

This museum is part of HemisFair Plaza, the site of the city's 1968 World's Fair. It contains exhibits about each of the twenty-five ethnic groups that make up the state of Texas, emphasizing their contributions to its development.

One of the uniquely black contributions to Texas life is the Juneteenth celebration, an annual holiday since June 19, 1865. Texas was remote from the main theaters of the Civil War and events that went on elsewhere seemed to have little relevance to life here. Union forces did not occupy Galveston to establish authority over the state until two months after the formal Confederate surrender. Major General Gordon Granger quickly announced that all acts of the legislature for the previous four years were null and void and that, under provisions of the Emancipation Proclamation, all slaves were free. That was the first news that Texas blacks had of their freedom, and since then the date has been been observed as a state holiday, with many celebrations scheduled during the week around it in the larger cities.

Location: HemisFair Plaza is just east of downtown, at the intersection of Market St. and Alamo St.

Hours: Tuesday to Sunday, 9-5.

Admission charge: Donation requested.

Telephone: (512) 226-7651.

Handicapped access: Yes.

U T A H

Salt Lake City

Brigham Young Monument, Pioneer Trail State Park

In view of the longtime friction that existed between blacks and The Church of Latter Day Saints over ordination of priests, it may be a bit surprising to see the names of three black pioneers inscribed on two monuments here. But in their early years the Mormons attracted several black converts who joined the overland treks to Utah. Others came less enthusiastically as slaves.

When the Saints were based in Nauvoo, Illinois, there was one instance of a black man ordained as a priest. Elijah Abel eventually came to Utah and, apparently, functioned in his religious capacity until his death in 1884. For the next ninety-four years, though, blacks were barred from the Mormon priesthood by church policy. As late as 1970, an official pronouncement stated that while the church opposed segregation and racial discrimination in any form, its teachings were based on revelation, which held that blacks "were not yet to receive the priesthood.... Sometime in God's eternal plan, the Negro will be given the right to hold the priesthood."

That right came just eight years later when the revelation was received by Church leaders. Within two days, Joseph Freeman, Jr., of Salt Lake City, was ordained as the first Mormon priest in this century.

There is some controversy over the status of the three black pioneers who were part of the founding party. Green Flake, Hark Lay, and Oscar Crosby all bore the last names of white members of the church, indicating that they were slaves at one time. All were thought to be Mormons, however, in 1847 when they were part of the 143-member pioneer trek to Salt Lake City. Lay eventually moved to California, while Flake is buried in suburban Union.

> **Location:** There are two monuments containing the names of the three black pioneers. The Brigham Young Monument is in the center of the city, at the southeast corner of Temple Square. The Pioneer Monument, also known as the "This Is the Place" Monument, is east of the city in Emigration Canyon. It is reached by heading out Fifth St. South.

Exhibits: There is a visitors' center at the Pioneer Monument, and nearby Deseret Village contains original and reconstructed dwellings of the first settlers.

Hours: Visitor Center, daily, 8-8, May to September; 8-4:30, the rest of the year. Deseret Village, daily, 9:30-4:30, May to September.

Admission charge: $1.

Telephone: (801) 584-8391.

W A S H I N G T O N

Centralia-Chehalis

George Washington Park, Chehalis County Museum

The name of the park doesn't honor the George Washington who was the father of his country but the George Washington who was the Father of Centralia. Both were born in Virginia. But the State of Washington's Washington arrived as a former slave, who not only made a new life but built a new community in the Pacific Northwest.

Born in 1817, he escaped from Virginia and was raised as a foster child by a white family in Missouri. Unable to attend school, he was tutored at home and by the time he was in his thirties ran a sawmill in St. Joseph, Missouri. But he chafed under the racial restrictions of that slave-holding state and in 1850 he joined a wagon train on the Oregon Trail.

Once again entering the lumber business, he established a homestead on the Chehalis River. But his farm lay in the path of the Northern Pacific Railroad, and with the settlement he received, Washington decided to plan a new town. He called it Centerville and laid out two thousand lots, setting some aside for parks and churches. The place thrived and even though the residents changed the name that Washington had selected, he spent the rest of his life there as an honored citizen. When he died in 1905 the town shut down for a day of mourning. His funeral service was held in a church that stood on land he donated, and he was buried in a cemetery that was also on land he donated.

> **Location:** Centralia is 30 miles south of Olympia by way of I-5. George Washington Park is in the heart of town, at Pearl St. and Harrison St. Washington is buried nearby in Centralia Cemetery. His grave is marked with a plaque installed by the county chapter of the Daughters of the American Revolution. Exhibits on Washington's life can be seen in the Lewis County Historical Museum in Chehalis, four miles north. The museum is at 599 N.W. Front St.
> **Exhibits:** The museum, in addition to the Washington material, has displays on the history of logging and pioneer life in the area.
> **Hours:** Tuesday to Saturday, 9-5, and Sunday, 1-5.

Admission charge: Donation requested.
Telephone: (206) 748-0831.
Handicapped access: Yes.

Seattle

Douglass-Truth Library

The best source for historical material regarding African Americans in the Pacific Northwest. While that is the focus of its collection, it also contains studies of the depiction of black characters in children's literature.

> **Location:** The library is at 2300 E. Yesler Wy., east of downtown.
> **Hours:** Monday to Wednesday, 1-9; Thursday, 10-9; and Saturday, 10-6.
> **Admission charge:** None.
> **Telephone:** (206) 684-4704

Mt. Zion Baptist Church

The congregation was established here in 1890, making it one of the oldest black churches in the Northwest. Its new building, erected in 1975, is an especially striking edifice, intended to heighten its congregation's racial awareness. African religious themes are carved into the pulpit and offering table and the stained-glass windows depict leading religious and historical figures from the black community. The church is supported by beams that have been left unfinished, as a symbol of African Americans as "an unfinished people."

> **Location:** The church adjoins an older building, erected in 1920, at 1634 Nineteenth Ave., east of downtown.
> **Hours:** Monday to Saturday, 9-5.
> **Telephone:** (206) 322-6500.

Tumwater

George Bush Exhibits in Henderson House Museum

George Washington may have been an early leader in this state (see above) but he was preceded by another black pioneer with a presidential name: George Bush. The older man's contributions may even have been more substantial in terms of national history.

Bush was born a free citizen of Pennsylvania, but like Washington he emigrated to Missouri as a young man. He had fought under Andrew Jackson at the battle of New Orleans and had prospered as a cattle trader. But increasingly onerous racial laws made him decide to join one of the first wagon trains setting forth on the Oregon Trail. Arriving in that territory in 1844, he learned to his disgust that Oregon had enacted racial laws prohibiting blacks from holding property, so he crossed the Columbia River and entered Washington. He settled in an area that is still known as Bush Prairie, to the south of the future state capital of Olympia.

While individuals like Bush were working out their own fortunes, the United States and Great Britain were wrangling over the great question of national destinies in the Northwest. The British claimed Washington, while Americans shouted "Fifty-Four-Forty or Fight," referring to a latitude far to the north, in present day British Columbia. A compromise had to be worked out, and it was because of the presence of Bush and a few other pioneers in this nearly empty land that the future state of Washington ended up on the American side of the border.

Bush went on to prosper on his farm. Ironically, it took a special act by the territorial legislature to secure his title to it in 1854.

> **Location:** Tumwater is on the southern outskirts of Olympia, by way of I-5. The Henderson House is at 602 DesChutes Wy.
> **Exhibits:** Besides its display on Bush, the museum features material relating to the settlement of this first town north of the Columbia River in Washington.
> **Hours:** Daily, 9-5.
> **Admission charge:** Donation requested.
> **Telephone:** (206) 753-8583.

Ontario

Lake Superior

Lake Michigan

Ontario

1. North American Black Historical Museum and Cultural Center, *Amherstburg*
2. Raleigh Township Centennial Museum, *Chatham*
3. Uncle Tom's Cabin, *Dresden*
4. Caribaña, *Toronto*

Ontario

Lake Huron

Lake Ontario

Lake Erie

O N T A R I O

Amherstburg

North American Black Historical Museum and Cultural Center

The town is situated on a strategic place on the Detroit River, near one of its narrowest points. It was a British shipyard and naval base during the War of 1812 and for half a century afterwards an unofficial port of entry for hundreds of slaves escaping on the Underground Railroad. Because the Detroit escape route was closely watched by slave hunters, many fugitives decided to risk everything and swim for freedom here. Others made their way across the frozen river in winter.

They established the Nazery African Methodist Episcopal Church here in the late 1850s, and a black community grew up in the area around it. Many descendants of these escaped slaves still live in Amherstburg and belong to the church. In 1966 they began raising funds for an adjacent museum to illustrate the story of blacks in Canada. This center opened fifteen years later. The primary exhibits concern the Underground Railroad routes into Canada and the history of the community that grew up here.

> **Location:** Amherstburg is 18 miles south of Windsor, by way of Ontario 18. The museum is at 277 King St., a few blocks east of the highway in the center of town.
> **Hours:** Wednesday to Friday, 10-5, and weekends 1-5, March to November.
> **Admission charge:** $2.
> **Telephone:** (519) 736-5433.

Chatham

Raleigh Township Centennial Museum

Many Canadian communities took the country's centennial celebration, in 1967, as an opportunity to explore their own past. As a result, museums throughout Canada bear the name "Centennial" in their title, such as this one a few miles outside of Chatham.

This city in southwestern Ontario was a major settlement for escaping slaves, many of whom maintained ties to the abolitionist community in the United States. John Brown attended meetings at the First Baptist Church here in the late 1850s, and it is supposed that much of the strategy for the raid on Harpers Ferry was laid out at the time (see entry on the National Historic Park at Harpers Ferry, West Virginia).

The Elgin (Buxton) Settlement was one of the havens for the Canadian freedmen, and this museum celebrates their history in their land of refuge under the leadership of Rev. William King.

> **Location:** The museum is in the village of North Buxton, 10 miles south of Chatham, by way of Kent County Hwy. 27 (Bloomfield Rd.) and then westbound County Hwy. 6. The Bloomfield Rd. exit on Hwy. 401 is 50 miles east of Windsor.
> **Hours:** Wednesday to Sunday, 1-5, May to September.
> **Admission charge:** $2.
> **Telephone:** (519) 352-4799.

Dresden

Uncle Tom's Cabin

The first antislavery law in Canada was passed in 1793 by the legislature of Upper Canada, which was what Ontario was called at that time. For the next sixty-eight years, escaping slaves understood that if they could get across the border they would be safe. The trickle of immigrants became a flood after 1850 when the Fugitive Slave Act went into effect in the United States, and former slaves who had lived freely for years in the North suddenly found themselves the prey of southern bounty hunters.

It is estimated that as many as fifty-thousand blacks may have entered Canada during this time. Among them was a fugitive slave from Kentucky named Josiah Henson (see the entry on the Josiah Henson Trail in Owensboro, Kentucky). In 1830, after his owner had doubled the price he was asking for his freedom when Henson accumulated the original amount, he escaped into Indiana. Making his way steadily northeast, he managed to enter Canada near Buffalo, New York.

A man of keen oratorical gifts and impressive intellect, Henson won many Canadian admirers. One of the things that concerned antislavery groups was how the blacks coming into the country would be able to support themselves. Henson proposed opening a trade school for both men and women to teach them useful occupations. His friends managed to purchase a tract of land for him in southwestern Ontario for the project, which became known as the British American

Josiah Henson

Institute. It opened in 1840 and offered a rudimentary education and instruction in such skills as carpentry and smithery. Women were taught to cook and sew.

To raise funds for his institute, Henson wrote a short pamphlet outlining his life story. It was published by the Anti-Slavery Society of Boston and circulated throughout the East, where it came to the attention of Harriet Beecher Stowe. The idea of a novel to dramatize the evils of slavery had already germinated in her mind, but Henson's pamphlet fleshed it out. Many of the incidents incorporated in her book were part of his story, and on a subsequent tour of New England Henson met with her and expanded on many of the events about which he had written.

Stowe never made any attempt to conceal Henson's influence, and after the publication of *Uncle Tom's Cabin* he became a celebrity. Henson lectured extensively and was introduced to Queen Victoria on a tour of Britain.

Henson's institute, however, never sustained itself financially and it closed down in the 1850s. After the Civil War, he continued to occupy a home on the site until his death in 1883. Eventually, he was forgotten by the outside world and the fictional character modeled after him came to represent something entirely different than the man Henson was. The person who lived in the real Uncle Tom's Cabin was decidedly no Uncle Tom.

> **Location:** Dresden is about 15 miles north of Chatham. From Ontario 401, exit at northbound Kent County Rd. 15, then left on Ontario 21. The site of the British American Institute is southwest of town on county road 40 (Park St.).
> **Exhibits:** Henson's residence, some of the original school buildings, and a cabin that housed newly arrived fugitives still stand on the site. There are also displays on the history of the novel *Uncle Tom's Cabin*.
> **Hours:** Daily 10-6, May to October.
> **Admission charge:** $2.50.
> **Telephone:** (519) 683-2978.

Toronto

Caribaña

After the Civil War era, most of Canada's black population came from the former British colonies in the West Indies. The black residents of the country's largest city celebrate their ethnic origins each August with a festival called Caribaña. It features parades, entertainment, reggae and steel band concerts, and Caribbean style cooking.

> **Location:** Most Caribaña activities are held on Toronto Islands park. This area is accessible by frequent ferryboat service from the docks at the foot of Bay St., downtown.
> **Dates:** The festival is usually held furing the first or second weekend of August. For specific dates, call Ontario Travel in Toronto at (800) 668-2746, toll free.

T I M E L I N E

1539	Estevanico leads the first party of exploration into what would become the American Southwest and is killed at Hawikuh, New Mexico.
1619	First black indentured servants arrive in Jamestown, Virginia.
1739	Slave revolt at Stono River, South Carolina.
1769	Richard Allen is named the first black minister in the American Methodist Church at St. George's, in Philadelphia.
1770	Crispus Attucks is killed in the Boston Massacre.
1775	Liberated slaves fight with the British at the Battle of Great Bridge, Virginia.
1777	Republic of Vermont passes the first constitution in America to prohibit slavery, in Windsor, Vermont.
1778	Black regiment fights as a unit at the battle of Portsmouth, Rhode Island.
1779?	Jean Baptiste Du Sable opens his trading post on the future site of Chicago.
1779	George Liele begins black Baptist services in Savannah, Georgia.
1781	Pioneer party of predominantly African descent arrives from Mexico to settle Los Angeles.
1783	George Washington bids farewell to his officers in a tavern owned by Samuel Fraunces in New York City.
1791	Benjamin Banneker publishes his first almanac and also helps to plan the future District of Columbia.
1793	Mother Bethel African Methodist Episcopal Church, under the ministry of Richard Allen, is organized in Philadelphia.
1796	Yucca House is built at Melrose Plantation, Louisiana.

1804	The Lewis and Clark Expedition, accompanied by the black servant York, leaves St. Louis to explore the territories acquired in the Louisiana Purchase.
1806	African Meeting House, the oldest black church building in the country, opens in Boston.
1811	Paul Cuffe begins a campaign to settle freed slaves in Sierra Leone.
1815	Black troops fight in the front lines with Andrew Jackson at the Battle of New Orleans.
1816	John Stewart opens the Methodist mission to the Wyandotte in Upper Sandusky, Ohio.
1816	American troops destroy an outpost manned by escaped slaves and rebellious Indians in Sumatra, Florida.
1817	Zephaniah Kingsley evades American laws banning the slave trade by setting up his plantation near Jacksonville, Florida.
1822	The planned Denmark Vesey uprising is crushed in Charleston, South Carolina.
1824	Interracial Neshoba Plantation is established near Memphis, Tennessee.
1825?	Stephen Bishop explores the depth of Mammoth Cave, Kentucky.
1825	Rev. John Rankin buys a home on a bluff above the Ohio River to hide escaping slaves in Ripley, Ohio.
1827	Levi Coffin sets up his Underground Railroad network from his home in Fountain City, Indiana.
1828	William Lloyd Garrison begins to publish his abolitionist newspaper in Bennington, Vermont.
1830	Bishop Richard Allen presides over the first national black convention, in Philadelphia.
1831	Nat Turner leads a slave rebellion that terrifies the South, in Courtland, Virginia.
1833	Oberlin College is founded in Ohio with a policy of admitting black students.
1835	Harriet Beecher Stowe visits a slave market in Washington, Kentucky, and experiences firsthand the horrors she would later fictionalize.
1836	Dred Scott arrives at Fort Snelling, Minnesota.
1839	Black mutineers seize the slave ship *Amistad*, which is sailed to New York.

1840	Escaped slave Josiah Henson opens the British-American Institute in Dresden, Ontario.
1841	Pioneer merchant William Liedesdorff arrives in San Francisco.
1842	Scout Jim Beckwourth opens a trading post at Pueblo, Colorado.
1846	Slave hunters pursuing the Crosswhite family are arrested and charged with kidnapping in Marshall, Michigan.
1847	Frederick Douglass begins to publish the *Northern Star* in Rochester, New York.
1847	Three black pioneers accompany the first Mormon party to Salt Lake City, Utah.
1847	First Dred Scott trial begins in St. Louis, Missouri.
1850	Harriet Tubman begins her journeys into the South to lead slaves to freedom.
1850	St. Andrew's becomes the first African Methodist Episcopal church on the west coast, in Sacramento, California.
1851	Serialization of *Uncle Tom's Cabin* in the periodical *National Era* begins.
1852	Sojourner Truth delivers her "Ain't I a Woman" address in Akron, Ohio.
1854	Lincoln University opens as the first college for black students, in Oxford, Pennsylvania.
1855	John Langston becomes the first black elected official in the United States, in Ohio.
1856	Wilberforce, in Ohio, opens as the first black-run college in the country.
1856	Antislavery song "Darling Nelly Gray" is written, in Westerville, Ohio.
1856	Guerilla war erupts between pro-slavery forces and abolitionists in Kansas.
1859	John Brown raids the arsenal at Harpers Ferry, West Virginia.
1859	The last slave ship, *Clothilde*, is scuttled, in Mobile, Alabama.
1861	General Benjamin Butler protects escaped slaves as contraband of war, at Fort Monroe, Virginia.
1862	First southern school for freed slaves is established, in Frogmore, South Carolina.

1862	Robert Smalls sails the Confederate ship *Planter* to the Federal lines, at Charleston, South Carolina.
1862	President Lincoln issues the Emancipation Proclamation after the Battle of Antietam, in Sharpsburg, Maryland.
1863	Kansas First Colored Volunteers becomes the first black unit in the Civil War, at Fort Scott, Kansas.
1863	The Massachusetts Fifty-fourth Colored Infantry wins distinction in an unsuccessful attack on Battery Wagner, South Carolina.
1864	Black units see action at Olustee, Florida.
1864	Black soldiers are massacred after surrendering at Fort Pillow, Tennessee.
1864	A last minute change of orders, withdrawing black assault troops, leads to a debacle at the Battle of the Crater, in Petersburg, Virginia.
1864	John Lawson wins the Congressional Medal of Honor at Mobile Bay, Alabama.
1864	Thirteen black soldiers win the Medal of Honor at the Battle of Chaffin's Farm, Richmond, Virginia.
1865	Atlanta University is founded in a railroad boxcar.
1866	Black infantry and cavalry units are organized within the U.S. Army, at Fort Leavenworth, Kansas.
1866-69	Black colleges open throughout the southern states including Fisk, Morehouse, and Hampton, as well as Howard University in Washington, D.C.
1868	Tenth Cavalry participates in the battle of Beecher Island, Colorado.
1870	Hiram Revels, of Mississippi, is appointed the first black U.S. Senator.
1871	Alcorn A&M opens as the first black land grant college, in Lorman, Mississippi.
1873	W. C. Handy is born, in Florence, Alabama.
1873	Jubilee Hall, in Nashville, Tennessee, is built from the proceeds of a concert tour by Fisk University students singing traditional spirituals.
1875	First Kentucky Derby is run with a black jockey on the winner, in Louisville, Kentucky.
1877	Fayetteville State opens as the first normal college in the South, in North Carolina.

1877 | The Nicodemus colony is founded in Kansas.

1878 | Minstrel performer James Bland writes "Carry Me Back to Old Virginny."

1881 | Booker T. Washington arrives to open Tuskegee Institute, in Alabama.

1882 | Henry O. Flipper, the first black graduate of West Point, is court martialed, in Fort Davis, Texas.

1883 | Jan Matzeliger patents the automatic lasting machine in Lynn, Massachusetts.

1886 | Fr. Augustine Tolton is ordained as the first American-born black priest.

1887 | Founding of the largest black community in the country, Mound Bayou, Mississippi.

1890 | Ninth Cavalry participates in the final battle of the Indian wars, at Pine Ridge, South Dakota.

1893 | Dr. Daniel H. Williams performs the first open heart surgery, in Chicago.

1896 | George Washington Carver joins the faculty at Tuskegee Institute, Alabama.

1896 | Poems of Paul Laurence Dunbar are acclaimed by New York critics.

1896 | The U.S. Supreme Court decision in Plessy v. Ferguson legally establishes the concept of racial segregation.

1897 | Scott Joplin publishes "The Maple Leaf Rag," in Sedalia, Missouri.

1898 | North Carolina Mutual Life Insurance is founded in Durham.

1900 | Louis Armstrong is born in New Orleans.

1903 | W. E. B. Du Bois publishes *Souls of Black Folk*, emerging as the leading opponent to the policies of Booker T. Washington.

1903 | Maggie Walker founds Consolidated Bank and Trust, in Richmond, Virginia.

1904 | Mary McLeod Bethune opens the school that would become Bethune-Cookman University, in Daytona Beach, Florida.

1905 | W. C. Handy writes "Memphis Blues."

1909 | Matthew Henson reaches the North Pole with the Robert Peary expedition.

1910 | Founding of the Allensworth colony, California.

1915	Karamu House is founded as a cultural center in Cleveland, Ohio.
1915	Carter G. Woodson establishes the Association for the Study of Negro Life and History.
1916	Tenth Cavalry pursues Pancho Villa into Mexico after a raid on Columbus, New Mexico.
1917	Fort Des Moines opens as a black officer training facility, Iowa.
1917	The black 369th Regiment lands in France.
1921	Eubie Blake and Noble Sissle open "Shuffle Along," the first black Broadway show.
1923	The traffic light is invented by Garrett Morgan.
1923	Adam Clayton Powell, Sr., dedicates a new church building and recreational center for the Abyssinian Baptist Church in New York City.
1925	Dr. Ossian Sweet is acquitted of murder after defending his home from a white mob, in Detroit.
1926	Schomburg Collection, an inspiration of the Harlem Renaissance, opens to the public in New York City.
1926	First observance of Black History Week, under the guidance of Carter Woodson, founder of the Association for the Study of Negro Life and History.
1929	Martin Luther King, Jr., is born, in Atlanta, Georgia.
1931	Trial of "Scottsboro Boys" begins, in Decatur, Alabama.
1935	National Council for Negro Women is founded by Mary McLeod Bethune.
1936	Jessie Owens wins four gold medals at the Olympic Games in Berlin.
1937	Joe Louis becomes heavyweight champion.
1939	Marian Anderson, barred from Constitution Hall, gives an Easter concert on the steps of the Lincoln Memorial, in Washington, D.C.
1941	Dr. Charles Drew sets up the first blood bank.
1941	Muddy Waters makes his first recordings with folklore researcher Alan Lomax, in Clarksdale, Mississippi.
1942	John H. Johnson launches the *Negro Digest* in Chicago.
1942	Black airmen go into training at Tuskegee, Alabama.

1944	Adam Clayton Powell, Jr., becomes the East's first black Congressman, from New York.
1948	In the Shelley Case, the U.S. Supreme Court rules that states may not enforce restrictive housing covenants.
1954	The U.S. Supreme Court decides, in Brown v. the Board of Education of Topeka, that segregation in public schools violates the Fourteenth Amendment to the Constitution.
1955-56	Boycott desegregates buses in Montgomery, Alabama.
1957	Federal troops enforce school desegregation orders in Little Rock, Arkansas.
1960	Lunch counter sit-ins begin in Greensboro, North Carolina.
1961	Leontyne Price becomes the first black singer to appear in a lead role with the Metropolitan Opera of New York.
1961	Motown Records registers its first number one hit, "Please, Mr. Postman," in Detroit.
1963	Four children are killed in the bombing of a church in Birmingham, Alabama.
1963	Dr. Martin Luther King, Jr., leads the civil rights march on Washington.
1964	Martin Luther King, Jr., receives the Nobel Peace Prize.
1964	Three civil rights workers are murdered in Philadelphia, Mississippi.
1965	Voting rights march from Selma to Montgomery, Alabama.
1968	Dr. Martin Luther King, Jr., is assassinated in Memphis, Tennessee.
1969	Studio Museum of Harlem opens in New York City.
1970	Two students are killed by police gunfire at Jackson State University, Mississippi.
1971	Congress funds the National Afro-American Museum in Wilberforce, Ohio.
1977	The TV miniseries "Roots" draws record ratings.
1989	The Civil Rights Memorial is dedicated in Montgomery, Alabama.

FURTHER READING

A

Anderson, James D. *The Education of Blacks in the South, 1860-1935*. Chapel Hill: University of North Carolina Press, 1988.

Aptheker, Herbert. *Abolitionism: A Revolutionary Movement*. Boston: G. K. Hall, 1989.

B

Baker, William J. *Jessie Owens: An American Life*. New York: Free Press/Macmillan, 1986.

Barrow Jr., Joe Louis and Munder, Barbara. *Joe Louis: 50 Years an American Hero*. New York: McGraw-Hill, 1988.

Bennett Jr., Lerone. *Wade in the Water*. Chicago: Johnson Publishing Co., 1979.

_____ . *Before the Mayflower: A History of Black America*. Chicago: Johnson Publishing Co., 1982.

Berry, Mary Frances and Blassingame, John W. *Long Memory: The Black Experience in America*. New York: Oxford University Press, 1982.

Blackett, R. J. M. *Building an Antislavery Wall: Black Americans in the Atlantic Abolitionist Movement, 1830-1860*. Ithaca, N.Y.: Cornell University Press, 1989.

Blassingame, J. W. *The Slave Community: Plantation Life in the Antebellum South*. New York, Oxford University Press, 1979.

Blockson, Charles L. *The Underground Railroad*. New York: Prentice Hall, 1987.

Bogle, Donald. *Toms, Coons, Mulattos, Mammies and Bucks: An Interpretive History of Blacks in American Film*. New York: Viking Press, 1989.

Branch, Taylor. *Parting the Waters: America in the King Years*. New York: Simon & Schuster, 1988.

Bringhurst, Newell G. *Saints, Slaves and Blacks: The Changing Place of Black People in Mormonism*. Westport, Conn.: Greenwood Press, 1981.

Brooks, Tilford. *America's Black Musical Heritage*. Englewood Cliffs, N.J.: Prentice Hall, 1984.

C

Cagin, Seth and Dray, Philip. *We Are Not Afraid: The Story of Goodman, Schwerner and Chaney and the Civil Rights Campaign for Mississippi.* New York: Macmillan, 1988.

Chambers, Bradford. *Chronicles of Negro Protest.* New York: Parents Magazine Press, 1968.

Collier, James Lincoln. *Louis Armstrong: An American Genius.* New York: Oxford University Press, 1983.

Cooper, Wayne F. *Claude McKay, Rebel Sojourner in the Harlem Renaissance: A Biography.* Baton Rouge: Louisiana State University Press, 1986.

Creel, Margaret Washington. *A Peculiar People: Slave Religion and Community Culture among the Gullahs.* New York: New York University Press, 1986.

D

Duberman, Martin Bauml. *Paul Robeson: A Biography.* New York: A. A. Knopf, 1989.

Dunbar, Paul Laurence. *Complete Poems.* New York: Dodd, Mead, 1980.

F

Fehrenbacher, Don E. *Slavery, Law and Politics: The Dred Scott Case in Perspective.* New York: Oxford University Press, 1978.

Fletcher, Marvin E. *The Black Soldier and Officer in the United States Army, 1891-1917.* Columbia: University of Missouri Press, 1985.

Foner, Eric. *Reconstruction: America's Unfinished Revolution, 1863-1877.* New York: Harper and Row, 1988.

Fox, Ted. *Show Time at the Apollo.* New York: Holt, Rinehart and Winston, 1983.

Franklin, John Hope and Meier, August (editors). *Black Leaders of the Twentieth Century.* Urbana: University of Illinois Press, 1982.

Franklin, John Hope and Moss Jr., Alfred A. *From Slavery to Freedom: A History of Negro Americans.* New York: A. A. Knopf, 1987.

G

Garrow, David J. *Bearing the Cross: Martin Luther King, Jr. and the Southern Christian Leadership Conference.* New York: William Morrow, 1986.

George, Nelson. *Where Did Our Love Go: The Rise and Fall of the Motown Sound.* New York: St. Martin's Press, 1985.

Gossett, Thomas F. *Uncle Tom's Cabin and American Culture.* Dallas: Southern Methodist University Press, 1985.

H

Harding, Vincent. *There Is a River: The Black Struggle for Freedom in America.* New York: Vintage Books, 1983.

Harlan, Louis R. *Booker T. Washington: The Wizard of Tuskegee, 1901-1915.* New York: Oxford University Press, 1986.

Harrison, Daphne Duval. *Black Pearls: Blues Queens of the 1920s.* New Brunswick, N.J.: Rutgers University Press, 1988.

Haskins, Jim and Mitgang, N. R. *Mr. Bojangles: The Biography of Bill Robinson.* New York: William Morrow, 1988.

Hill, Daniel G. *Blacks in Early Canada: The Freedom Seekers.* Concord, Ontario: Irwin, 1981.

Hine, Darlene Clark. *Black Victory: The Rise and Fall of the White Primary in Texas.* Millwood, N.Y.: KTO Press, 1979.

Hooks, Bell. *Ain't I a Woman: Black Women and Feminism.* Boston: South End Press, 1981.

Huckaby, Elizabeth. *Crisis at Central High: Little Rock, 1957-58.* Baton Rouge: Louisiana State University Press, 1982.

Huggins, Nathan; Karlson, Martin; and Fox, Daniel M. (editors). *Key Issues in the Afro-American Experience.* New York: Harcourt, Brace, Jovanovich, 1971.

J

Johnson, John H. *Succeeding against the Odds: The Autobiography of John H. Johnson.* New York: Warner Books, 1989.

Jones, Howard. *Mutiny on the Amistad: The Saga of a Slave Revolt and Its Impact on American Abolition, Law and Diplomacy.* New York: Oxford University Press, 1986.

K

Katz, William Loren. *Black Indians: A Hidden Heritage.* New York: Atheneum, 1986.

————. *The Black West.* Seattle: Open Hand Publishing, Inc., 1987.

Kremer, Gary R. *George Washington Carver in His Own Words.* Columbia: University of Missouri Press, 1984.

L

Lewis, David Levering. *When Harlem Was in Vogue.* New York: Oxford University Press, 1989.

Linnemann, Russell J. (editor). *Alain Locke: Reflections on a Modern Renaissance Man.* Baton Rouge: Louisiana State University Press, 1982.

Litwack, Leon F. *North of Slavery: The Negro in the Free States, 1790-1860.* Chicago: University of Chicago Press, 1965.

Lofton, John. *Denmark Vesey's Revolt: The Slave Plot That Lit a Fuse to Fort Sumter.* Kent, Ohio: Kent State University Press, 1983.

Longstreet, Stephen. *Storyville to Harlem: Fifty Years in the Jazz Scene.* New Brunswick, N.J.: Rutgers University Press, 1985.

M

Martin, B. Edman. *All We Want Is Make Us Free .....La Amistad and the Reform Abolitionists.* Lanham, Md.: University Press of America, 1986.

Mays, Joe H. *Black Americans and Their Contributions towards Union Victory in the American Civil War.* Lanham, Md. University Press of America, 1984.

McGovern, James R. *Black Eagle: General Daniel "Chappie" James, Jr.* University: University of Alabama Press, 1985.

Morris, Robert C. *Reading, 'Riting and Reconstruction: The Education of Freedmen in the South, 1861-1870*. Chicago: University of Chicago Press, 1981.

Moses, Wilson Jeremiah. *The Golden Age of Black Nationalism, 1850-1925*. New York: Oxford University Press, 1988.

O

Oates, Stephen B. *The Fires of Jubilee: Nat Turner's Fierce Rebellion*. New York: Mentor, New American Library, 1976.

————— . *Let the Trumpet Sound: The Life of Martin Luther King, Jr*. New York: Plume, 1983.

P

Painter, Nell Irvin. *Exodusters: Black Migration to Kansas after Reconstruction*. New York: Knopf, 1977.

Pearson Jr., Nathan W. *Goin' to Kansas City*. Urbana: University of Illinois Press, 1988.

Perry, Margaret. *The Harlem Renaissance: An Annotated Bibliography and Commentary*. New York: Garland Publishing, 1982.

Piersen, William D. *Black Yankees: The Development of an African- American Subculture in Eighteenth-Century New England*. Amherst: University of Massachusetts Press, 1987.

Q

Quarles, Benjamin. *The Negro in the American Revolution*. Chapel Hill: University of North Carolina Press, 1961.

R

Rabinowitz, Howard N. (editor). *Southern Black Leaders of the Reconstruction Era*. Urbana: University of Illinois Press, 1982.

Rable, George C. *But There Was No Peace: The Role of Violence in the Politics of Reconstruction*. Athens: University of Georgia Press, 1984.

Rawley, James A. *The Transatlantic Slave Trade: A History*. New York: W. W. Norton, 1981.

S

Sawyer, Charles. *B. B. King: The Authorized Biography*. New York: DaCapo, 1982.

Sinnette, Elinor Des Verney. *Arthur Alfonso Schomburg, Black Bibliophile and Collector, a Biography*. Detroit: Wayne State University Press, 1989.

Smith, Edward D. *Climbing Jacob's Ladder: The Rise of Black Churches in Eastern American Cities, 1740-1877*. Washington: Smithsonian Institution Press, 1988.

Summerville, James. *Educating Black Doctors: A History of Meharry Medical College*. University: University of Alabama Press, 1983.

W

Weinstein, Allen and Gutell, Frank Otto (editors). *The Segregation Era.* New York: Oxford University Press, 1970.

West, Hollie I. *Afro-American Culture and Traditions.* Washington: Howard University Press.

Wheeler, Edward L. *Uplifting the Race: The Black Minister in the New South, 1865-1902.* Lanham, Md.: University Press of America, 1986.

Williams, Juan. *Eyes on the Prize: America's Civil Rights Years, 1954-1965.* New York: Viking Press, 1986.

Williamson, Joel. *The Crucible of Race: Black-White Relations in the South since Emancipation.* New York: Oxford University Press, 1984.

Wink, Robin W. *The Blacks in Canada: A History.* New Haven, Conn.: Yale University Press, 1971.

Wood, Peter H. *Black Majority: Negroes in Colonial South Carolina from 1670 through the Stono Rebellion.* New York: Norton, 1975.

Woodward, C. Vann. *The Strange Career of Jim Crow.* New York: Oxford University Press, 1974.

I N D E X

Abel, Elijah, 334
Abernathy, Rev. Ralph, 273
Abiel Smith School, 70
abolitionists, 9, 13, 33, 35, 44,
    46, 48, 54, 58, 69-70, 100,
    108, 114, 187-88, 306, 309,
    316
Abyssinian Baptist Church, 93,
    95
Adams, John, 71, 73
Adams, John Quincy, 54
Africa Town, 130
African American National
    Historic Site, 70
African Baptist Church,
    Nantucket, Massachusetts, 77
African Meeting House, 70
African Methodist Episcopal
    Church, 46, 59, 83, 109, 139,
    216, 232
African Zion Baptist Church,
    Malden, West Virginia, 278
African-American Museum,
    Cleveland, 36
Afro-American Historical and
    Cultural Museum,
    Philadelphia, 107
Afro-American Historical
    Museum, Jersey City, New
    Jersey, 83
Afro-American Life Insurance
    Company, 209
Afro-American Museum,
    Chattanooga, Tennessee, 192
A. G. Gaston Gardens, 120, 122
Alabama State University, 130-
    131
Alcorn, James I., 168

Alcorn State University, 168,
    267
Alex Haley House, 194
All-Wars Memorial to Black
    Soldiers, Philadelphia, 107
Allen, Rev. Richard, 59, 107,
    109
Allensworth, Col. Allen, 290
Allensworth State Park, 290
American Beach, 209
American Missionary Association,
    55, 254
American Negro Academy, 275
American Red Cross, 247
Amherst College, 247
Amistad, 54-5, 139
Amistad Research Center, 160-61
The Amistad Trials, 54
Anacostia Museum, 266
Anderson, C. Alfred, 143
Anderson, Marian, 272
Anthony, Susan B., 101
Antietam, 40, 69
Antietam National Battlefield, 69
Apaches, 287-88, 321
APEX Museum, Atlanta, 215
Apollo Theater, 95-7
Arapahos, 301
Arlington National Cemetery, 62,
    64
Armstrong, Louis, 91, 163, 165-
    66
Armstrong, Gen. Samuel, 254-55
Arnold, Benedict, 56
Asbury, Francis, 60, 109
Asbury Methodist Episcopal
    Church, 60
ASCAP, 103, 190

Association for the Study of Negro Life and History, 269-70

Atlanta Compromise, 75, 141-42, 218

Atlanta Constitution, 223

Atlanta Life Insurance Company, 216, 218

Atlanta University, 216, 218-19

Attucks, Crispus, 72-3

Atwater, Lee, 272

Avery Research Center, 236-37

Baker, Josephine, 65

Banneker, Benjamin, 245-46

Banneker-Douglass Museum, 62

Baptist Tabernacle Church, Beaufort, S.C., 235

Barrow, Joseph Louis (see Louis, Joe)

Basie, Count, 185-86

Battery Wagner, 74, 222, 241, 313

Battle of New Orleans, 161-63, 166, 337

Battle of the Crater, 257

Baumfree, Isabella (see Truth, Sojourner)

Beale Street, 198-99

Beale Street Baptist Church, 199

Bearden, Romare, 218

Beck Cultural Exchange Center, 197

Beckwourth, Jim, 291-92, 299

Beckwourth Pass, 291-92

Beecher Island, 301-02

Beecher, Rev. Henry Ward, 58, 203

Beecher, Rev. Lyman, 34, 155

Bell, Thomas, 274

Bennett, Lerone Jr., 230

Bennington Museum, 114-15

Berea College, 149

Bethune-Cookman College, 208-09, 274

Bethune, Mary McLeod, 208-09, 266-67, 274

Bethune Museum and Archives, 266

Biltmore Estate, 226-27

Bishop, Stephen, 153-54

Black American West Museum amd Heritage Center, 299

Black Archives History and Research Foundation, Miami, 210

Black Archives of MidAmerica, 184

Black Civil War Veterans Memorial, Norfolk, Virginia, 257

Black Confederate Memorial, 169-70

Black Doughboy Monument, 11

Black Fashion Museum, New York, 97

Black Heritage Trail, 71

Black History Week, 270

Black Laws, 310

Black Regiment Memorial, Portsmouth, Rhode Island, 112-13

Blair, Ezell, 230

Blake, Eubie, 65-6, 99-100, 191

Bland, James, 103-04

Blue Jacket, 47

Booker, Fannye, 177

Booker T. Washington National Monument, 262-63

Booker-Thomas Museum, 177

Boot Hill Cemetery, 287, 288

Boston Common, 73-4

Boston Massacre, 71, 73

Bowdoin College, 61

Boyne, Sgt. Thomas, 320

Braden, Dr. John W., 204

Brigham Young Monument, 334

British American Institute, 343, 345

Brooke, Sen. Edward, 268

Brown AME Chapel, 139

Brown, Charlotte Hawkins, 233-34

Brown, Clara, 297-98

Brown, John, 68, 101, 276, 277-78, 296, 309-10, 316, 343

Brown, Linda, 312

Brown, Tarlee W., 143

Brown v. Board of Education, 134, 310-11

Bruce, Sen. Blanche, 267

Bryan, Andrew, 224

Buchanan, James, 188

Bunch, Lonnie G., III, 292-93

Burleigh, Harry T., 91-2

Bush, George, 337-38

Bush, Pres. George, 272

Butler, Benjamin, 252-53, 261-62

Cab Calloway Jazz Institute, 64

Caesar, 47

California Afro-American
Museum, 292
Calloway, Cab, 64-5
Campbell, Sally, 316
Canada, 13, 21, 28, 30, 43, 58,
88, 109, 155, 316, 342-43
Caribaña, 345
Carnegie, Andrew, 255
Carney, Sgt. William H., 241-42
"Carry Me Back to Old
Virginny," 103
Carver, George Washington, 17-
18, 141-42, 182-83, 305, 308
Carver Museum, 143
Cass, Lewis, 30
Castaneda, Pedro de, 320-21
Castillo de San Marcos, 212-13
Castro, Fidel, 95
Catfish Row, 237
Catlett, Elizabeth, 166
Cato, 243
Catton, Bruce, 196, 253
Centennial Hill Historic District,
131
Central City Opera House, 297-
98
Central High School, Little
Rock, Arkansas, 146-47
Central State University, 46
Chamberlain, Rev. Jeremiah, 168
Chambliss, Robert E., 122
Chaney, James Earl, 178, 180
Chehalis County Museum, 336
Chesapeake and Ohio Railroad,
278
Chesnutt, Charles W., 228
Cheyennes, 287, 301
Chicago Historical Society, 5
Chicago Medical College, 9
Chicago River, 4, 5
Chief Billy Bowlegs, 213
Chiricahua Apaches, 284
Churchill Downs, 151, 153
Churchill, Winston, 99
Cinque, 54-5
Civil Rights Act of 1964, 137,
230
Civil Rights Memorial, 132-33
Civil War, 14-16, 40, 43, 45,
48, 69, 74, 76, 83, 88, 103,
105, 109, 124, 137, 150,
153, 163, 168-69, 183, 198-
99, 227, 231, 240, 252-53,
257, 263, 270, 290, 298,
307-09, 330, 333

Clafflin's Farm, 262
Claiborne, William C. C., 162
Clark College, 216
Clark, George Rogers, 5
Clark, Sheriff Jim, 137
Clark, William, 326
Clay, Cassius M., 149
Clay, Henry, 30
Clothilde, 129-30
Cobo Convention Center, 25
Cochise, 284
Coffin House, 13
Coffin, Levi, 13-14
Coincoin, Marie Therese, 158-59
Colgate University, 94
College of Charleston, 236
Collins, Addie May, 120
Columbia University, 84, 247
Communist Party, 86, 126
Confederates, 144, 166, 182,
196, 211, 235, 241, 253,
257, 261-62, 268, 277, 306,
322, 333
The Confessions of Nat Turner,
250
Congress of Racial Equality, 50,
178, 230
Congressional Medal of Honor,
8, 74, 125, 243, 258, 261,
304, 307, 319, 328
Connor, Eugene, 122
Consolidated Bank and Trust
Company, 260
Constitution House, Windsor,
Vermont, 115-16
Cook, Will Marion, 99
Coppin, Fannie Jackson, 65
Coppin State College, 64-5
Coronado, Francisco Vasquez de,
285, 313, 321
Coronado National Memorial,
285-86
Cosby, Bill, 217
Creeks, 213, 322
Croix de Guerre, 10, 328
Crosby, Oscar, 334
Crosswhite, Adam, 30
Crosswhite Boulder, 29
Crows, 291-99
The Crucible, 80
Crummell, Alexander, 275
Crump, Edward H., 127
Crunelle, Leonard, 11
Cuba, 54
Cuffe Memorial, 80-1

Cuffe, Paul, 80-1
Custer, Gen. George, 318
"Darling Nelly Gray," 45
Darrow, Clarence, 22-3
Daughters of the American
  Revolution, 273, 336
Davis, Jefferson, 170, 177, 253,
  261, 267
Day, Tom, 231
"Deep River," 91
Dees, Morris, 133
Delta Blues Museum, 170, 172
Denny, Sgt. John, 320
DePriest, Oscar, 268
Detroit River, 342
DeVoto, Bernard, 291
Dexter Avenue Baptist Church,
  133-35
Dr. Martin Luther King, Jr.,
  National Historic Site, 215,
  219-21
Dorsey, Sgt. Decatur, 258
Douglass, Frederick, 21, 28, 100-
  02, 270-71
Douglass House, 270-71
Douglass-Truth Library, Seattle,
  337
Drexel, Sister Catherine, 169
Du Bois, W. E. B., 11, 29, 34,
  74-6, 142, 290
Du Sable Museum of African-
  American History and Art, 6
Du Sable, Jean Baptiste Pointe,
  4-5
Dunbar House, 38-9
Dunbar, Paul Laurence, 38-9
Duncanson, Robert, 36
Dunmore, Lord, 250-51
Dutch East Indies, 77
Ebenezer Baptist Church, 220-21
Ebony, 7
Ebony Museum of Art, 293
Eighth U.S. Colored Troops, 211
Eisenhower, Dwight D., 128, 147
El Pueblo Museum, 301
Elaine Riots, 146
Ellington, Duke, 99
Elmwood Cemetery, Norfolk,
  Virginia, 257
Emancipation Festival, 40
Emancipation Proclamation, 40,
  69, 253, 271, 333
The Emperor Jones, 86
Estevanico, 286, 313, 320-21,
  331

Eubie Blake Cultural Center, 65-
  6
Evers, Medgar, 133
Fairvue Plantation, 193
Fall, Albert, 331
Farragut, Admiral David, 124-25
Faubus, Orville, 147-48
Fayetteville State University, 228
FBI, 178-79
Fee, John G., 149
feminists, 34, 100
Fields, Mary, 316
Fifteenth Amendment, 87, 297
Fifty-fourth Massachusetts
  Regiment, 73, 106, 211, 222,
  241, 305,313
Fifty-fourth Regiment Memorial,
  73
First African Baptist Church,
  Savannah, Georgia, 224-25
First Baptist Church, Selma,
  Alabama, 139
First Bryan Baptist Church,
  Savannah, Georgia, 224-25
First Church of Christ,
  Farmington, Connecticut, 54-5
First Kansas Colored Infantry,
  305-06
First Kansas Colored Regiment,
  144
First Parish Church, Brunswick,
  Maine, 61
Fisk University, 202-04, 254
The Fist, 25
Five Civilized Tribes, 322-23
Flake, Green, 334
Flatheads, 314
Flipper, Lt. Henry O., 330-31
Ford, Barney, 296-97
Ford, Henry, 142
Forrest, Gen. Nathan Bedford,
  196
Fort Apache, 284
Fort Bowie, 284
Fort Clatsop, 326-27
Fort Concho, 332
Fort Davis National Historic Site,
  330-32
Fort Des Moines, 10, 17
Fort Gadsden, 213
Fort Gaines, 124-25
Fort Griswold, 56
Fort Griswold State Park, 56
Fort Huachuca, 287, 318
Fort Leavenworth, 307

Fort Missoula, 315
Fort Monroe, 252-53
Fort Moosa, 212-13
Fort Pillow, 144, 196
Fort Pillow State Park, 196
Fort Scott National Historic Site, 305-06
Fort Shaw, 313
Fort Smith and Western Railroad, 322
Fort Snelling, 31-32, 187
Fort Stanton, 319-20
Fort Wallace, 301-02
Fortune, Amos, 82
Fortune, T. Thomas, 87
Fourteenth Amendment, 105, 312
France, 4-5, 10, 112
Frances Ellen Watkins Harper House, 107
Franklin and Armfield, 244
Fraunces, Samuel, 89
Fraunces Tavern, 89-90
Frederick Douglass Memorial and Grave, 100
Free Staters, 309
Freedman's Aid Society, 36
Freedmans Hospital, 9
Freedmen's Bureau, 203, 254, 272, 322
Freeman, Jordan, 56-57
Freeman, Joseph, Jr., 334
French, Daniel Chester, 274
Fugitive Slave Act, 30, 41, 88, 156, 253, 343
Gage, Mrs. Frances, 34
Gaines, Lloyd L., 184
Gambia, 239
Gamble, James, 208
Garfield, James, 255
Garrison Marker, 115
Garrison, William Lloyd, 114-15
George Washington Carver National Monument, 182-83
Geronimo, 284
Gershwin, George, 237
Ghana, 106
Gibbs, Phillip I., 174
The Gift of Black Folk, 34
Glory, 73, 243, 306
"Go Down, Moses," 67
Gold Coast, 239
Gold Rush, 294, 296
Goodman, Andrew, 178, 180
Goodrich, Joseph, 48

Gordy, Berry, Jr., 25-27
Graham, Robert, 25
Granary Burial Ground, 73
Granger, Maj. Gen. Gordon, 333
Grant, Gen. U. S., 199, 257-58, 261-62
Great Awakening, 60
Great Blacks in Wax Museum, 67
Great Bridge Battlefield, 250-52
Great Britain, 243, 247, 255, 338, 342
    and the American Revolution, 5, 56, 71, 73, 90, 112, 115, 212, 250-51
    and the slave trade, 54-5
    and the War of 1812, 107, 161-62, 213
Great Depression, 94
Great Plains Black Museum, 316-17
Great Red Scare, 146
Greeley, Horace, 297
Green, James F., 174
Greene, Gen. Nathanael, 112-13
Grierson, Gen. Benjamin, 318, 330
Guinea (and slave trade), 129
Gullahs, 236-37
Guy Family, 150
Haley, Alex, 194-95
Haley House, 195
Hamilton, Ed, 25
Hammonds, Dr. O. T., 218
Hampton Institute, 141, 253-55
Hampton Springs Cemetery, Carthage, Arkansas, 145
Hanby, Benjamin, 45
Hanby House, 44-45
Handy Birthplace, Museum, and Library, 128
Handy, W. C., 99, 127-28, 198
Harlem, 11, 92-5, 97, 99
Harlem Renaissance, 92, 97
Harper, Frances Ellen Watkins, 107
Harper's Magazine, 38
Harpers Ferry National Historic Park, 276-77
Harriet Tubman Association, 69
Harriet Tubman Historical and Cultural Museum, Macon, Georgia, 224
Harriet Tubman House, 88-9
Harris, Joel Chandler, 222-23

Harrison, Benjamin, 271
Harvard University, 269
Hawikuh Pueblo, 320
Hawkins, Erskine, 123
Haynes, Rev. Lemuel, 115
Henderson House Museum, 337-
  38
Henry, Cammie Garrett, 159
Henry, John, 278-79
Henry O. Tanner House, 107
Henson, Josiah, 154, 343-44
Henson, Matthew, 61-4
Henson Trail, 155
Herndon, Alonzo, 218
Herndon Home, 219
Herndon, Jessie Gillespie, 218
Herndon, Norris, 218
Heyward, DuBose, 237
Hitler, Adolf, 136
Holy Rosary Mission, 328
Hoover, Herbert, 209, 266
Horace King Marker, 136
Horton, Judge James F., 126
Hotel Theresa, 95, 97
House Un-American Activities
  Committee, 86
Houston, Charles, 17
Howard, Gen. Oliver O., 272
Howard University, 17, 40, 103,
  247, 271-72
Howells, William Dean, 38
Hughes, Langston, 92, 106
Hunter, Clementine, 158-59
Huntsville A & M, 127
Idlewild, 29
Illinois Central Railroad, 180
Indiana State Museum, 14
Institute of Texas Cultures, 333
Iowa State University, 18, 142
Isaac Murphy Memorial, 151
Jackson, Andrew, 161-62, 166,
  213, 337
Jackson, Jimmie Lee, 137
Jackson State University, 174-76
Jackson Ward, 258, 260-61
Jamaica, 224
James Bland Grave, 103
James, Gen. Daniel, 143
James, Jesse, 184
Jamestown Colony, 255-56
Jasper, Rev. John, 260
Jefferson, Thomas, 245
Jenkins Ferry, 145
Jesse Owens Monument, 135
Jim Crow, 94, 141, 230

Joe Louis Arena, 25
John Brown's Caves, 316
John M. Langston House, 40
Johnson, Andrew, 106
Johnson, Anthony, 255
Johnson, Pvt. Henry, 10
Johnson House, 108
Johnson, Jack, 23
Johnson, James Weldon, 75, 99-
  100
Johnson, John H., 7-8
Johnson, Lyndon B., 138, 179
Johnson Publishing Corporation,
  6, 8
Johnson, Samuel, 108
Jones, Absalom, 110
Jones, Casey, 180
Jones, John, 5
Jones, John W., 131
Joplin, Scott, 65, 188-91
Jubilee Singers, 203
Juneteenth, 333
Karamu House, 37
Kelly-Ingram Park, 120, 123
Kennedy, John F., 122
Kentucky Derby, 151-53
Kentucky Derby Museum, 153
Kentucky Horse Park, 151-52
Kentucky Military History
  Museum, 149
Key, Marshall, 155
King, Horace, 136-37
King, Dr. Martin Luther, Jr., 27,
  61, 122-23, 131-35, 138, 200,
  202, 217-21, 273
King, Rev. William, 343
Kingsley Plantation, 209-10
Kingsley, Zephaniah, 209
King-Tisdell Cottage, 225
Kinzie, John, 5
Korean War, 328
Ku Klux Klan, 22, 122, 138,
  178-79
Lafitte, Jean, 161
Lake Michigan, 5
Lane Theologicial Seminary, 34
Langston, John M., 40, 322
Langston University, 322
Latham, Lambert, 56
Laveau, Marie, 167
Lawnside, 83
Lawson, John, 125
Lay, Hark, 334
Ledyard, Col. William, 56
Lee, Gen. Robert E., 257, 262

Lee, Spike, 217
Lee, Tom, 198
Leibowitz, Samuel, 126-27
Leidesdorff, William, 294
l'Enfant, Pierre Charles, 245
Letter from Birmingham Jail, 122
Lewis and Clark Expedition, 276,
  313-5, 326
Lewis County Historical Museum,
  336
Lewis, Cudjoe, 130
The Liberator, 114
Liberia, 80, 106, 109, 228, 266
Liele, George, 224
Lin, Maya, 132
Lincoln, Abraham, 5, 21, 40, 48,
  69, 105, 197, 253, 270, 272-
  74
Lincoln Memorial, 272-73
Lincoln Park, 274
Lincoln University, Missouri,
  183-84
Lincoln University, Pennsylvania,
  106
Liuzzo, Viola, 138
Livingstone College, 232
Livingstone, Robert, 232
Locke, Alain, 272
Loeb, Henry, 200
Lomax, Alan, 170
Lorraine Motel, 200-02
Louis Armstrong House, 91
Louis Armstrong Park, 163, 166
Louis, Joe, 23-5
Louisiana Purchase, 31, 313
Love, Nat, 299-300
lunch counter sit-ins, 229-30
Lyrics of Lowly Life, 38-9
Madame Walker Urban Life
  Center, 15
Malcolm X, 195
Mammoth Cave National Park,
  153-5
Mandans, 314
Mandela, Nelson, 93
Mann, Celia, 239
Mann, Horace, 228
Mann-Simons Cottage, 239
Mardi Gras, 166-67
Mark's Mill, 144-45
Marshall, Thurgood, 106, 311-12
Martin Luther King, Jr., Street
  Church of God, Selma,
  Alabama, 139
Marvelettes, 26

Matthew Henson Memorial, 62
Matzeliger, Jan, 76-7
Mayhew, Allen B., 316
Mayhew Cabin, 316
Mays, Benjamin, 217
McCabe, E. P., 322
McCain, Franklin E., 230
McCarthy, Joseph, 80, 86
McGill University, 247
McKay, Claude, 99
McKinley, William, 268
McLellan, Gen. George, 262
McNair, Denise, 120, 122
McNeill, Joseph A., 230
Meharry Medical School, 203-04
Meharry, Samuel, 204
Melrose Plantation, 158-60
Melville, Herman, 77
"Memphis Blues," 128
Merion Cemetery, Bala Cynwyd,
  Pennsylvania, 103
Mescalero Apaches, 320
Methodist Church, 44, 60, 109-
  11
Methodist Episcopal Church, 18,
  155
Methodists, 238
Metoyer, Thomas Pierre, 159
Mexican War, 286
Mexico, 286, 292, 294, 306,
  318, 320-21, 330-31
Miller, Arthur, 80
Miller, Dorrie, 303
Miller, Zack, 324-25
Mills, Florence, 100
Milton House, 48-9
Milton Olive Park, 8
Mission Dolores, 294
Mississippi Burning, 178
Mississippi River, 4, 31, 127,
  157, 161, 196, 198
Missouri Compromise, 188, 309
Moby Dick, 77
Monroe, James, 163, 252
Montana Historical Museum,
  313, 315
Montgomery, Isaiah T., 177-78
Moody Bible Institute, 208
Morehouse College, 216-18
Morgan, J. P., 91
Morgan, Garrett A., 36-7
Morgan State University, 67
Mormons, 334
Morrill Land Grant Act, 168
Morris Brown College, 216, 219

Mother Bethel AME Church,
    109-10
Motown Museum, 26-7
Motown Records, 27
Mound Bayou, 177-78
Mount Hope Cemetery,
    Rochester, New York, 101-02
Mount Nebo Cemetery, Jackson,
    Alabama, 129
Mount Pisgah AME Church,
    Lawnside, New Jersey, 83
Mount Zion Baptist Church,
    Seattle, 337
Mount Zion United Methodist
    Church, Neshoba County,
    Mississippi, 178, 180
Murphy, Judge Frank, 23
Murphy, Isaac, 151-52
Museum of African American
    History, Detroit, 27-8
Museum of Afro-American
    History, Boston, 70-1, 77
Mutual Musicians Association,
    186
NAACP, 22-3, 50, 75, 92, 94,
    100, 133, 142, 200, 222,
    228, 230, 277, 311
Nashoba Plantation, 202
Natchez Indians, 159
National Afro-American Museum
    and Cultural Center, 45-6
National Archives, 195
National Association of Colored
    Women's Clubs, 271
National Council of Negro
    Women, 209, 266
National Geographic Society, 63
National Museum of African Art,
    274-75
National Museum of the
    Tuskegee Airmen, 28
National Park Service, 73, 219,
    221, 277
Navahos, 321
Negro Digest, 6
Negro History Bulletin, 270
Nell, William C., 70
Neshoba County Courthouse,
    179-80
Nettles, Isaac, 129
New York Metropolitan Opera
    Company, 172
New Orleans Rhythm Kings, 165
New York Age, 87
New York Sun, 87

New York Times, 65, 120
Nez Percés, 315
Niagara Movement, 87
Nicodemus, 307-08
Ninety-second Division, 287
Ninth U.S. Cavalry, 184, 284,
    287, 307, 328
Nixon Archives, 132
Nixon, E. D., 131
Niza, Fray Marcos de, 286, 320
Nkrumah, Kwame, 106
North American Black Historical
    Museum and Cultural Center,
    342
North Carolina A & T State
    University, 229, 231
North Carolina Mutual Life
    Insurance Company, 227
Northern California Center for
    Afro-American History and
    Life, 293
Northern Pacific Railroad, 336
Northwest Ordinance, 31, 43,
    187
Oakland Memorial Chapel, 168-
    69
Oberlin University, 40-1, 106
Oglala Sioux, 301
Ohio River, 13, 35, 40-2, 149,
    155
Ohio State University, 135
Old Courthouse, Decatur,
    Alabama, 127
Old Courthouse, St. Louis,
    Missouri, 186-88
Old Mint Museum, New Orleans,
    166-67
Old Slave Market, Washington,
    Kentucky, 155-56
Old Slave Mart, Charleston,
    South Carolina, 238
Olive, Milton, III, 8
Oliver, King, 165
Olustee Battlefield, 211
Olympic Games, 135-36
101 Ranch, 323-24
O'Neill, Eugene, 86
Oregon Trail, 336, 338
Original Dixieland Jazz Band,
    165
Osceola, 213
Owens, Jesse, 135-36
Pakenham, Sir Edward, 162
Palmer Institute, 234
Paradise Club, 29

Parkman, Francis, 291, 301
Parks, Rosa, 133-35
Paul Robeson Center, 84
Pea Island Coast Guard Station, 232
Peake, Mary, 253-54
Peary, Admiral Robert E., 61-3
Peary-McMillan Arctic Museum, 61
Penn School, 240
Pershing, Gen. John J., 318-19
Petersburg National Battlefield, 257, 261
Peterson, Thomas M., 87
Pettis Bridge, 137-38
Pickens County Courthouse, Carrollton, Alabama, 124
Pickett, Bill, 324-25
Pico, Pio, 293
Pioneer Monument, 334
Plessy v. Ferguson, 133-34, 311
Pointer, Jonathan, 44
Poison Spring, 144-45
Porgy and Bess, 65, 237
Potomac River, 276-77
Powell, Rev. Adam Clayton, Jr., 93-5
Presbyterian Mission Board, 168
Preservation Hall, 164, 166
Prestwould Plantation, 248
Price, Joseph C., 232
Price, Leontyne, 172-73
Prince George Winyah Church, 241
Princeton University, 106
Progressive Farmers and Household Union of America, 146
Provident Hospital, 9-10
Pueblo de Los Angeles, 292-93
Pullman, George, 297
Puritans, 56
Quakers, 13, 80, 83, 107-08, 240
Queen Victoria, 344
Rainy, Ma, 192
Raleigh Township Centennial Museum, 342-43
Randolph, Thomas Jefferson, 244
Rangel, Charles, 95
Rankin House, 41-3
Rankin, Rev. John, 41, 43
Ray, James Earl, 200

Reconstruction, 105, 148, 168, 177, 235, 267, 271, 330
Red River Campaign, 145
Reed, Rev. James, 138
Rendall, Isaac N., 106
Resurrection City, 273
Revels, Sen. Hiram, 267
Revolutionary War, 5, 56, 60, 90, 112, 155, 212, 224, 250, 252
Rhode Island Black Heritage Society, 113
Richard Allen Marker, 59
Richmond, David, 230
Richmond National Battlefield, 261-62
Roberts, Pvt. Needham, 10
Robertson, Carol, 120
Robertson, Smith, 176
Robeson, Paul, 84-6
Robinson, Bill "Bojangles," 260
Robinson, Smokey, 26
Rockefeller, John D., 218
Rockefeller, John D., Jr., 265
Rockwell, Norman, 148
Rogers, Randolph, 21
Roman Nose, 301
Roosevelt, Eleanor, 7, 86, 266
Roosevelt, Franklin D., 266
Roosevelt, Theodore, 101, 142, 307
Roots, 194-95
Russell, Charles, 314
Rust College, 172, 174
Rutgers University, Newark, 84, 86
St. Andrew's AME Church, Sacramento, 294
St. Andrew's Episcopal Church, Darien, Georgia, 222
St. Augustine Seminary, 169
Saint-Gaudens, Augustus, 74
St. George's Episcopal Church, New York, 91-2
St. George's Methodist Church, Philadelphia, 110
St. Louis Cemetery Number One, New Orleans, 167
St. Luke's Episcopal Church, Washington, 275
St. Paul AME Zion Church, Florence, Alabama, 129
St. Phillip's Episcopal Church, New York, 92
San Carlos Apaches, 285

Santa Fe Trail, 306
Saunders, Wallace, 180
Savery, William, 139
Schmeling, Max, 24
Schomburg, Arthur A., 97
Schomburg Center for Research
    in Black Culture, 97-8
Schuller, Gunther, 189
Schwerner, Michael, 178, 180
Scott, Dred, 31-2, 186-88
Scott, Emmett J., 10
Scott Joplin House, 190
Scott Joplin Ragtime Festival,
    191
Scott, S. H., 322
Scottsboro Boys, 126
Seminole War, 213
Seminoles, 212-13
Shaw, Col. Robert Gould, 73,
    222, 241, 313
Shawnees, 47
Shelley House, 190
Shenandoah River, 277
Sherman, Gen. William, 197,
    223
Shreiner's Cemetery, Lancaster,
    Pennsylvania, 106
Shuffle Along, 65, 100
Sierra Leone, 54, 80, 203
Simpson College, 18
Singleton, Benjamin, 308
Sioux, 328
Sissle, Noble, 65-6, 99-100
Sixteenth Street Baptist Church,
    Birmingham, Alabama, 120-22
Sixth Mt. Zion Baptist Church,
    260
Slaughter, John, 288
slave trade, 28, 129-30, 209,
    239, 244, 251, 255
Smalls, Robert, 235-36
Smith, Bessie, 192-93
Smith, Bragg, 221
Smith, Dr. E. E., 228
Smith Robertson Museum, 176
Smithsonian Institution, 266, 274
Sojourner Truth Monument, 33
Soldiers and Sailors Monument,
    Detroit, 21
Song of the South, 222
The Souls of Black Folk, 75
Southern Christian Leadership
    Conference, 120, 220, 273
Southern Poverty Law Center,
    132

Southern University, 157
Soviet Union, 237
Spain, 54, 209, 212-13, 243,
    252, 255, 286
Spanish-American War, 125, 257,
    284, 307, 315, 318, 328
Spelman College, 217
Sports Illustrated, 25
Stagville Preservation Center,
    227
State Fair Community College,
    191
Steele, Gen. Frederick, 144
Stevens, Thaddeus, 105
Stewart, John, 43-4
Stewart, Paul W., 299
Stieglitz, Alfred, 203
Still, William G., 83-4, 108
Stono River National Historic
    Landmark, 243
Storer College, 277
Stowe, Dr. Calvin, 35, 61, 155
Stowe, Harriet Beecher, 13, 34,
    43, 58, 61, 155, 344
Stowe House, Brunswick, Maine,
    35, 61
Strivers' Row, 99
Student Nonviolent Coordinating
    Committee, 230
Studio Museum of Harlem, 100-
    01
Styron, William, 250
Sumner Elementary School, 310,
    312
Supremes, 27
Susan B. Anthony House, 100,
    102
Sutton, Percy, 143
Swails, Sgt. Stephen A., 211
Swain, John, 287-88
Sweet, Henry, 23
Sweet, Dr. Ossian, 21-3
Taft Museum, 36
Taft, William Howard, 36, 255
Talladega College, 139
Tallman House, 49
Tallman Restorations, 48-9
Tallman, William M., 48
Tandy, Vertner Woodson, 89
Taney, Roger B., 188
Tanner, Henry O., 107-08
Taylor, Gen. Zachary, 213
Temple Emanu-El, New York,
    92
Temple, Lewis, 78

Tenth U.S. Cavalry, 184, 284, 287, 301-02, 307, 318-19, 328, 330,332
Thaddeus Stevens Tomb, 105
Thirteenth Amendment, 69
369th Regiment, 10-11
Tituba, 80
Tolton, Fr. Augustine, 11
Tougaloo College, 174
Townsend Acts, 73
Treemonisha, 189
Truman, Harry S., 65, 266
Truth, Sojourner, 19-21, 33-4
Tubman, Harriet, 67-8, 88, 108
Tulane University, 160
Turner, Nat, 238, 248-50
Tuskegee Airmen, 28, 143
Tuskegee Institute, 28, 139, 141-43, 182, 255, 263, 305
Tuxedo Junction, 123-24
Tuxedo Park, 123
Twenty-fourth Infantry, 290, 307
Twenty-fifth Infantry, 307, 313, 315
Uncle Remus, 222-23
Uncle Tom's Cabin, 13, 35, 43, 61, 155-56, 343-45
Underground Railroad, 13-14, 21, 28, 33, 43, 45, 48, 67-8, 83,88, 108, 150, 155, 296, 316, 342
Union Army, 144
Union Literary Institute, 16
United Church-on-the-Green, 56, 58
United Nations, 266, 273
University of Alabama, 134
University of California, 217
University of Chicago, 6, 269
Up from Slavery, 262
USS Arizona, 303-04
U.S. Congress, 30, 45, 54, 63, 69, 93-4, 100, 103, 129, 138, 168, 188, 235, 268, 274, 307
U.S. Constitution, 70, 114, 126, 188
U.S. Military Academy, 330
U.S. Navy, 235, 303-04
U.S. Shoe Company, 77
U.S. Supreme Court, 54, 95, 106, 126-27, 133-34, 146, 148, 176, 184, 186, 188, 190, 311-12
Utes, 301
Vaca, Cabeza de, 286

Valentine, Edward W., 261
Van Buren, Martin, 54
Vance, Zebulon, 228
Vanderbilt, George, 226
Vaughn Cultural Center, St. Louis, Missouri, 190
Vesey, Denmark, 238
Vietnam, 328
Vietnam War, 8, 174, 230
Villa, Pancho, 285, 307, 318
Vinson, Fred, 311
Virgin Islands, 294
Virginia Union University, 258
Vittorio, 320, 330
Voting Rights Act of 1965, 87, 138, 230
Walker, A'Lelia, 15
Walker, Mme. C. J., 15, 89
Walker, Maggie Lena, 259-61
Wallace, George, 122, 138
Wall Street Journal, 217
War of 1812, 84, 154, 161, 213
Warren, Earl, 311-12
Washington, Booker T., 10, 74-5, 87, 140-43, 234, 255, 262-63, 278
Washington, George, 336
Washington, Pres. George, 89-90, 251, 276
Waters, Muddy, 170-71
W. E. B. Du Bois Memorial, 74
Wells, Louis, 124
Wesley, Cynthia, 120
West Indies, 211, 238, 255, 345
Whaling Museum, New Bedford, Massachusetts, 77
Wilberforce University, 46-7, 106
Wilkins, Roy, 94
Williams, Dr. Daniel Hale, 9-10, 29
Williamsburg Corporation, 265
Wilson, Corp. William O., 328
Wilson, Woodrow, 146
Wisconsin Historical Society, 50
Witch House, Salem, 78-9
Woodruff, Hale, 139
Woodson, Carter, 269-70
World War I, 10-11, 17, 47, 257, 319, 328
World War II, 24, 28, 46, 100, 143, 247, 287, 328
Wounded Knee, 328
Wright, Dr. Charles, 27-8
Wright, Frances, 202

Wyandotte Indian Missionary
    Church, 43
Wyandotte Indians, 43-4
Yazoo and Mississippi Valley
    Railroad, 177
Yellow Tavern, 231

York, 313-14, 326-27
Young, Col. Charles, 47
Young, Coleman A., 25, 28, 143
Young Men's Institute, 226
Zunis, 320-21